Mathematics 600
Teacher's Guide

CONTENTS

Author: **Carol Bauler, B.A.**
Editor: Alan Christopherson, M.S.
Graphic Design: JoAnn Cumming, A.A.

Alpha Omega Publications®

804 N. 2nd Ave. E., Rock Rapids, IA 51246-1759
© MCMXCIX by Alpha Omega Publications, Inc. All rights reserved.
LIFEPAC is a registered trademark of Alpha Omega Publications, Inc.

OVERVIEW

MATHEMATICS

Curriculum Overview
Grades K-12

■——————————————————————■

Kindergarten

Lessons

1-40	41-80	81-120	121-160
Directions-right, left, high,low,etc.	**Directions**-right,left, high,low,etc.	**Directions**-right,left, high,low,etc.	**Directions**-right,left, high,low,etc.
Comparisons-big, little,alike,different	**Comparisons**-big, little,alike,different	**Comparisons**-big, little,alike,different	**Comparisons**-big, little,alike,different
Matching	**Matching**	**Matching**	**Matching**
Cardinal Numbers-to 9	**Cardinal Numbers**-to 12	**Cardinal Numbers**-to 19	**Cardinal Numbers**-to 100
Colors-red,blue,green, yellow, brown,purple	**Colors**-orange	**Colors**-black,white	**Colors**-pink
Shapes-circle,square, rectangle,triangle	**Shapes**-circle,square, rectangle,triangle	**Shapes**-circle square, rectangle,triangle	**Shapes**-circle,square, rectangle,triangle
Number Order	**Number Order**	**Number Order**	**Number Order**
Before and After	**Before and After**	**Before and After**	**Before and After**
Ordinal Numbers-to 9th	**Ordinal Numbers**-to 9th	**Ordinal Numbers**-to 9th	**Ordinal Numbers**-to 9th
Problem Solving	**Problem Solving**	**Problem Solving**	**Problem Solving**
	Number Words-to nine	**Number Words**-to nine	**Number Words**-to nine
	Addition-to 9	**Addition**-to 10 and multiples of 10	**Addition**-to 10 and multiples of 10
		Subtraction-to 9	**Subtraction**-to 10
		Place Value	**Place Value**
		Time/Calendar	**Time/Calendar**
			Money
			Skip Counting-2's, 5's, 10's
			Greater/ Less than

Mathematics LIFEPAC Overview

	Grade 1	Grade 2	Grade 3
LIFEPAC 1	**NUMBERS TO 99** • Number order, skip-count • Add, subtract to 9 • Story problems • Measurements, shapes	**NUMBERS TO 100** • Numbers and words to 100 • Operation symbols +, −, =, >, < • Add, subtract, story problems • Place value, fact families	**NUMBERS TO 999** • Digits, place value to 999 • Add, subtract, time • LInear measurements, dozen • Operation symbols +, −, =, ≠, >, <
LIFEPAC 2	**NUMBERS TO 99** • Add, subtract to 10 • Number words • Place value, shapes • Patterns, sequencing, estimation	**NUMBERS TO 200** • Numbers and words to 200 • Add, subtract, even and odd • Skip-count 2's, 5's, 10's, shapes • Ordinal numbers, fractions, money	**NUMBERS TO 999** • Fact families, patterns, fractions • Add, subtract - carry, borrow • Skip count 2's, 5's, 10's • Money, shapes, lines, even, odd
LIFEPAC 3	**NUMBERS TO 100** • Number sentences, • Fractions, oral directions • Story problems • Time, symbols =, ≠	**NUMBERS TO 200** • Add w/ carry to 10's place • Subtract, standard measurements • Flat shapes, money, AM/PM • Rounding to 10's place	**NUMBERS TO 999** • Add 3 numbers w/ carry • Coins, weight, volume, AM/PM • Fractions, oral instructions • Skip count 3's, subtract w/ borrow
LIFEPAC 4	**NUMBERS TO 100** • Add to 18, place value • Skip-count, even and odd • Money • Shapes, measurement	**NUMBERS TO 999** • Numbers and words to 999 • Add, subtract, place value • Calendar, making change • Measurements, solid shapes	**NUMBERS TO 9,999** • Place value to 9,999 • Rounding to 10's, estimation • Add and subtract fractions • Roman numerals, 1/4 inch
LIFEPAC 5	**NUMBERS TO 100** • Add 3 numbers - 1 digit • Ordinal numbers, fractions • Time, number line • Estimation, charts	**NUMBERS TO 999** • Data and bar graphs, shapes • Add, subtract to 100's • Skip-count 3's, place value to 100's • Add fractions, temperature	**NUMBERS TO 9,999** • Number sentences, temperature • Rounding to 100's, estimation • Perimeter, square inch • Bar graph, symmetry, even/odd rules
LIFEPAC 6	**NUMBERS TO 100** • Number words to 99 • Add 2 numbers - 2 digit • Symbols >, < • Fractions, shapes	**NUMBERS TO 999** • Measurements, perimeter • Time, money • Subtract w/ borrow from 10's place • Add, subtract fractions	**NUMBERS TO 9,999** • Add, subtract to 9,999 • Multiples, times facts for 2 • Area, equivalent fractions, money • Line graph, segments, angles
LIFEPAC 7	**NUMBERS TO 200** • Number order, place value • Subtract to 12 • Operation signs • Estimation, graphs, time	**NUMBERS TO 999** • Add w/ carry to 100's place • Fractions as words • Number order in books • Rounding and estimation	**NUMBERS TO 9,999** • Times facts for 5, missing numbers • Mixed numbers - add, subtract • Subtract with 0's in minuend • Circle graph, probability
LIFEPAC 8	**NUMBERS TO 200** • Addition, subtract to 18 • Group counting • Fractions, shapes • Time, measurements	**NUMBERS TO 999** • Add, subtract, measurements • Group count, 'think' answers • Convert coins, length, width • Directions-N, S, E, W	**NUMBERS TO 9,999** • Times facts for 3, 10 - multiples of 4 • Convert units of measurement • Decimals, directions, length, width • Picture graph, missing addend
LIFEPAC 9	**NUMBERS TO 200** • Add 3 numbers - 2 digit • Fact families • Sensible answers • Subtract 2 numbers - 2 digit	**NUMBERS TO 999** • Area and square measurement • Add 3 numbers - 20 digit w/ carry • Add coins and convert to cents • Fractions, quarter-inch	**NUMBERS TO 9,999** • Add, subtract whole numbers, fractions, mixed numbers • Standard measurements, metrics • Operation symbols, times facts for 4
LIFEPAC 10	**NUMBERS TO 200** • Add, subtract, place value • Directions - N, S, E, W • Fractions • Patterns	**NUMBERS TO 999** • Rules for even and odd • Round numbers to 100's place • Time - digital, sensible answers • Add 3 numbers - 3 digit	**NUMBERS TO 9,999** • Add, subtract, times facts 2,3,4,5,10 • Rounding to 1,000's, estimation • Probability, equations, parentheses • Perimeter, area

Grade 4	Grade 5	Grade 6	
WHOLE NUMBERS & FRACTIONS • Naming whole numbers • Naming fractions • Sequencing patterns • Numbers to 1,000	**WHOLE NUMBERS & FRACTIONS** • Operations & symbols • Fraction language • Grouping, patterns, sequencing • Rounding & estimation	**WHOLES, FRACTIONS, DECIMALS** • Numbers to billions, number order • Whole number operations, symbols • Add, subtract fractions, decimals • Equations, missing number problems	LIFEPAC 1
WHOLE NUMBERS & FRACTIONS • Operation symbols • Multiplication - 1 digit multiplier • Fractions - addition & subtraction • Numbers to 10,000	**WHOLE NUMBERS & FRACTIONS** • Multiplication & division • Fractions - +, −, simplify • Plane & solid shapes • Symbol language	**WHOLES, FRACTIONS, DECIMALS** • Estimation, patterns - even and odd • Prime factors, exponential notation • Fractions, decimals - add, subtract, convert, write in number order	LIFEPAC 2
WHOLE NUMBERS & FRACTIONS • Multiplication with carrying • Rounding & estimation • Sequencing fractions • Numbers to 100,000	**WHOLE NUMBERS & FRACTIONS** • Short division • Lowest common multiple • Perimeter & area • Properties of addition	**WHOLES, FRACTIONS, DECIMALS** • Rounding, average, symbols $\geq$, $\leq$ • Ratios, patterns in addition • Geometric symbols, plane shapes • Multiply fractions, decimals	LIFEPAC 3
LINES & SHAPES • Plane & solid shapes • Lines & line segments • Addition & subtraction • Multiplication with carrying	**WHOLE NUMBERS** • Lines - shapes - circles • Symmetric - congruent - similar • Decimal place value • Properties of multiplication	**WHOLES, FRACTIONS, DECIMALS** • Divide fractions, decimals • Perimeter, area, distance, amount • Simplify standard measurements • Brackets, order of operations	LIFEPAC 4
WHOLE NUMBERS • Division - 1 digit divisor • Families of facts • Standard measurements • Number grouping	**WHOLE NUMBERS & FRACTIONS** • Multiply & divide by 10, 100, 1,000 • Standard measurements • Rate problems • Whole number & fraction operations	**WHOLES, FRACTIONS, DECIMALS** • Large numbers, calculators, statistics • Metric units, Roman numerals • Circle (pi), solid shapes, volume • Patterns in multiplication	LIFEPAC 5
WHOLE NUMBERS & FRACTIONS • Division - 1 digit with remainder • Factors & multiples • Fractions - improper & mixed • Equivalent fractions	**FRACTIONS & DECIMALS** • Multiplication of fractions • Reading decimal numbers • Adding & subtracting decimals • Multiplication - decimals	**FRACTIONS, DECIMALS, PERCENT** • Variables, function tables • Divisibility rules, circle - area • Metric units, square and cubic units • Percent - convert fraction, decimal	LIFEPAC 6
WHOLE NUMBERS & FRACTIONS • Multiplication - 2 digit multiplier • Simplifying fractions • Averages • Decimals in money problems	**WHOLE NUMBERS & FRACTIONS** • Division - 2-digit divisor • Metric units • Multiplication - mixed numbers • Multiplication - decimals	**WHOLES, PERCENT** • Properties - addition, multiplication • Integers, coordinate graph • Time zones, square root, polygons • Percent as a mixed number	LIFEPAC 7
WHOLE NUMBERS & FRACTIONS • Division - 1 digit division • Fractions - unlike denominators • Metric units • Whole numbers - +, −, x, ÷	**WHOLE NUMBERS** • Calculators & whole numbers • Calculators & decimals • Estimation • Prime factors	**PROBABILITY, METRICS, GRAPHS** • Problem solving - data, probability, norm, random selection, sample • Convert metric and standard units • Graphs - bar, line, circle, picture	LIFEPAC 8
DECIMALS & FRACTIONS • Reading and writing decimals • Mixed numbers - +, − • Cross multiplication • Estimation	**FRACTIONS & DECIMALS** • Division - fractions • Division - decimals • Ratios & ordered pairs • Converting fractions to decimals	**WHOLES, FRACTIONS** • Relate whole number to integer, fraction to decimal, ratio, percent • Calculators, perfect square • Symbols, measurements, shapes	LIFEPAC 9
PROBLEM SOLVING • Estimation & data gathering • Charts & Graphs • Review numbers to 100,000 • Whole numbers - +, −, x, ÷	**PROBLEM SOLVING** • Probability & data gathering • Charts & graphs • Review numbers to 100 million • Fractions & decimals - +, −, x, ÷	**WHOLES, FRACTIONS** • Mental arithmetic, number lines • Division w/ 3-digit divisor • Variables, missing numbers • Short cuts in multiplication	LIFEPAC 10

Mathematics LIFEPAC Overview

	Grade 7	Grade 8	Grade 9
LIFEPAC 1	**WHOLE NUMBERS** • Number concepts • Addition • Subtraction • Applications	**WHOLE NUMBERS** • The set of whole numbers • Graphs • Operations with whole numbers • Applications with whole numbers	**VARIABLES AND NUMBERS** • Variables • Distributive Property • Definition of signed numbers • Signed number operations
LIFEPAC 2	**MULTIPLICATION AND DIVISION** • Multiplication and division facts • Properties • Exponents • Weights and measures	**NUMBERS AND FACTORS** • Numbers and bases • Sets • Factors and multiples • Least common multiples	**SOLVING EQUATIONS** • Sentences and formulas • Properties • Solving equations • Solving inequalities
LIFEPAC 3	**GEOMETRY** • Segments, lines, and angles • Triangles • Quadrilaterals • Circles and hexagons	**RATIONAL NUMBERS** • Proper and improper fractions • Mixed numbers • Decimal fractions • Per cent	**PROBLEM ANALYSIS AND SOLUTION** • Words and symbols • Simple verbal problems • Medium verbal problems • Challenging verbal problems
LIFEPAC 4	**RATIONAL NUMBERS** • Common fractions • Improper fractions • Mixed numbers • Decimal fractions	**FRACTIONS AND ROUNDING** • Common fraction addition • Common fraction subtraction • Decimal fractions • Rounding numbers	**POLYNOMIALS** • Addition of polynomials • Subtraction of polynomials • Multiplication of polynomials • Division of polynomials
LIFEPAC 5	**SETS AND NUMBERS** • Set concepts and operations • Early number systems • Decimal number system • Factors and multiples	**FRACTIONS AND PER CENT** • Multiplication of fractions • Division of fractions • Fractions as per cents • Per cent exercises	**ALGEBRAIC FACTORS** • Greatest common factor • Binomial factors • Complete factorization • Word problems
LIFEPAC 6	**FRACTIONS** • Like denominators • Unlike denominators • Decimal fractions • Equivalents	**STATISTICS, GRAPHS, & PROBABILITY** • Statistical measures • Types of graphs • Simple probability • And–Or statements	**ALGEBRAIC FRACTIONS** • Operations with fractions • Solving equations • Solving inequalities • Solving word problems
LIFEPAC 7	**FRACTIONS** • Common fractions • Decimal fractions • Per cent • Word problems	**INTEGERS** • Basic concepts • Addition and subtraction • Multiplication and division • Expressions and sentences	**RADICAL EXPRESSIONS** • Rational and irrational numbers • Operations with radicals • Irrational roots • Radical equations
LIFEPAC 8	**FORMULAS AND RATIOS** • Writing formulas • A function machine • Equations • Ratios and proportions	**FORMULAS AND GEOMETRY** • Square root • Perimeter, circumference, and area • Rectangular solid • Cylinder, cone, and sphere	**GRAPHING** • Equations of two variables • Graphing lines • Graphing inequalities • Equations of lines
LIFEPAC 9	**DATA, STATISTICS AND GRAPHS** • Gathering and organizing data • Central tendency and dispersion • Graphs of statistics • Graphs of points	**ALGEBRAIC EQUATIONS** • Variables in formulas • Addition and subtraction • Multiplication and division • Problem solving	**SYSTEMS** • Graphical solution • Algebraic solutions • Determinants • Word problems
LIFEPAC 10	**MATHEMATICS IN SPORTS** • Whole numbers • Geometry, sets, and systems • Fractions • Formulas, ratios, and statistics	**NUMBERS, FRACTIONS, ALGEBRA** • Whole numbers and fractions • Fractions and per cent • Statistics, graphs and probability • Integers and algebra	**QUADRATIC EQUATIONS AND REVIEW** • Solving quadratic equations • Equations and inequalities • Polynomials and factors • Radicals and graphing

Grade 10	Grade 11	Grade 12	
A MATHEMATICAL SYSTEM • Points, lines, and planes • Definition of definitions • Geometric terms • Postulates and theorems	SETS, STRUCTURE, AND FUNCTION • Properties and operations of sets • Axioms and applications • Relations and functions • Algebraic expressions	RELATIONS AND FUNCTIONS • Relations and functions • Rules of correspondence • Notation of functions • Types of functions	LIFEPAC 1
PROOFS • Logic • Reasoning • Two-column proof • Paragraph proof	NUMBERS, SENTENCES, & PROBLEMS • Order and absolute value • Sums and products • Algebraic sentences • Number and motion problems	SPECIAL FUNCTIONS • Linear functions • Second-degree functions • Polynomial functions • Other functions	LIFEPAC 2
ANGLES AND PARALLELS • Definitions and measurement • Relationships and theorems • Properties of parallels • Parallels and polygons	LINEAR EQUATIONS & INEQUALITIES • Graphs • Equations • Systems of equations • Inequalities	TRIGONOMETRIC FUNCTIONS • Definition • Evaluation of functions • Trigonometric tables • Special angles	LIFEPAC 3
CONGRUENCY • Congruent triangles • Corresponding parts • Inequalities • Quadrilaterals	POLYNOMIALS • Multiplying polynomials • Factoring • Operations with polynomials • Variations	CIRCULAR FUNCTIONS & GRAPHS • Circular functions & special angles • Graphs of sin and cos • Amplitude and period • Phase shifts	LIFEPAC 4
SIMILAR POLYGONS • Ratios and proportions • Definition of similarity • Similar polygons and triangles • Right triangle geometry	RADICAL EXPRESSIONS • Multiplying and dividing fractions • Adding and subtracting fractions • Equations with fractions • Applications of fractions	IDENTITIES AND FUNCTIONS • Reciprocal relations • Pythagorean relations • Trigonometric identities • Sum and difference formulas	LIFEPAC 5
CIRCLES • Circles and spheres • Tangents, arcs, and chords • Special angles in circles • Special segments in circles	REAL NUMBERS • Rational and irrational numbers • Laws of Radicals • Quadratic equations • Quadratic formula	TRIGONOMETRIC FUNCTIONS • Trigonometric functions • Law of cosines • Law of sines • Applied problems	LIFEPAC 6
CONSTRUCTION AND LOCUS • Basic constructions • Triangles and circles • Polygons • Locus meaning and use	QUADRATIC RELATIONS & SYSTEMS • Distance formulas • Conic sections • Systems of equations • Application of conic sections	TRIGONOMETRIC FUNCTIONS • Inverse functions • Graphing polar coordinates • Converting polar coordinates • Graphing polar equations	LIFEPAC 7
AREA AND VOLUME • Area of polygons • Area of circles • Surface area of solids • Volume of solids	EXPONENTIAL FUNCTIONS • Exponents • Exponential equations • Logarithmic functions • Matrices	QUADRATIC EQUATIONS • Conic sections • Circle and ellipse • Parabola and hyperbola • Transformations	LIFEPAC 8
COORDINATE GEOMETRY • Ordered pairs • Distance • Lines • Coordinate proofs	COUNTING PRINCIPLES • Progressions • Permutations • Combinations • Probability	PROBABILITY • Random experiments & probability • Permutations • Combinations • Applied problems	LIFEPAC 9
REVIEW • Proof and angles • Polygons and circles • Construction and measurement • Coordinate geometry	REVIEW • Integers and open sentences • Graphs and polynomials • Fractions and quadratics • Exponential functions	CALCULUS • Mathematical induction • Functions and limits • Slopes of functions • Review of 1200 mathematics	LIFEPAC 10

LIFEPAC

MANAGEMENT

STRUCTURE OF THE LIFEPAC CURRICULUM

The LIFEPAC curriculum is conveniently structured to provide one teacher handbook containing teacher support material with answer keys and ten student worktexts for each subject at grade levels two through twelve. The worktext format of the LIFEPACs allows the student to read the textual information and complete workbook activities all in the same booklet. The easy to follow LIFEPAC numbering system lists the grade as the first number(s) and the last two digits as the number of the series. For example, the Language Arts LIFEPAC at the 6th grade level, 5th book in the series would be LAN0605.

Each LIFEPAC is divided into 3 to 5 sections and begins with an introduction or overview of the booklet as well as a series of specific learning objectives to give a purpose to the study of the LIFEPAC. The introduction and objectives are followed by a vocabulary section which may be found at the beginning of each section at the lower levels, at the beginning of the LIFEPAC in the middle grades, or in the glossary at the high school level. Vocabulary words are used to develop word recognition and should not be confused with the spelling words introduced later in the LIFEPAC. The student should learn all vocabulary words before working the LIFEPAC sections to improve comprehension, retention, and reading skills.

Each activity or written assignment has a number for easy identification, such as 1.1. The first number corresponds to the LIFEPAC section and the number to the right of the decimal is the number of the activity.

Teacher checkpoints, which are essential to maintain quality learning, are found at various locations throughout the LIFEPAC. The teacher should check 1) neatness of work and penmanship, 2) quality of understanding (tested with a short oral quiz), 3) thoroughness of answers (complete sentences and paragraphs, correct spelling, etc.), 4) completion of activities (no blank spaces), and 5) accuracy of answers as compared to the answer key (all answers correct).

The self test questions are also number coded for easy reference. For example, 2.015 means that this is the 15th question in the self test of Section II. The first number corresponds to the LIFEPAC section, the zero indicates that it is a self test question, and the number to the right of the zero the question number.

The LIFEPAC test is packaged at the centerfold of each LIFEPAC. It should be removed and put aside before giving the booklet to the student for study.

Answer and test keys have the same numbering system as the LIFEPACs and appear at the back of this handbook. The student may be given access to the answer keys (not the test keys) under teacher supervision so that he can score his own work.

A thorough study of the Curriculum Overview by the teacher before instruction begins is essential to the success of the student. The teacher should become familiar with expected skill mastery and understand how these grade level skills fit into the overall skill development of the curriculum. The teacher should also preview the objectives that appear at the beginning of each LIFEPAC for additional preparation and planning.

TEST SCORING and GRADING

Answer keys and test keys give examples of correct answers. They convey the idea, but the student may use many ways to express a correct answer. The teacher should check for the essence of the answer, not for the exact wording. Many questions are high level and require thinking and creativity on the part of the student. Each answer should be scored based on whether or not the main idea written by the student matches the model example. "Any Order" or "Either Order" in a key indicates that no particular order is necessary to be correct.

Most self tests and LIFEPAC tests at the lower elementary levels are scored at 1 point per answer; however, the upper levels may have a point system awarding 2 to 5 points for various answers or questions. Further, the total test points will vary; they may not always equal 100 points. They may be 78, 85, 100, 105, etc.

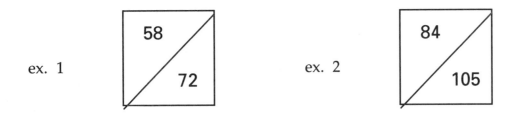

ex. 1   58 / 72   ex. 2   84 / 105

A score box similar to ex.1 above is located at the end of each self test and on the front of the LIFEPAC test. The bottom score, 72, represents the total number of points possible on the test. The upper score, 58, represents the number of points your student will need to receive an 80% or passing grade. If you wish to establish the exact percentage that your student has achieved, find the total points of his correct answers and divide it by the bottom number (in this case 72.) For example, if your student has a point total of 65, divide 65 by 72 for a grade of 90%. Referring to ex. 2, on a test with a total of 105 possible points, the student would have to receive a minimum of 84 correct points for an 80% or passing grade. If your student has received 93 points, simply divide the 93 by 105 for a percentage grade of 89%. Students who receive a score below 80% should review the LIFEPAC and retest using the appropriate Alternate Test found in the Teacher's Guide.

The following is a guideline to assign letter grades for completed LIFEPACs based on a maximum total score of 100 points.

LIFEPAC Test = 60% of the Total Score (or percent grade)
Self Test   = 25% of the Total Score (average percent of self tests)
Reports   = 10% or 10* points per LIFEPAC
Oral Work   = 5% or 5* points per LIFEPAC
*Determined by the teacher's subjective evaluation of the student's daily work.

Example:

LIFEPAC Test Score	=	92%	92	x	.60	=	55 points
Self Test Average	=	90%	90	x	.25	=	23 points
Reports						=	8 points
Oral Work						=	4 points

_____

TOTAL POINTS	=	90 points

Grade Scale based on point system:

100	–	94	=	A
93	–	86	=	B
85	–	77	=	C
76	–	70	=	D
Below		70	=	F

TEACHER HINTS and STUDYING TECHNIQUES

LIFEPAC Activities are written to check the level of understanding of the preceding text. The student may look back to the text as necessary to complete these activities; however, a student should never attempt to do the activities without reading (studying) the text first. Self tests and LIFEPAC tests are never open book tests.

Language arts activities (skill integration) often appear within other subject curriculum. The purpose is to give the student an opportunity to test his skill mastery outside of the context in which it was presented.

Writing complete answers (paragraphs) to some questions is an integral part of the LIFEPAC Curriculum in all subjects. This builds communication and organization skills, increases understanding and retention of ideas, and helps enforce good penmanship. Complete sentences should be encouraged for this type of activity. Obviously, single words or phrases do not meet the intent of the activity, since multiple lines are given for the response.

Review is essential to student success. Time invested in review where review is suggested will be time saved in correcting errors later. Self tests, unlike the section activities, are closed book. This procedure helps to identify weaknesses before they become too great to overcome. Certain objectives from self tests are cumulative and test previous sections; therefore, good preparation for a self test must include all material studied up to that testing point.

The following procedure checklist has been found to be successful in developing good study habits in the LIFEPAC curriculum.

1. Read the introduction and Table of Contents.
2. Read the objectives.
3. Recite and study the entire vocabulary (glossary) list.
4. Study each section as follows:
    a. Read the introduction and study the section objectives.
    b. Read all the text for the entire section, but answer none of the activities.
    c. Return to the beginning of the section and memorize each vocabulary word and definition.
    d. Reread the section, complete the activities, check the answers with the answer key, correct all errors, and have the teacher check.
    e. Read the self test but do not answer the questions.
    f. Go to the beginning of the first section and reread the text and answers to the activities up to the self test you have not yet done.
    g. Answer the questions to the self test without looking back.
    h. Have the self test checked by the teacher.
    i. Correct the self test and have the teacher check the corrections.
    j. Repeat steps a–i for each section.

5. Use the SQ3R* method to prepare for the LIFEPAC test.
6. Take the LIFEPAC test as a closed book test.
7. LIFEPAC tests are administered and scored under direct teacher supervision. Students who receive scores below 80% should review the LIFEPAC using the SQ3R* study method and take the Alternate Test located in the Teacher Handbook. The final test grade may be the grade on the Alternate Test or an average of the grades from the original LIFEPAC test and the Alternate Test.

   *SQ3R: Scan the whole LIFEPAC.
   Question yourself on the objectives.
   Read the whole LIFEPAC again.
   Recite through an oral examination.
   Review weak areas.

GOAL SETTING and SCHEDULES

Each school must develop its own schedule, because no single set of procedures will fit every situation. The following is an example of a daily schedule that includes the five LIFEPAC subjects as well as time slotted for special activities.

Possible Daily Schedule

8:15	–	8:25	Pledges, prayer, songs, devotions, etc.
8:25	–	9:10	Bible
9:10	–	9:55	Language Arts
9:55	–	10:15	Recess (juice break)
10:15	–	11:00	Mathematics
11:00	–	11:45	Social Studies
11:45	–	12:30	Lunch, recess, quiet time
12:30	–	1:15	Science
1:15	–		Drill, remedial work, enrichment*

*Enrichment: Computer time, physical education, field trips, fun reading, games and puzzles, family business, hobbies, resource persons, guests, crafts, creative work, electives, music appreciation, projects.

Basically, two factors need to be considered when assigning work to a student in the LIFEPAC curriculum.

The first is time. An average of 45 minutes should be devoted to each subject, each day. Remember, this is only an average. Because of extenuating circumstances a student may spend only 15 minutes on a subject one day and the next day spend 90 minutes on the same subject.

The second factor is the number of pages to be worked in each subject. A single LIFEPAC is designed to take 3 to 4 weeks to complete. Allowing about 3-4 days for LIFEPAC introduction, review, and tests, the student has approximately 15 days to complete the LIFEPAC pages. Simply take the number of pages in the LIFEPAC, divide it by 15 and you will have the number of pages that must be completed on a daily basis to keep the student on schedule. For example, a LIFEPAC containing 45 pages will require 3 completed pages per day. Again, this is only an average. While working a 45 page LIFEPAC, the student may complete only 1 page the first day if the text has a lot of activities or reports, but go on to complete 5 pages the next day.

Long range planning requires some organization. Because the traditional school year originates in the early fall of one year and continues to late spring of the following year, a calendar should be devised that covers this period of time. Approximate beginning and completion dates can be noted on the calendar as well as special occasions such as holidays, vacations and birthdays. Since each LIFEPAC takes 3-4 weeks or eighteen days to complete, it should take about 180 school days to finish a set of ten LIFEPACs. Starting at the beginning school date, mark off eighteen school days on the calendar and that will become the targeted completion date for the first LIFEPAC. Continue marking the calendar until you have established dates for the remaining nine LIFEPACs making adjustments for previously noted holidays and vacations. If all five subjects are being used, the ten established target dates should be the same for the LIFEPACs in each subject.

FORMS

The sample weekly lesson plan and student grading sheet forms are included in this section as teacher support materials and may be duplicated at the convenience of the teacher.

The student grading sheet is provided for those who desire to follow the suggested guidelines for assignment of letter grades found on page 3 of this section. The student's self test scores should be posted as percentage grades. When the LIFEPAC is completed the teacher should average the self test grades, multiply the average by .25 and post the points in the box marked self test points. The LIFEPAC percentage grade should be multiplied by .60 and posted. Next, the teacher should award and post points for written reports and oral work. A report may be any type of written work assigned to the student whether it is a LIFEPAC or additional learning activity. Oral work includes the student's ability to respond orally to questions which may or may not be related to LIFEPAC activities or any type of oral report assigned by the teacher. The points may then be totaled and a final grade entered along with the date that the LIFEPAC was completed.

The Student Record Book which was specifically designed for use with the Alpha Omega curriculum provides space to record weekly progress for one student over a nine week period as well as a place to post self test and LIFEPAC scores. The Student Record Books are available through the current Alpha Omega catalog; however, unlike the enclosed forms these books are not for duplication and should be purchased in sets of four to cover a full academic year.

WEEKLY LESSON PLANNER

Week of:

	Subject	Subject	Subject	Subject
Monday				
Tuesday				
Wednesday				
Thursday				
Friday				

WEEKLY LESSON PLANNER

Week of:

	Subject	Subject	Subject	Subject
Monday				
	Subject	Subject	Subject	Subject
Tuesday				
	Subject	Subject	Subject	Subject
Wednesday				
	Subject	Subject	Subject	Subject
Thursday				
	Subject	Subject	Subject	Subject
Friday				

Student Name _____   Year _____

Bible

LP #	Self Test Scores by Sections					Self Test Points	LIFEPAC Test	Oral Points	Report Points	Final Grade	Date
	1	2	3	4	5						
01											
02											
03											
04											
05											
06											
07											
08											
09											
10											

History & Geography

LP #	Self Test Scores by Sections					Self Test Points	LIFEPAC Test	Oral Points	Report Points	Final Grade	Date
	1	2	3	4	5						
01											
02											
03											
04											
05											
06											
07											
08											
09											
10											

Language Arts

LP #	Self Test Scores by Sections					Self Test Points	LIFEPAC Test	Oral Points	Report Points	Final Grade	Date
	1	2	3	4	5						
01											
02											
03											
04											
05											
06											
07											
08											
09											
10											

Student Name _____   Year _____

Mathematics

| LP # | Self Test Scores by Sections | | | | | Self Test Points | LIFEPAC Test | Oral Points | Report Points | Final Grade | Date |
	1	2	3	4	5						
01											
02											
03											
04											
05											
06											
07											
08											
09											
10											

Science

| LP # | Self Test Scores by Sections | | | | | Self Test Points | LIFEPAC Test | Oral Points | Report Points | Final Grade | Date |
	1	2	3	4	5						
01											
02											
03											
04											
05											
06											
07											
08											
09											
10											

Spelling/Electives

| LP # | Self Test Scores by Sections | | | | | Self Test Points | LIFEPAC Test | Oral Points | Report Points | Final Grade | Date |
	1	2	3	4	5						
01											
02											
03											
04											
05											
06											
07											
08											
09											
10											

**N
O
T
E
S**

INSTRUCTIONS FOR SIXTH GRADE MATHEMATICS

The LIFEPAC curriculum from grades two through twelve is structured so that the daily instructional material is written directly into the LIFEPACs. The student is encouraged to read and follow this instructional material in order to develop independent study habits. The teacher should introduce the LIFEPAC to the student, set a required completion schedule, complete teacher checks, be available for questions regarding both content and procedures, administer and grade tests, and develop additional learning activities as desired. Teachers working with several students may schedule their time so that students are assigned to a quiet work activity when it is necessary to spend instructional time with one particular student.

Mathematics is a subject that requires skill mastery. But skill mastery needs to be applied toward active student involvement. Measurements require measuring cups, rulers, empty containers. Boxes and other similar items help the study of solid shapes. Construction paper, beads, buttons, beans are readily available and can be used for counting, base ten, fractions, sets, grouping, and sequencing. Students should be presented with problem situations and be given the opportunity to find their solutions.

Any workbook assignment that can be supported by a real world experience will enhance the student's ability for problem solving. There is an infinite challenge for the teacher to provide a meaningful environment for the study of mathematics. It is a subject that requires constant assessment of student progress. Do not leave the study of mathematics in the classroom.

The Teacher Notes section of the Teacher's Guide lists the required or suggested materials for the LIFEPACs and provides additional learning activities for the students. Additional learning activities provide opportunities for problem solving, encourage the student's interest in learning and may be used as a reward for good study habits.

MATHEMATICS TERMS

acute angle   An angle that is less than a right angle or less than 90 degrees.

addend   A number to be added in an addition problem.

angle   The distance between two rays or line segments with a common end point.

arc   A curved section (line segment) of the perimeter of a circle.

area   The measurement of a flat surface.   A = l x w (rectangle) A = πr² (circle) A = $\frac{1}{2}$ b x h (triangle)

associative property   No matter how numbers are grouped in addition and multiplication, the answer is always the same.

average   The total of a group divided by the number in the group.

bar graph   A graph that uses bars to show data.

base   The part of a geometric figure on which the figure rests.
The number used as a factor in exponential notation.

brackets   Signs used to enclose digits and symbols. []

cancelling   Simplifying a problem in multiplication or division of fractions within the problem.

cardinal numbers   Numbers used for counting. 1, 2, 3, 4.....

Celsius   Metric unit of measurement for temperature. Freezing 0° C., Boiling 100 °C.

chart   An arrangement of data in a logical order.

chord   A straight line (line segment) drawn between two points on a circle.

circle   A continuous closed line always the same distance from a center point.

circle graph   A circular graph that always represents the whole of the data.

circumference   The distance around (perimeter) a circle.   C = 2πr   or C = πd

common denominator   Fractions must have the same or common denominator to be added or subtracted.

commutative property   No matter what order numbers are added or multiplied, the answer is always the same.

compass   An instrument having two hinged legs used for drawing circles, curved lines, and measuring distances.

composite number   A number that can be divided by 1, by itself, and other numbers.

concentric   Having the same center as in concentric circles.

congruent   Figures that have the same size and shape.

coordinate graph   A system of lines for positioning a fixed point using coordinate numbers or ordered pairs

cross multiplication   Multiplying the numerators and denominators of two fractions.

cube   A solid shape with six square faces.

cylinder   A round shape with flat ends.

data   A list of facts from which a conclusion may be drawn.

decimal number   A fraction with an understood denominator of 10, 100, 1,000...

decimal point   A dot separating the whole number from the fractional part of a decimal number.

degree   The unit of measurement for angles.

denominator   The bottom number of a fraction. This number represents the whole.

diagonal   A line segment connecting two vertices of a polygon that are not next to each other.

diameter   The distance across a circle straight through the middle.

difference The answer to a subtraction problem.

digit Symbols 0, 1, 2, 3, 4, 5 ,6, 7, 8, 9 which when used alone or in combinations represent a value.

distributive property The same product results in multiplication whether numbers are multiplied individually or as a set.

dividend The number being divided in a division problem.

divisibility rules Rules that determine whether a number can be divided evenly by 2, 3, 5, 6, and 9.

divisible Capable of being divided by.

division bar The line that separates the numerator from the denominator of a fraction.

divisor The number doing the dividing in a division problem.

end points Dots that show the beginning and end of a line segment.

equal to Has the same value as. equal = (not equal ≠)

equation A number sentence that contains an equal sign.

equilateral triangle A triangle whose sides are all equal in length.

equivalent fractions Two or more fractions of equal value. To make an equivalent fraction, multiply or divide the numerator and denominator by the same number.

estimate To find an approximate answer.

even number Any number divisible by two.

expanded form Expressing a number by showing the sum of the digits times the place value of each digit.

exponent The number that tells how many times a base number is used as a factor.

exponential notation Writing a number with a base and its exponent.

face The surfaces of a solid figure.

factor(s) Numbers which when multiplied together form a product or multiple.

Fahrenheit U.S. standard measurement for temperature. Freezing 32°F. Boiling 212°F.

fraction A number that represents all or part of a whole.

fraction bar Also called the division bar.

frequency distribution The number of times data falls within a particular classification.

function table A relationship between two sets of numbers when one number is associated with a single variable.

gram Metric unit of the measurement of weight.

graph A special kind of chart. The most common are bar, line, picture, and circle.

greater than Has larger value than. 2 > 1

greatest common factor The largest factor that can be divided into two numbers.

hexagon A six-sided polygon.

horizontal Level to or parallel to the horizon.

improper fraction A fraction that is greater than or equal to 1. The numerator is larger than or equal to the denominator.

input Data entered into a calculator (computer).

integers A set of positive and negative whole numbers.

International Date Line The 180th meridian. People who cross the line going west, gain a day. People who cross going east, lose a day.

intersecting lines Lines that cross each other.

inverse operations Opposite mathematics operations also known as fact families - addition and subtraction, multiplication and division.

invert   To turn around the positions of the numerator and denominator of a fraction.

isosceles triangle   A triangle that has two sides of equal length.

least common multiple   The smallest multiple that two numbers have in common.

legend   Explanation of symbols on a map or diagram.

less than   Has smaller value than. 1 < 2

light-year   A unit of length, about six trillion miles, used to measure astronomical distances.

line   A continuous set of dots that has no beginning and no end.

line graph   A graph that shows data by connecting points with lines.

line segment The part of a line that has a beginning and an end.

liter   Metric unit of liquid or dry measurement.

mean   The same as the average.

median   The number located exactly in the middle of a list of numbers.

meridian   A circle or half-circle passing through or to and from the earth's poles

meter   Metric unit of linear (line) measurement.

minuend   The number from which another number is being subtracted in a subtraction problem.

mixed number   A number that combines a whole number and a fraction.

mode   The number that appears most often in a list of numbers.

multiple   A multiple of a number is a product of that number.

multiplicand   The number being multiplied in a multiplication problem.

multiplier   The number doing the multiplying in a multiplication problem.

negative number   A number with a value less than zero.

norm   A standard for a particular group.

number line A line with even spaces used to represent certain values.

numeral   A figure that stands for or represents a number.

numerator   The top number of a fraction. This number represents the parts being described.

obtuse angle An angle greater than a right angle (90 degrees) but less than a straight line (180 degrees).

octagon   An eight-sided polygon.

odd number Any number that cannot be divided by two.

ordered pairs   Two numbers written in a particular order so that one can be considered the first number and the other the second number.

order of operations   In a multi-operation problem without parentheses or brackets, multiplication and division are completed first, addition and subtraction second

ordinal numbers   Numbers that show position. 1st, 2nd, 3rd, 4th.....

output   The answer to data entered into a calculator (computer).

oval   A flattened circle - egg shaped.

parallel lines   Lines that are always the same distance apart.

parallelogram   A quadrilateral with opposite sides equal.

parentheses A set of characters used to group operations. (7 + 6) x 2

pattern   A set arrangement or design of forms, colors or numbers.

pentagon   A five-sided polygon.

per cent   The relationship between a part and a whole. The whole is always 100.

perfect square   A number whose square root is an even number.

perimeter   The distance around the outside of a closed figure.

perpendicular lines   Lines that form right or 90 degree angles.

pi (π)   3.14   Used to solve for the circumference or area of a circle.

pictograph   A graph that uses pictures to represent data.

place value   The value of a digit determined by its position in a number.

plane shape   A flat shape. A plane shape is two-dimensional.

point of intersection   The one and only point that intersecting lines have in common.

polygon   A closed plane figure with three or more sides.

positive number   A number with a value greater than zero.

prediction   To tell something in advance.

prime factorization   Prime factors of a number expressed in exponential notation.

prime meridian   The meridian (0 degrees) that passes through Greenwich, England. Greenwich Time is the basis for setting standard time elsewhere. Noon is determined when the sun is directly over the prime meridian.

prime number   A number divisible by only 1 and itself.

prism   A solid figure whose bases have the same size and shape and are parallel to each other. Each of its sides is a parallelogram.

probability   The study of the likelihood of events.

product   The answer to a multiplication problem.

proper fraction   A fraction greater than 0 but less than 1. The numerator is smaller than the denominator.

property of zero   In addition, any number added to zero will have itself as an answer. In multiplication, any number multiplied by zero will have zero as an answer.

proportion   An equation stating that two ratios are equal.

protractor   A semi-circular instrument marked in degrees used to find the measure of an angle.

pyramid   A solid figure with a polygon as a base and triangular faces that meet at a point.

quadrilateral   A four-sided polygon.

quotient   The answer to a division problem.

radical sign   Used to express square root.

radius   The distance from the center of a circle to the edge of a circle. The radius is half of the diameter.

random sample   A sample in which every member of a large group has an equal chance of being chosen.

ratio   The relationship of two numbers to each other written 1:2 or $\frac{1}{2}$.

ray   A line with one end point.

reciprocal   The fraction that results from inverting a fraction.

rectangle   A four-sided polygon with four right angles.

rectangular solid   A solid figure with six rectangular faces.

reduced fraction   A fraction equivalent to another fraction that has been written in smaller numbers. This is also called simplifying a fraction or reducing to lowest terms.

reflection   Moving a plane shape to show a mirror image.

related operations   Mathematics operations showing that multiplication is repeated addition and division is repeated subtraction.

remainder   The amount that remains when a division problem has been completed.

repeated factor   In prime factorization, a prime factor that is used as a factor more than once.

repeating decima   A decimal in which the same number or series of numbers repeats itself indefinitely. $\frac{1}{3}$ = .333

rhombus A parallelogram with four equal sides.
right angle An angle that measures 90 degrees.
right triangle A triangle with one right angle.
Roman numerals The ancient Roman numeral system.
I = 1   V = 5   X = 10   L = 50   C = 100   D = 500   M = 1,000

rotation Moving a plane shape around its center or axis resulting in an inverse image
scale The size of a map compared to what it represents.
scalene triangle A triangle with no equal sides.
sequence Numbers arranged in a certain pattern.
similar Figures that have the same shape but not necessarily the same size.
solid shape A shape that takes up space. A solid shape is three-dimensional.
sphere A geometric solid in a round shape.
square A rectangle with all sides equal.
square root A number which when multiplied by itself produces a given number.
straight angle An angle that measures 180 degrees.
subtrahend The number being taken away or subtracted in a subtraction problem.
sum The answer to an addition problem.
symmetry Shapes with equal halves.
terminating decimal A decimal number that does not have a remainder.
translation Moving a plane shape by sliding from one point to another.
triangle A three-sided polygon.
variable A letter that represents a quantity in an algebraic expression.
vertex The point at which two rays or line segments meet.
vertical Straight up and down. Perpendicular to the horizon.
volume The measurement of space that a solid figure occupies. $V = l \times w \times h$
whole numbers Digits arranged to represent a value equal to or greater than a whole.

Metric Chart of Prefixes

smallest	_ milli _	- a unit contains 1,000
	__ centi __	- a unit contains 100
	___ deci ___	- a unit contains 10
	____ unit ____	- unit (meter, liter, gram)
	_____ deca _____	contains 10 units
	_____ hecto _____	contains 100 units
largest	_____ kilo _____	contains 1,000 units

···

English System of Weights and Measures

Length	Weight	Dry Measure	Liquid Measure
12 inches = 1 foot	16 ounces = 1 pound	2 cups = 1 pint	16 fl ounces = 1 pint
3 feet = 1 yard	2,000 lb. = 1 ton	2 pints = 1 quart	2 cups = 1 pint
36 inches = 1 yard		8 quarts = 1 peck	2 pints = 1 quart
5,280 ft. = 1 mile	**Square**	4 pecks = 1 bushel	4 quarts = 1 gallon
320 rods = 1 mile	144 sq. in. = 1 sq. ft		
	9 sq. ft. = 1 sq. yd.		**Cubic** (Volume)
	4,840 sq. yd. = 1 acre		1,728 cu. in. = 1 cu. ft.
	640 acres = 1 sq. mi.		27 cu. ft. = 1 cu. yd.

···

Time Measurement

60 seconds = 1 minute	60 minutes = 1 hour	24 hours = 1 day
30/31 days = 1 month	12 months = 1 year	365 days = 1 year
1 decade = 10 years	1 score = 20 years	1 century = 100 years
1 millennium = 1,000 years	6×10^{12} mi. = 1 light year	

···

Conversion Chart

To convert linear measure	To	Multiply by	To convert	To	Multiply by
centimeters	inches	.394	inches	centimeters	2.54
meters	yards	1.0936	yards	meters	.914
kilometers	miles	.62	miles	kilometers	1.609
liquid measure					
liters	quarts	1.057	quarts	liters	.946
dry measure					
liters	quarts	.908	quarts	liters	1.101
weight					
grams	ounces	.0353	ounces	grams	28.35
kilograms	pounds	2.2046	pounds	kilograms	.4536

INTRODUCTION OF SKILLS

Introduction of Skills is a quick reference guide for the teacher who may be looking for a rule or explanation that applies to a particular skill or to find where or when certain skills are introduced in the LIFEPACs. The first number after the skill identifies the LIFEPAC, and the second number identifies the section. 505/3 refers to LIFEPAC number ML505, Section 3.

average			603/1	604/4
base ten system	601/3	602/1, 2		
calculators				
using whole numbers				
decimals, fractions				
percent				
cardinal, ordinal numbers	601/1, 5		603/5	
composite, prime numbers	601/1, 5	602/1, 2, 3, 5	603/3	
decimals				
add, subtract	601/3	602/1, 4, 5	603/5	604/5
borrow to subtract		602/1		
convert to fractions	601/3	602/1, 5	603/2, 5	604/2
convert to percent				
divide				
by 10, 100, 1,000			603/4, 5	604/2
by a whole number			603/3	604/2, 5
by a decimal number				604/3, 5
equivalent	601/3, 5	602/1, 5	6032, 5	604/3
horizontal		602/4, 5		
multiply		602/4, 5	603/2	604/2, 5
by 10, 100, 1,000			603/4, 5	604/2, 3
read and write	601/3			
repeating, terminating				604/2
understood decimal point		602/1	603/4	604/2
written in number order	601/3, 5		603/2	
digits	601/1, 5		603/5	
divisibility rules				
equations	601/3	602/4	603/1	604/2
estimation				
add, subtract	601/4	602/3, 5	603/3	604/4
multiply, divide	601/4			604/4
fraction				
probability				
even, odd numbers	601/1, 5	602/3, 5	603/2	
expanded numbers				
exponential notation		602/2, 3	603/3, 4, 5	604/3
base factor, repeated factor		602/2, 5	603/3, 4	604/3
exponent		602/2	603/3, 4	
powers of ten		602/2	603/4	604/4, 5

605	606	607	608	609	610
605/4					
				609/1	
605/4		607/5		609/2	
				609/2	
605/5	606/5			609/5	
605/5	606/1, 2, 5			609/1, 5	
605/3	606/1, 2, 5	607/4	608/1, 2, 5	609/1, 5	
				609/1	
605/1	606/2, 3	607/2, 4, 5	608/4	609/1, 4	610/4
	606/3	607/2, 4, 5	608/4	609/1, 4	610/4
605/5		607/5		609/5	610/5
605/3	606/1, 5	607/4		609/5	
605/3	606/1, 5	607/4	608/4, 5	609/5	
605/4, 5	606/2, 3	607/5			
	606/1, 2, 5	607/4	608/3, 5	609/5	
605/5	606/1, 2			609/5	610/5
605/5	606/1		608/1		610/2, 5
605/1, 4	606/2, 3	607/2			
605/5				609/5	
605/4	606/2			609/1	
		607/1		609/1, 5	
	606/1, 2	607/3	608/5	609/5	610/3
	606/5	607/2	608/4		610/4
605/5				609/2	
605/5				609/2	
				609/2	
				609/2	
605/5	606/5		608/5	609/5	610/4
		607/1, 5	608/1		
	606/2, 5	607/1, 5	608/1	609/1	
			608/1	609/1	
			608/1	609/1	
605/1, 2			608/1	609/1	

fact families	601/2, 3, 4		
factors	601/1, 2, 5	602/1	603/1, 5
prime factors		602/1, 2, 3, 5	603/3, 4	604/3
factor boxes		602/1, 3, 5	603/3, 4	604/3
GCF (see fractions)			
fractions			
add/subtract w/ like,			
unlike denominators	601/2, 5	602/2, 3, 4, 5	603/3, 4	604/3, 5
borrow to subtract		602/4, 5		
compare for =, ≠, >, <			
w/ equivalent fractions				604/3
w/ cross multiplication		602/3	603/2, 5	604/3, 4
convert to decimals	601/3		603/3	604/2
convert to percent			
divide				604/1, 2, 5
checking				604/5
reciprocal				604/1, 2
equal to 1	601/2	602/4		
equivalent	601/2, 5	602/2, 5	603/2, 3, 5	604/3
GCF, LCM	601/2	602/2, 3, 5	603/1, 3	604/1, 3
multiply			603/1, 2, 5	604/1, 5
checking				604/5
simplify in the problem			603/1	604/1
times multi-digit number			
using the word 'of'			603/1	604/1, 5
part of whole or set		602/2		
proper, improper, mixed	601/2, 5	602/3, 4, 5		
numerator, denominator			
fraction bar	601/2		
read and write	601/2		603/2	
simplify	601/2, 5	602/2	603/1	
understood denominator		603/1	604/1	
write in number order	601/5	602/3, 5	603/2, 5	604/3
function tables			
geometry			
angles			
identifying			603/4	604/1, 3, 5
measuring				604/1, 3
vertex, vertices				604/1
circle			
identifying				604/1, 3
concentric			
congruent, similar			603/4	604/1
line segment, ray, end point			603/4	604/1, 5
lines			
identifying types of			603/4	604/1, 5

605	606	607	608	609	610
		607/1			
605/3, 5			608/3	609/1	
605/3, 5	606/2	607/3, 5	608/3	609/1, 5	
605/3, 5	606/2	607/3, 5	608/3	609/1, 5	
605/3	606/2, 5	607/3	608/1, 2, 5	609/1	610/2
				609/1	
				609/3	
605/1	606/2, 3	607/2	608/3	609/1, 4	610/4
	606/3	607/2, 3, 5	608/4	609/1, 4	610/4
605/3	606/2, 5	607/3	608/4, 5		610/2
605/5	606/2, 5				
605/3	606/2	607/3, 5	608/3	609/5	610/2
605/3	606/2, 5	607/3	608/3, 5		610/2
					610/2
			608/4		610/2
		607/2			610/2
605/3					
605/5			608/1		610/2, 5
605/3				609/1	
605/4	606/2, 5			609/1, 2	
	606/3	607/1, 5	608/1, 5	609/4, 5	610/3
605/1, 3, 5				609/2	610/5
605/3	606/4, 5			609/2	
605/1, 3, 5				609/2	
605/3	606/4		608/5	609/2	
	606/4		608/5	609/2, 5	
605/1, 2, 3	606/4	607/2		609/2, 3	
605/5				609/2	
605/5				609/2	610/5

605	606	607	608	609	610
Celsius		607/3, 5			
				609/2	
		607/3, 5	608/5	609/2	
605/3	606/3	607/3	608/5	609/2	610/5
					610/3
605/2	606/4	607/4		609/2	
605/2				609/2	610/5
605,5					
605/2, 5		6073, 5		609/2	610/5
605/4	606/5	607/5	608/2	609/5	610/4
		607/1, 2		609/4	
		607/2			
		607/2	608/1	609/4	
					610/3
	606/5	607/1, 5	608/3	609/3	610/4
		607/4		609/2	
605/2	606/5			609/2	
605/2	606/3	607/4			
		607/4		609/2	
		607/4			
605/2, 4		607/4			
605/5	606/3			609/3	
605/3, 5	606/3, 4	607/1, 3	608/5	609/3	610/4, 5
605/2					
		607/1, 3			
605/2	606/3	607/1, 3	608/5	609/3	610/4, 5
605/3, 5	606/3	607/3	608/5	609/3	
605/5	606/3			609/3	610/4, 5
	606/4	607/5	608/3		
	606/4	607/5	608/3	609/5	610/3
605/2	606/4	607/5	608/3	609/5	
			608/3		

	601	602	603	604
standard measurements				
add, subtract, multiply, divide				604/4
convert to metric				
convert to simplest terms				604/4
degrees and minutes				
directions - N, S, E, W				
Fahrenheit				
linear/square units		602/5	603/5	
to 16th inch				
scale drawings				
time, A.M., P.M., light year,				
24-hr. clk., time zones		602	603/5	
weight/volume		602/5	603/5	
mental arithmetic				
whole numbers, decimals				
fractions				
missing number problems	601/3, 5	602/4, 5	603/1	604/2, 3
fractions -				
w/ cross multiplication				604/4, 5
whole numbers -				
(see inverse operations)				
w/ two missing numbers				
w/ range of numbers				
multi-operation problems	601/3, 5	602/5	603/5	
order of operations				604/4
brackets				604/4
multiples	601/1, 4, 5	602/1, 2, 3, 4, 5	603/1, 2, 4	604/3
LCM (see fractions)				
number sentences	601/3, 5	602/4	603/2, 3	
patterns and sequence	601/2, 5		603,5	
percent				
definition				
solving problems				
as ratios,				
fractions, decimals				
using the word 'of'				
write in number order				
place value chart	601/1, 3			
problem solving				
data				
mean, median, mode				
prediction				
probability, norm				
random selection, sample				
properties of (patterns)				
addition			603/2	

multiplication

		607/4		609/5	610/3
			608/3		
605/5	606/4			609/5	610/3
	606/5				
	606/4				
			608/3		
605/2	606/4			609/5	
	606/4				
	606/4				
605/3, 5	606/5	607/5		609/3, 5	
	606/4			609/3, 5	
					610/1
					610/2
	606/3, 4, 5	607/3, 5	608/4	609/3	
605/1	606/4	607/3		609/3	610/4
	606/5			609/3	
					610/3
605/2, 4			608/5	609/3	
605/4				609/3	
605/2, 4	606/5			609/3	
	606/2	607/1, 5	608/1, 3	609/5	610/1
605/5	606/5			609/2	610/5
	606/3	607/4		609/1	
	606/5	607/2, 4		609/1	
	606/3	607/2, 4, 5	608/2, 4, 5	609/1, 4	610/4
					610/5
				609/1	
			608/2	609/4	
605/4		607/3		609/4	610/4
			608/2		610/4
			608/2, 5	609/4	610/4
			608/2	609/4	
		607/1, 2	608/1, 5		610/3
605/2		607/1, 2	608/1, 5		610/3

ratio, proportion				
equivalent to fraction,				
decimal, percent			603/4, 5	604/3, 4
simplifying			603/4	
write in number order				
related operations				
Roman, Arabic numerals				
rounding				
decimals			603/2	604/2, 3
mixed number fractions			603/3, 5	
money				
whole numbers	601/4, 5	602/3, 5	603/1, 3, 4	604/4
square root				
variables				
whole numbers				
add				
addend, sum	601/1, 5			
checking	601/3, 5			
problems	601/2		603/1, 5	604/5
divide				
by 10, 100, 1,000			603/4	
dividend, divisor, quotient	601/1, 5			
checking	601/4, 5			
1-digit divisor	601/1, 2	602/4		604/5
2-digit divisor	601/4	602/2	603/1, 3	604/5
3-digit divisor				
short division			603/1, 3, 5	
multiply				
by 10, 100, 1,000		602/1, 3, 4, 5	603/2, 4	
multiplicand, multiplier,				
product	601/1, 5			
checking	601/4, 5			
2-digit multiplier	601/1, 2	602/3	603/2	604/5
3-digit multiplier	601/4	602/3	603/2	
numbers to				
millions	601/1, 2			
billions	601/3	602/1, 4, 5	603/1, 4, 5	604/3
greater than billions				
subtract				
difference, minuend				
subtrahend	601/1, 5			
checking	601/3, 5			
problems	601/2	602/1, 5	603/5	604/5
zero				
as a multiple	601/1, 4	602/2		
as a place holder	601/1, 3, 5	602/1, 5		

605	606	607	608	609	610
	606/3, 4, 5	607/2, 4	608/4	609/1, 4	610/4
605/2					
				609/1	
		607/1	608/1, 5	609/5	610/1, 3
605/2, 5	606/5			609/5	
	606/1, 3		608/4	609/1, 5	
605/4	606/1		608/4	609/1, 5	
					610/2
605/1, 2			608/4	609/1, 5	610/1
		607/1	608/1	609/4	
	606/3, 5	607/1, 5	608/1, 4	609/3	610/3
605/5					
	606/5		608/1, 5	609/1, 5	610/1
605/5	606/4			609/5	610/5
605/5	606/1				
		607/1	608/4, 5	609/5	
605/2	606/1, 5	607/1	608/4, 5	609/5	
605/2	606/1, 5				
605/5	606/4			609/5	610/5
605/5					
	606/1, 5	607/2	608/3, 5	609/5	
	606/1, 5	607/2		609/5	
605/1, 2, 5				609/1, 5	
605/5					
	606/5		608/2, 5	609/1, 5	

ADDITIONAL ACTIVITIES

1.   Plan **regular drill** periods for **mathematics facts**. These should occasionally be timed. They may be either oral or written.

2.   **Manipulatives, hand-held objects,** are basic to developing a relationship between the written problem and an understanding by the child of the problem solution. Manipulatives are both appropriate and essential at all grade levels. A majority of the manipulatives used in problems may be developed from material already available in the classroom or home. Measurements require measuring cups, rulers, and empty containers. Boxes and other similar items help the study of solid shapes. Construction paper, beads, buttons, beans are readily available to use for counting, base ten, fractions, sets, grouping, sequencing and plane figures. **Manipulatives may extend to drawings.** For example, students may draw the shape of a polygon when solving for area or perimeter. Have the students use colored pencil or crayons to show the polygon's dimensions and flat surface. Then have them explain the logic of their answers.

3.   **Dictation** strengthens comprehension. Dictate problems with answers for students to write on paper. (Five plus six equals eleven or $5 + 6 = 11$.) This will help them to develop vocabulary and spelling of mathematics terms. Problems may be written numerically or in words.

4.   Keep a **log book of terms** with which the student is having difficulty. These may be identified from the *Introduction of Skills* or the *Mathematics Terms*. Quiz the student regularly until the term is mastered.

5.   An **oral arithmetic bee** can be held in which problems are given orally and must be solved mentally. Selected LIFEPAC pages may be used for this exercise. Teach grouping of numbers for easier problem solving as well as estimation in the same way.

6.   The student may create **number patterns** for others to solve.

When studying geometry,

7.   Create 2- and 3-dimensional figures out of construction paper or cardboard.

8.   Create figures that are congruent and/or similar. Form circles, squares, and rectangles from triangles. Try making octagons and pentagons from triangles, squares and rectangles. Cut figures into geometric shapes similar to a jigsaw puzzle and then put back together.

9.   Allow students to use the protractor and compass to develop individual designs.

10.   Use building blocks to show how many cubes in a rectangle and how many cubes in a rectangular solid with the same size base as the rectangle but different heights.

11.   Construct polygons with a given number of sides and use a protractor to measure the angles. Complete the following table. Use the information to develop a chart or graph. Develop a rule for a figure with N sides.

Number of Sides	3	4	5	6	7	8	N
The sum of the measure of all angles							

When studying measurements,

12. Use groups of coins to show what combination of coins may be worth a certain amount of money.

13. Using local newspaper advertisements, have students make a collage of the items they could buy if they had $100.00 to spend. Prices should be included on the clippings.

14. Have students fill containers and then use a combination of measurers such as cup, quarts, liters, tablespoons, and/or teaspoons to determine quantity.

15. Have the students measure their height, length of arms, legs and feet, the lengths around their heads, arms wrists and ankles. Either use metric measurements or English measurements and then convert them.

16. Have your student read Roman numerals on buildings, monuments and similar locations. Discuss when the events occurred in our history.

When studying ratios,

17. Measure the rooms of a building and then develop a scale drawing.

18. Use a ratio chart to enlarge or reduce the size of any picture. Draw the picture. (ML509)

19. Use a state map to determine the number of miles from one city to another. Develop a similar map using a different ratio or scale.

When studying statistics,

20. Gather data to form charts and graphs. Begin with gathering the data, then decide how the data could be most effectively presented. Choose between charts, bar and line graphs, picture graphs, and circle graphs. Suggestions for data collection would be number of people living in each home, students eye color, shoe size, height, weight, food preferences. Other suggestions would be weather patterns, classified ads, ratio of windows to doors in a home, car colors or styles, transportation schedules, food costs.

21. Provide a set of solid-color marbles. Put the marbles in a sack. Have the student take a random selection of marbles from the sack and count them. Find all the possible ratios between the marbles. Develop a chart of probabilities. Compare the ratios to the random selections. Use the random selection method to develop other data.

When studying calculators,

22. Select a group of appropriate problems from a LIFEPAC or supply the student with problems to be solved on a calculator. Calculator skills are necessary because they are both time saving and accurate but basic understanding of mathematics concepts is the ultimate goal of the classroom teacher.

To develop a unit study,

23. Tell your student that you are going to turn a part of the housekeeping duties over to him/her for a week. Provide an imitation check book, ledger book and other appropriate items. The student may set up a budget including purchasing of groceries, payment of household utilities, automobile requirements, and larger budget items. Food coupons, newspaper advertisements, unit prices, metric and standard measurements may all be compared for value. The student should participate in meal preparation to learn quantity measurement. Recipes may be cut in half or doubled to challenge the students use of fractions. A final report should be developed between the teacher and the student regarding the value of the assignment.

24.   LIFEPAC **word problems** often reflect everyday experiences of the student. If a problem relates to the distance, rate and time of travel when a family visits friends or relatives, develop a similar problem the next time an actual trip is taken. Use all possible opportunities to translate word problems into similar real experiences.

TESTS

Reproducible Tests
for use with the Mathematics
600 Teacher's Guide

MATHEMATICS 601: Alternate LIFEPAC TEST

Name _____

Date _____

Score _____

80 / 100

1. Write … (each answer, 1 point)

   a. the ten digits. _____

   b. why zero is used in a number. _____

2. Write commas in the numbers. Write the underlined part of the number in words. (this question, 4 points)

   a. 3 5 4 2 8 1 6 0 5 9 _____

   b. 8 6 7 9 5 2 8 3 0 1 5 _____

3. Circle the numbers … (each letter, 1 point)

   a. even.   4   17   35   32   b. odd.   3   25   54   70

   c. cardinal. 6th   21   33rd   46   d. ordinal.   8th   39   41   69th

   e. prime.   5   9   11   16   f. composite. 4   17   21   29

4. Circle the correct symbols. (each answer, 1 point)

   a. $8 \cdot 3$ (=, ≠) 6×4 $12 + 8$ (=, ≠) $3(10)$

   b. $\frac{56}{7}$ (>, <) $\frac{72}{8}$ $5\overline{)40}$ (>, <) $36 \div 9$

5. Write the missing symbols. (this question, 2 points)

   18 _____ 3 = 2 _____ 3   18 _____ 6 = 2 _____ 12

6. Write a fact family using the numbers 5, 8, and 13. (this question, 2 points)

   _____   _____   _____   _____

7. Write the answer. (each answer, 1 point)

   a. The addends are 26, 53, 75 and 32. What is the sum?   _____

   b. The minuend is 75. The subtrahend is 48. What is the difference?   _____

   c. The multiplicand is 28. The multiplier is 65. What is the product?   _____

   d. The dividend is 92. The divisor is 4. What is the quotient?   _____

8. Solve the problems. Check each answer. *Show work.* (this question, 8 points)

   a.   287   b.   8,031   c.   39   d.
           364   − 2,975   × 63   5)631
        + 529

   check:
      (a.)   (b.)   (c.)   (d.)

9. Solve. (each answer, 2 points)

   a.   4,839   b.   609   c.   d.
         × 45   × 314   31)659   49)928

10. Write the factors for each set of numbers. Circle the GCF. (each answer, 1 point)

    10 _____ and 15 _____

11. Write the largest multiple of 6 that is equal to or less than ... (this question, 2 points)

    38 _____   12 _____   61 _____   29 _____

12. Describe each number as ... (each answer, 1 point)
                       a. proper   b. improper   c. mixed number

    $\frac{5}{8}$ _____ $9\frac{1}{4}$ _____ $\frac{10}{3}$ _____

13. Write numbers in words or digits. (each answer, 1 point)
    a. $8\frac{2}{3}$ _____   thirteen-fifteenths _____
    b. $\frac{3}{5}$ _____   six and one- fourth _____

14. Write missing numbers. (each answer, 1 point)

    $\frac{3}{7} = \frac{}{14}$ $\frac{}{9} = \frac{10}{18}$ $\frac{}{24} = \frac{5}{6}$

15. Add or subtract. *Simplify answers.* (each answer, 1 point)

a.

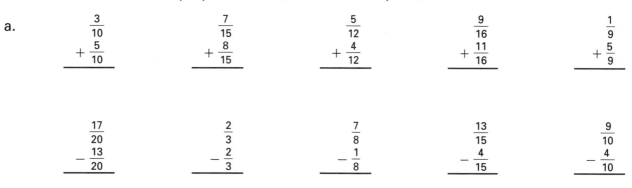

$$\begin{array}{r} \frac{3}{10} \\ +\frac{5}{10} \\ \hline \end{array} \qquad \begin{array}{r} \frac{7}{15} \\ +\frac{8}{15} \\ \hline \end{array} \qquad \begin{array}{r} \frac{5}{12} \\ +\frac{4}{12} \\ \hline \end{array} \qquad \begin{array}{r} \frac{9}{16} \\ +\frac{11}{16} \\ \hline \end{array} \qquad \begin{array}{r} \frac{1}{9} \\ +\frac{5}{9} \\ \hline \end{array}$$

$$\begin{array}{r} \frac{17}{20} \\ -\frac{13}{20} \\ \hline \end{array} \qquad \begin{array}{r} \frac{2}{3} \\ -\frac{2}{3} \\ \hline \end{array} \qquad \begin{array}{r} \frac{7}{8} \\ -\frac{1}{8} \\ \hline \end{array} \qquad \begin{array}{r} \frac{13}{15} \\ -\frac{4}{15} \\ \hline \end{array} \qquad \begin{array}{r} \frac{9}{10} \\ -\frac{4}{10} \\ \hline \end{array}$$

16. Write numbers in words. (each answer, 1 point)

a. 8.3 _____   .065 _____

b. .13 _____   .204 _____

17. Write equivalent decimals with a common denominator. Compare.
    Write the first set in number order. (each answer, 1 point)

.24   .3   .379   .186   .4

_____   _____   _____   _____   _____

_____   _____   _____   _____   _____

18. Solve. (each answer, 1 point)

a. $4.36 + .02 + 1.004 =$ _____ $.95 + .06 + .581 =$ _____ $82.5 + .63 + .09 =$ _____

b. $9.54 - 6.38 =$ _____ $8.49 - 1.763 =$ _____ $5.07 - 2.584 =$ _____

19. Round and estimate. Write the answer. (each answer, 2 points)

a. The youth group had received a donation of $615 for sports equipment.
   If they divided the money evenly between three sports that they sponsored,
   about how much money would each sport receive? _____

b. The second grade class was saving pennies for a charity donation.
   Over a 38 day period, they brought in an average of 293 pennies per day.
   About how many pennies did the class have after the 38 days? _____

c. Jason's family bought a new car that was priced at $22,975.
   The broker gave the family a discount of $1,925.
   About how much money did the family pay for the car? _____

20. Complete multi-operation problems. (each answer, 1 point)

a. $6 + (2 \times 4) + 9 =$ $(36 \div 9) + (36 \div 6) =$

b. $(5 \times 0) + (2 \times 4) + 8 =$ $18 \div (9 - 3) =$

21. Solve for missing numbers. *Prove.* (this question, 4 points)

a. $N + 36 = 81$ b. $N - 27 = 68$

Prove:

22. Write the next two numbers in the sequence. Explain the pattern. (this question, 2 points)

2, 4, 6, 12, 14, 28, _____ , _____

Explain.   _____

MATHEMATICS 602: Alternate LIFEPAC TEST

Name _____

Date _____

Score _____

80 / 100

1. Write in words. (this question, 1 point)

   47,306,210,435 _____

   _____

2. Circle the correct symbols. Circle the equation. (this question, 4 points)

   7 + 0 (>, <) 7 × 0   7 + 8 (=, ≠) 3 × 5   12 ÷ 4 (=, ≠) 8 ÷ 2   3 × 6 (>, <) 4 × 5

3. Solve. (each answer, 1 point)

   25,000   409   631
   − 18,635   × 58   × 297   4)‾837‾   37)‾5,831‾

4. Round to one billions' place. Drop the zeros. Find the total. (each answer, 1 point)

   32,817,369,104 _____   21,953,004,281 _____   10,318,635,472 _____

   _____ billions + _____ billions + _____ billions = _____ billions

5. Write the understood decimal point in each of
   the whole numbers. (this question, 2 points)   629,536   11   520   4,103

6. Describe the pattern. Write (E) even or (O) odd. (each answer, 1 point)

   E + E = ____   O + O = ____   E + O = ____   E − E = ____   O − O = ____   O − E = ____

7. Simplify. (each answer, 1 point)

   $\frac{15}{20}$ = $\frac{9}{9}$ = $\frac{14}{3}$ =

8. Write a fraction equal
   to 1 with a denominator
   of 6. (this question, 1 point)   _____

9. Express numbers as fractions. (each answer, 1 point)

   a. Adam divided the banana
      into 3 parts.
      He gave 1 part to his friend. _____

   b. Adam had 3 bananas.
      He gave 1 to his friend.   _____

55

10. Solve. Simplify. (each answer, 1 point)

a.
$$7\frac{3}{8}$$
$$+\ 6$$
_____

$$9$$
$$+\ 3\frac{2}{5}$$
_____

$$6\frac{1}{4}$$
$$-\ 4$$
_____

$$\frac{1}{6}$$
$$+\ \frac{3}{8}$$
_____

$$\frac{3}{4}$$
$$+\ \frac{7}{12}$$
_____

b.
$$6\frac{1}{3}$$
$$+\ 4\frac{1}{2}$$
_____

$$8\frac{7}{8}$$
$$+\ 4\frac{1}{4}$$
_____

$$11$$
$$-\ \frac{5}{6}$$
_____

$$7\frac{1}{5}$$
$$-\ \frac{2}{5}$$
_____

$$13\frac{3}{8}$$
$$-\ 11\frac{5}{8}$$
_____

$$8\frac{1}{3}$$
$$-\ 2\frac{5}{9}$$
_____

11. Change to equivalent fractions. Write the original set in number order.
(this question, a. 4 points & b. 1 point)

a. $\frac{7}{10} =$ _____ $\frac{3}{4} =$ _____ $\frac{4}{5} =$ _____ $\frac{13}{20} =$ _____

b. _____   _____   _____   _____

12. Match equivalent numbers from each of the three columns. (this question, 9 points)

a. five tenths _____ _____ _____   .05 $\frac{5}{100}$ .0050

b. five hundredths _____ _____ _____   .5 $\frac{5}{10}$ .50

c. five thousandths _____ _____ _____   .005 $\frac{5}{1,000}$ .050

13. Solve. (each answer, 1 point)

a. $9 + 4.6 + .038 =$ $6.43 + 5.18 + .831 =$ $.128 - .05 =$

b. $5.8 - 3.94 =$ $.36 \times .05 =$ $2.7 \times 8.3 =$

14. (a. and b. each 1 point)

a. Write the factors of 20.   b. Write six multiples of 8.

_____   ___ ___ ___ ___ ___ ___

15. Solve multi-operation problems. (each answer, 1 point)

$47 - (7 \times 6) =$ _____ $(26 - 5) \div 3 =$ _____ $(14 \times 2) + 5 =$ _____ $36 + (9 \times 4) =$ _____

56

16. Write ... (each answer, 1 point)

    in words. $6 + 8 \neq 3 \times 5$ _____

    in digits and operation symbols.
              Five times four is less than five times five.   _____

17. Solve missing number problems. (this question, 8 points)

    $N + 38 = 71$ $283 = N + 109$ $N - 49 = 86$ $112 = N - 289$

    Prove.

18. Write the answers. (each answer, 1 point)

    a. _____ ounces = 1 pound _____ square inches = 1 square foot _____ months = 1 year

    b. _____ units = 1 dozen   _____ years = 1 score   _____ quarts = 1 gallon

    c. How many ...
       inches in 4 feet? _____   pints in 3 quarts? _____   weeks in 63 days? _____

    d. Joseph left the house at 11:03 A.M. and returned at 12:18 P.M.
       How many minutes was Joseph gone from the house?   _____

19. Fill in the blanks for each set of prime factors. (each answer, 1 point)

Base Factor(s)	Exponent(s)	Exponential Notation	Product
$2 \times 2 \times 3 \times 3$ _____	_____	_____	_____

20. Fill in the blanks for each number written in exponential notation. (each answer, 1 point)

	Number Words	Repeated Factor	Product
a. 2^5	_____	_____	_____
b. 10^2	_____	_____	_____

21. Find the prime factors of 108. (this question, 2 points)
    Express your answer in exponential notation.

                          Prime factors
                          of 108 are ...

                          _____ $\times$ _____

MATHEMATICS 603: Alternate LIFEPAC TEST

80 / 100

Name _____

Date _____

Score _____

1. Write decimals in number order. (this question, 1 point)

   .4   .2   .8   .3   .7   _____ _____ _____ _____ _____

2. Write equivalent decimals. Write the first set in number order. (this question, 5 points)

   .6 _____   .37 _____   .504 _____   .63 _____   .4 _____   _____ _____ _____ _____ _____

3. Write in words. (this question, 1 point)

   5.043 _____

4. Solve. (each answer, 1 point)

   a. $2.09 + .847 =$ _____   b. $9.5 - 2.67 =$ _____   c. $.09 \times .430 =$ _____

5. The number is 2^4. (each answer, 1 point))

   a. The base factor is _____.   b. The exponent is _____.   c. The repeated factor is _____.

   d. The product is _____.   e. Write the expression in words. _____

6. Use the factor boxes to find the prime factors. Write the prime factors in exponential notation. (this question, 6 points)

   15   factors

   _____

   18   factors

   _____

7. Find the LCM of 15 and 18 using prime factors. (this question, 2 points)

   Write the prime factors of the numbers. $15 =$ _____ $18 =$ _____

   Select the highest power of each factor.   _____

   Multiply the selected factors.   _____ $\times$ _____ $\times$ _____ $=$ _____

8. Circle the equations. (this question, 2 points)

   $8 \times 12 = 96$ $\frac{36}{6} = 24$ $7 \cdot 5 = 42$ $5^2 = 25$

9. Solve multi-operation problems. (this question, 4 points)

$(12 - 4) \times 6 = N$ $\quad$ $27 - (3 \cdot 5) = N$ $\quad$ $(12 - 3) + (16 - 10) = N$ $\quad$ $(5 \times 9) - (18 \div 3) = N$

$\qquad = N$ $\qquad\qquad = N$ $\qquad\qquad\qquad = N$ $\qquad\qquad\qquad = N$

10. Solve missing number problems. Prove. (this question, 4 points)

$N \times 7 = 112$ $\qquad\qquad\qquad\qquad$ $N \div 9 = 13$

$\qquad N =$ $\qquad\qquad\qquad\qquad\qquad$ $N =$

Prove.

11. Compare. Use cross multiplication.
(this question, 2 points)

$\frac{2}{4}$ (>, =, <) $\frac{6}{12}$ $\qquad$ $\frac{6}{9}$ (>, =, <) $\frac{3}{5}$

12. Convert fractions to decimals and round to the hundredth's place. (this question, 2 points)

$\frac{2}{9} =$ $\qquad\qquad$ $\frac{3}{5} =$

13. Write in words. (this question, 1 point) $\quad 7\frac{2}{3}$ _____

14. Write equivalent fractions. Write the first set in number order. (this question, 5 points)

$\frac{5}{8}$ _____ $\qquad$ $\frac{3}{4}$ _____ $\qquad$ $\frac{1}{2}$ _____ $\qquad$ $\frac{9}{16}$ _____ $\qquad$ _____ _____ _____ _____

15. A bag of candy has 12 pieces. 2 are orange, 4 are lemon, and 6 are grape.
(this question, 6 points)

   a. Write each flavor as a ratio simplified. $\qquad$ orange _____ lemon _____ grape _____

   b. Another bag has 18 pieces in the same ratio.
   Write the number of each flavor. $\qquad$ orange _____ lemon _____ grape _____

16. Solve. Simplify. (each answer, 1 point)

$\begin{array}{r} 6\frac{5}{8} \\ + 4\frac{7}{12} \\ \hline \end{array}$ $\qquad$ $\begin{array}{r} 8 \\ - 3\frac{5}{9} \\ \hline \end{array}$ $\qquad$ $20 \times 3\frac{3}{4} =$ $\qquad$ $2\frac{3}{8} \times 24 =$ $\qquad$ $\frac{14}{25} \times \frac{15}{28} =$

$\frac{9}{10} \times 3\frac{1}{3} =$ $\qquad\qquad$ $6\frac{2}{3} \times \frac{3}{4} =$ $\qquad\qquad$ $9\frac{1}{3} \times 4\frac{1}{2} =$

17. Match. (each answer, 1 point)

_____ a. ray   1. line AB

_____ b. vertical   2. a line parallel to the horizon

_____ c. $\overleftrightarrow{AB}$ 3. congruent to

_____ d. ⊥   4. line segment AB

_____ e. ≅   5. perpendicular to

_____ f. angle   6. identical in form, different in size

_____ g. horizontal   7. distance between two rays with a common end point

_____ h. ∥   8. a line with one end point

_____ i. similar   9. a line straight up and down

_____ j. $\overline{AB}$ 10. parallel to

(Name) _____

18. Complete the line graph.
(this question, 5 points)

Number of Drinks Sold at the Game
    Sodas 45   Coffee 32
    Water 10   Shakes 25
    Lemonade 18   Slurpies 28

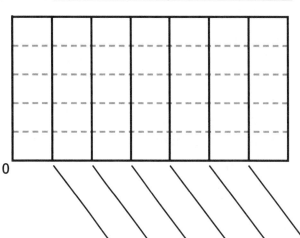

19. Use patterns of addition to simply problem solving. Rewrite and add.
(2 points each, a. and b.)

a. 25 + 0 + 12 + 15 = _____ = _____   b. 7 + 14 + 0 + 56 = _____ = _____

20. How many ... (each answer, 1 point)

feet in 48 inches? _____   weeks in 2 years? _____   pints in 8 quarts? _____

        decades in 60 years? _____   tons in 4,000 lb. _____

21. Find the average of 7, 15, and 26. (this question, 1 point)   _____

22. Multiply or divide. (each answer, 1 point)

100 × 50 = _____   10 × 5.08 = _____   86 ÷ 100 = _____   37.4 ÷ 1,000 = _____

23. Divide. Use short division for 1-digit divisors.
    Round answers to the nearest whole number. (each problem, 2 points)

    9)615   4)807   39)587   67)839

24. Write a number sentence for ... (1 point each, a. and b.)

 a. the set of numbers that are *equal to*
    or *less than* 18 but *greater than* 15.   18 ≥ _____ > 15

 b. the set of odd numbers that are *equal to*
    or *greater than* 21 but *less than* 27.   21 ≤ _____ < 27

25. (each answer, 1 point)
    Round to ten billions' place.   846,275,390,488 _____

    Describe the number ...   in words. _____

                                  in powers of ten. _____

26. Round to thousands' place. Add or subtract. Compare. (2 points each, a. and b.)

 a.   7,138   b.   5,105
        + 6,942   + _____   − 1,936   − _____
        ─────────   ─────────

MATHEMATICS 604: Alternate LIFEPAC TEST

Name_____

Date _____

Score _____

$\dfrac{80}{100}$

1. Solve. (each answer, 2 points)

.9 2.53 + .467	9.2 − 4.63	69.5 × .08	.803 × .71

2. Solve. (each answer, 1 point)

$100 \times 4.1 =$ _____ $1{,}000 \times 3.62 =$ _____ $8.7 \div 10 =$ _____ $.91 \div 100 =$ _____

3. Divide. Round answers to the nearest decimal place. (each answer, 2 points)

$8\overline{)4.39}$ $5\overline{).451}$ $.06\overline{).583}$ $.9\overline{)18.37}$

4. Change to a common denominator. Compare.
Write the original set in number order. (this question, 4 points)

$.5 =$ _____ $.52 =$ _____ $.35 =$ _____ $.513 =$ _____

_____   _____   _____   _____

5. Solve. Simplify. (each answer, 2 points)

a. $\dfrac{3}{8}$ $4\dfrac{5}{6}$ $9\dfrac{7}{12}$ $7\dfrac{2}{5}$
$+\dfrac{7}{10}$ $+5\dfrac{3}{4}$ $-2\dfrac{3}{8}$ $-4\dfrac{9}{10}$

b. $\dfrac{5}{6} \times \dfrac{9}{25} =$ $7\dfrac{1}{3} \times 4\dfrac{1}{2} =$ $4\dfrac{1}{8} \div 11 =$ $6\dfrac{1}{4} \div 2\dfrac{1}{2} =$

63

6. Change to a common denominator. Compare.
   Write the original set in number order. (this question, 4 points)

   $\frac{7}{9} =$ _____ $\frac{5}{6} =$ _____ $\frac{1}{2} =$ _____ $\frac{2}{3} =$ _____

   _____   _____   _____   _____

7. Convert fractions to decimals.   a. $\frac{7}{8} =$ _____   b. $\frac{2}{3} =$ _____
   Divide until numbers terminate or repeat.
   Write repeating decimals with a bar over
   the repeating numbers.
   (each lettered answer, 2 points)

8. Use cross multiplication ... (each answer, 1 point)

   a. to compare.   b. to find the missing numbers.

   $\frac{3}{8}$ (>, =, <) $\frac{1}{8}$ $\frac{4}{10}$ (>, =, <) $\frac{6}{15}$ $\frac{N}{6} = \frac{3}{9}$ $\frac{2}{8} = \frac{3}{N}$

   $N =$ _____ $N =$ _____

9. Write the value of the number. (each answer, 1 point)

   4^2 _____ 2^4 _____ 3^3 _____ 7^2 _____

10. Find the prime factors.
    Write in exponential notation.
    (this question, 4 points)

    Prime Factors of 12 _____

    Prime Factors of 16 _____

11. Find the GCF of 12 and 16. (each answer, 1 point)

    Write the prime factors of the numbers.   12 = _____   16 = _____

    Select the factors *common* to both numbers.   _____

    Multiply the factors. The GCF of 12 and 16 is ...   _____

12. Identify each triangle as ... (each answer, 1 point)

(E) equilateral, (I) isosceles, or (S) scalene.

a. _____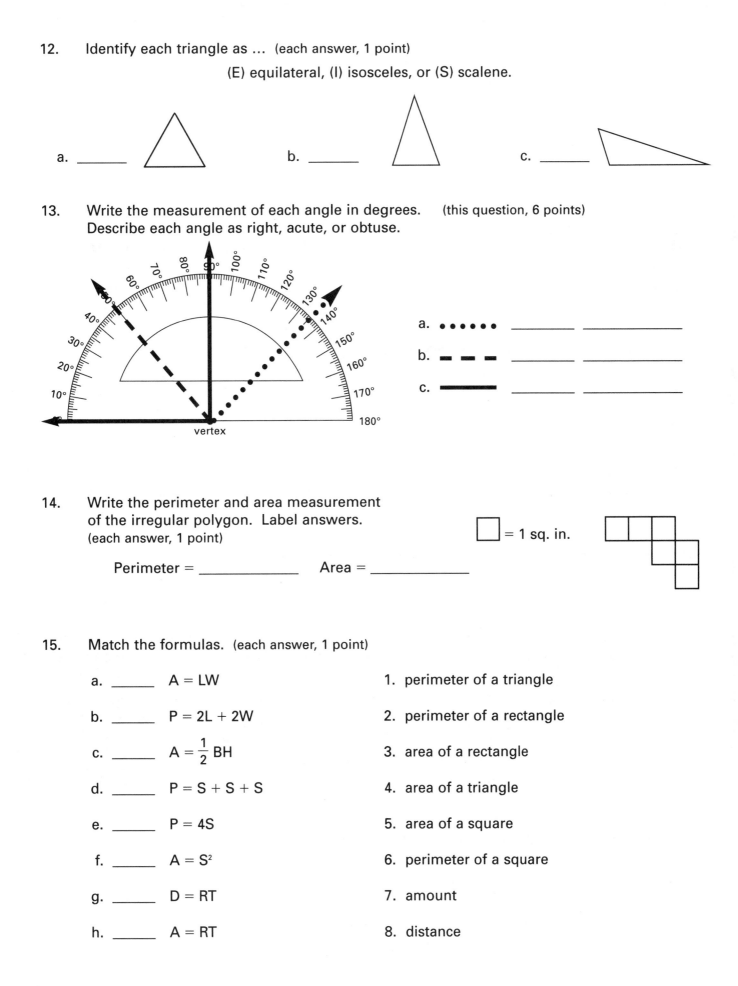

b. _____

c. _____

13. Write the measurement of each angle in degrees. (this question, 6 points)
    Describe each angle as right, acute, or obtuse.

vertex

a. • • • • • • _____ _____

b. – – – – _____ _____

c. ▬▬▬▬ _____ _____

14. Write the perimeter and area measurement
    of the irregular polygon. Label answers.
    (each answer, 1 point)

    ☐ = 1 sq. in.

    Perimeter = _____   Area = _____

15. Match the formulas. (each answer, 1 point)

    a. _____ A = LW   1. perimeter of a triangle

    b. _____ P = 2L + 2W   2. perimeter of a rectangle

    c. _____ A = $\frac{1}{2}$ BH 3. area of a rectangle

    d. _____ P = S + S + S   4. area of a triangle

    e. _____ P = 4S   5. area of a square

    f. _____ A = S^2 6. perimeter of a square

    g. _____ D = RT   7. amount

    h. _____ A = RT   8. distance

65

16. Find the missing numbers. Use the formulas from the previous problem. *Label answers.*
(each answer, 1 point)

a. Base = 6 ft.   Height = 4 ft.   Area = _____

b. Rate = 48 mph   Time = 5 hr.   Distance = _____

c. Area = 48 sq. in.   Length = 8 in.   Width = _____

17. Solve multi-operation problems using ... (each answer, 1 point)

a. brackets and parentheses.   b. order of operation

$3 \times [18 - (2 \times 5)] =$ $[(6 + 8) \div 7] \times 9 =$ $5 + 21 \div 3 - 6 =$ $8 \times 2 - 13 + 24 \div 6 =$

18. The ratio of dimes to quarters is 2:3.
Write the missing number of coins, given the following information:
(each answer, 1 point)

a. 8 dimes _____.   15 quarters _____.

19. Cross out the numbers that do not belong in the set. Write in correct order.
(each answer, 1 point)

the set of odd numbers that are
equal to or less than 15 but $15 \geq 18$ 13   17   11   14   15 > 9
greater than 9

_____

20. Add and simplify.   21. Subtract.   22. Simplify.
(this question, 2 points)   (this question, 1 point)   (this question, 1 point)

   8 hr. 25 min.   6 ft. 3 in.
+ 6 hr. 38 min.   − 2 ft. 7 in. $4 \overline{) 8 \text{ lb. 5 oz.}}$

23. Find the actual and estimated totals. Check by comparing. (this question, 2 points)

The school was raising money   Mark counted the   actual   estimated
pennies collected by the 3rd, 4th, 5th, and 6th grades.
He counted 318, 295, 172, and 211 pennies.   _____   _____

MATHEMATICS 605: Alternate LIFEPAC TEST

Name _____

Date _____

Score _____

80/100

> You will need a calculator for question 5 only.

billion 9   trillion 12   quadrillion 15   quintillion 18   sextillion 21   septillion 24

1. Write each number in digits using the correct number of zeros. (each answer, 1 point)
   (*Remember to use commas to separate the periods (thousands, millions, ...)*

   a. 832×10^{15} _____

   b. 431 quintillion _____

2. Round the number to its largest period. (each answer, 1 point)

   a. Write it in exponential notation using powers of 10.   354,921,683 _____

   b. Drop the zeros. Write in digits and words.   241,387,506,119 _____

3. What unit of measure is used for the vast distances of space?
   (this question, 1 point) _____

4. Complete each problem. Then, check the problem using the opposite operation.
   (this question, 8 points)

   a.   34
         62
       + 19
      _____

   b.   508
       − 369
      _____

   c.   82
       × 56
      _____

   d.   7)‾3‾0‾1‾

5. Complete these problems using a calculator. (each answer, 1 point)

   a. $429 + 63 + 218 =$ _____ $327 \times 490 =$ _____ $11.7 - 4.38 =$ _____

   b. $17.28 \div 5.4 =$ _____ $7\frac{3}{4} - 2\frac{5}{8} =$ _____ $4\frac{3}{5} \times 5\frac{1}{2} =$ _____

6. Match the rule to the problem. (each answer, 1 point)

_____ a. Multiplying by zero (0) results in an answer of zero.   1. $(2 \times 4) \times 6 = 2 \times (4 \times 6)$

_____ b. Multiplying by one (1) does not change the number.   2. $5 \times 4 = 4 \times 5$

_____ c. Changing the order of numbers does not change the answer.   3. $54 \times 1 = 54$

_____ d. Changing the grouping of numbers does not change the answer.   4. $36 \times 0 = 0$

_____ e. When applied to addition, changing the grouping of numbers   5. $(3 \times 5) + (3 \times 4) = 3(5 + 4)$
        does not change the answer.

7. Convert to Arabic or Roman numerals. (each answer, 1 point)

a. LXIX _____   b. MCCV _____   c. 26 _____   d. 519 _____

8. Write the decimal equivalents. (each answer, 1 point)

a. $\frac{1}{2} =$ _____ $\frac{1}{4} =$ _____ $\frac{3}{4} =$ _____ $\frac{2}{5} =$ _____ $\frac{4}{5} =$ _____

b. $\frac{1}{8} =$ _____ $\frac{3}{8} =$ _____ $\frac{5}{8} =$ _____ $\frac{1}{3} =$ _____ $\frac{1}{6} =$ _____

9. Match. (each answer, 1 point)

_____ a. chord   1. used to solve for the circumference of a circle

_____ b. circle   2. the distance between two rays with a common end point

_____ c. vertex   3. identical in size and shape

_____ d. arc   4. perimeter of a circle

_____ e. angle   5. curved section of the perimeter of a circle

_____ f. congruent   6. straight line joining two points on a circle

_____ g. circumference   7. the point at which two rays meet

_____ h. pi   8. continuous closed line always the same distance from a center point

10. (each answer, 1 point)
Write the formula and solve for the
circumference of a circle with a diameter of 7 in.

formula = _____

circumference = _____

11. Find the perimeter and area
of the irregular polygon.
(this question, 4 points)

perimeter = _____

area = _____

2 in. ↑

4 in. →

← 8 in.

5 in. ↓

68

12. Shade the bases. Choose from (R) *rectangular*, (S) *square* or (T) *triangular* and (Py) *pyramid* or (PR) *prism* to name the shapes. (this question, 8 points)

a. _____ _____   b. _____ _____   c. _____ _____   d. _____ _____

13. Write the formula and solve for the volume of a rectangular prism measuring: length 6 ft., width 3 ft., height 5 ft. (each answer, 1 point)

formula = _____

volume = _____

14. Write the formula and solve for the volume of a square prism measuring: 2 yd. each side. (each answer, 1 point)

formula = _____

volume = _____

15. Draw a reflection of the shape. Then, combine into a single shape. (this question, 6 points) Describe the new shape that you have made. Reflect so that ...

    a. $\overline{AC}$ is the line of symmetry.   b. $\overline{BC}$ is the line of symmetry.   c. $\overline{AB}$ is the line of symmetry.

B _____ C

A

_____   _____   _____

16. Match. (each answer, 1 point)

_____ a. median   1. has the same meaning as average

_____ b. mode   2. the number located exactly in the middle of a group of numbers

_____ c. mean   3. the number that appears most often in a group of numbers

17. The numbers are: 15 3 12 10 2 15 6 Find the ...

a. median _____   b. mode _____   c. mean _____

69

18. Answer questions about the metric system (SI). (each answer, 1 point)

a. How do we describe the number pattern that we use? _____

          What number is the metric system based on? _____

b. Write the names of the basic units in the metric system for ...

       length _____ , liquid and dry units _____ , weight _____ .

c. Each metric unit has standard prefixes. Which prefix represents the ...

       smallest unit of measure? _____   largest unit of measure? _____

d. What English Standard is similar in size to the ...

          meter? _____   liter? _____   gram? _____

e. To change a meter to centimeters, multiply by _____ ; to kilometers, divide by _____ .

19. Complete a circle graph about a Lincoln Penny collection.
(this question, 12 points)

a. Write a ratio comparing the number of coins by year to the total number of coins.
Reduce the ratios to simplest terms. Convert to a common denominator.

    1950 – 2   1951 – 4   1952 – 8   1953 – 4   1954 – 6

    _____   _____   _____   _____   _____

b. Based on the common denominator, how many
parts should the circle graph be divided into? _____

c. Write how many parts for each year.
Complete the graph.
Select a color for each box.
Color graph.

☐	1950	_____
☐	1951	_____
☐	1952	_____
☐	1953	_____
☐	1954	_____

MATHEMATICS 606: Alternate LIFEPAC TEST

Name _____

Date _____

Score _____

80 / 100

1. Solve. *Note:* Division answers should be rounded to nearest whole number or decimal place. (each answer, 1 point)

   a.
   $$\begin{array}{r} 750 \\ 291 \\ 536 \\ + 178 \\ \hline \end{array}$$
   $$\begin{array}{r} 9{,}000 \\ - 2{,}746 \\ \hline \end{array}$$
   $$\begin{array}{r} 389 \\ \times 75 \\ \hline \end{array}$$
   $$7\overline{)586}$$
   $$49\overline{)887}$$

   b.
   $$\begin{array}{r} 6.048 \\ + 3.86 \\ \hline \end{array}$$
   $$\begin{array}{r} 8.7 \\ - 2.84 \\ \hline \end{array}$$
   $$\begin{array}{r} .513 \\ - .08 \\ \hline \end{array}$$
   $$6\overline{).077}$$
   $$5.2\overline{).156}$$

   c.
   $$\begin{array}{r} 9\frac{5}{6} \\ + 4\frac{3}{8} \\ \hline \end{array}$$
   $$\begin{array}{r} 14 \\ - 6\frac{2}{3} \\ \hline \end{array}$$
   $$7\frac{1}{5} \times 3\frac{3}{4} =$$
   $$16 \div 3\frac{5}{9} =$$
   $$2\frac{5}{8} \div 5\frac{1}{4} =$$

2. Complete the rules of divisibility by writing the missing words or number. (each answer, 1 point)

   a. Any number that ends in …

   _____ is divisible by 2.   _____ is divisible by 5.   _____ is divisible by 10.

   b. Any number whose digits …

   _____ is divisible by 3.   _____ is divisible by 9.

   _____ is divisible by 6.

3. Write the prime factors of each number two times.   (this question, 4 points)
   In the first group, circle the factors to multiply for the LCM. Write the LCM.
   In the second group, circle the factors to multiply for the GCF. Write the GCF.

	PF		PF	LCM		PF		PF	GCF
6		10			6		10		
12		16			12		16		

4. A letter that stands for a missing number is called a _____. (this answer, 1 point)

5. Find the missing number using opposite operations or cross multiplication.
   (each answer, 1 point)

   a. $x + 39 = 84$ b. $y \div 8 = 13$ c. $\dfrac{n}{6} = \dfrac{6}{9}$ d. $\dfrac{4}{8} = \dfrac{5}{c}$

6. Complete the function tables using inverse operations. The variable is $x = 4$.
   (each answer, 1 point)

add	5		3		subtract
x		9		15	x

multiply	4		7		divide
x		24		32	x

7. Measure. (each answer, 1 point)

   ├───────┤   _____

   ├───────────────┤   _____

8. Write the measurement as a fraction and as a decimal. (each answer, 1 point)

   ├───────┤   _____ _____

9. Write the missing numbers. (640, 27, 144, 9) (each answer, 1 point)

   _____ sq. in. = 1 sq. ft.   _____ sq. ft. = 1 yd.   _____ acres = 1 sq. mi.   _____ cu. ft. = 1 cu. yd.

10. The scale on a map reads $\frac{1}{2}$ in. = 1 mi.
    What are 3 inches on a map equal to?
    (this question, 1 point)   _____ miles

11. If one side of each angle is
    on 0°, what is the measure
    of the angle that is marked   a? _____   b? _____
    (each answer, 1 point)

mm - millimeter	cm - centimeter	dm - decimeter	m - meter	km - kilometer
mL - milliliter	cL- centiliter	dL - deciliter	L - liter	kL - kiloliter
mg - milligram	cg - centigram	dg - decigram	g - gram	kg - kilogram

←—————— *multiply* ——————
—————— *divide* ——————→

12. Write M (multiply) or D (divide) to change units. (each answer, 1 point)

    a. dm to mm _____   b. dL to L _____   c. kg to g _____

72

13. Write the standard measure that is closest to the meter _____, liter _____, gram _____.
(each answer, 1 point)

14. Write the multiplier or divisor (10, 100, 1,000). (each answer, 1 point)

a. cm to mm _____   b. mL to L _____   c. g to cg _____

15. Write the value. (each answer, 1 point)

a. 5 cm = _____ m   b. 4L = _____ dL   c. 7 g = _____ mg

16. Match. (each answer, 1 point)

_____ a. $P = 2l + 2w$ 1. perimeter of triangle

_____ b. $A = rt$ 2. area of square

_____ c. $P = 4s$ 3. area of triangle

_____ d. $V = s^3$ 4. volume of rectangular prism

_____ e. $A = \frac{1}{2}bh$ 5. measure amount

_____ f. $A = s^2$ 6. perimeter of rectangle

_____ g. $V = lwh$ 7. volume of square prism

_____ h. $P = s + s + s$ 8. perimeter of square

17. Solve for the missing number. Label answer. (each answer, 1 point)

a. The perimeter of the triangle is 29.
Two sides measure 11 in. each.
What is the measure of the third side?

b. The perimeter of the square is 36 in.,
What is the width?

_____   _____

18. Which set of circles
is concentric?
(this question, 1 point)   _____   a.   b.   c.

73

19. What is the measure of
    the radius of the circle? _____ the diameter? _____
    (each answer, 1 point)

    3" ↓

20. Find the circumference
    of the circle? _____ area? _____
    (each answer, 1 point)

21. Write the values in percent. (each answer, 1 point)

    a. .08 _____   b. 23:100 _____   c. $\frac{5}{100}$ _____   d. .94 _____

22. Write each percent as a ratio, fraction, and decimal. (this question, 6 points)

    a. 45% _____ _____ _____   b. 9% _____ _____ _____

23. Write each fraction as a decimal with a denominator of 100.
    Round, if necessary. Write the fraction in percent. (this question, 6 points)

    a. $\frac{3}{4}$ = _____ = _____%   b. $\frac{1}{5}$ = _____ = _____%   c. $\frac{3}{8}$ = _____ = _____%

24. Write 24-hour time in standard time.   25. Write standard time in 24-hour time.
    (each answer, 1 point)   (each answer, 1 point)

    a. 9.46 _____   b. 18.00 _____   a. 7:15 A.M. _____   b. 9:30 P.M. _____

26. Solve missing number problems with two variables. (each answer, 1 point)

    a. Lisa had saved 3 more dimes than Joseph.
       Together, they had saved 27 dimes.
       How much did each one save?

                                    Lisa _____   Joseph _____

    b. Mary had baked 12 more cupcakes for the
       bake sale than Julie. Together, they baked
       44 cupcakes. How many cupcakes did
       each one bake?

                                    Mary _____   Julie _____

74

MATHEMATICS 607: Alternate LIFEPAC TEST

Name_____

Date_____

Score_____

80/100

1. Write each number as ...   a. an expanded number.   (this question, 4 points)
   b. expanded notation using powers of ten.

   783,290,538   a. _____

   _____

   b. _____

   _____

2. Describe each set of numbers as (C) cumulative, (A) associative, or (D) distributive.
   Write the value of each set on the second line. (each answer, 1 point)

   a. _____ $4(2 + 3)$ $(4 \times 2) + (4 \times 3)$ _____   b. _____ $(3 + 4) + 6$ $3 + (4 + 6)$ _____

   c. _____ 5×9 9×5 _____   d. _____ $(2 \times 5) \times 3$ $2 \times (5 \times 3)$ _____

3. Rewrite the problem using its distributive property.
   Solve the problem as it is rewritten. (this question, 2 points)

   $(9 \times 2) + (9 \times 5) =$ _____ = _____

4. Write the problem in ...   You *must* show work. (this question, 4 points)

   a. repeated addition and multiplication.   b. repeated subtraction and division.
   How much is four 14's?   How many 17's in 68?

5. Rewrite or convert each expression. (each answer, 1 point)

	ratio	fraction	decimal	percent
a.	3:10	_____	_____	_____
b.	2:5	_____	_____	_____

6. Solve. Label answers. (each answer, 1 point)

   a. 39%   b. 83%   c. 21%   d.   e. 32% of 25 =
      + 56%   − 67%   × 3   8)48%
      _____   _____   _____

7. Write the percent as a decimal and as a fraction. (each answer, 1 point)

225% _____ _____

8. Solve the problem in proportion. (this question, 2 points)

The baseball team decided to supply 5 balls for every
8 team members. If there were 24 members,
how many balls did the team need to supply?
Let x equal the number of balls.

_____

9. Select numbers from the second and third column. Match to the first column.
Each number may be used only once. Look for the best match. (this question, 10 points)

_____ _____   a. quadrilateral   1.   ⬭

6. 4-sided polygon, opposite sides parallel and equal, having 4 right angles

_____ _____   b. parallelogram   2.   □

7. 4-sided polygon

_____ _____   c. rhombus   3.   ▱

8. polygon with 4 equal sides, opposite sides parallel, having 4 right angles

_____ _____   d. rectangle   4.   ▭

9. 4-sided polygon, opposite sides parallel and equal

_____ _____   e. square   5.   ⬭

10. polygon with 4 equal sides, opposite sides parallel, usually having 2 acute and 2 obtuse angles

10. Write the formula for the area of each plane shape. Solve. Label answers.
(this question, 10 points)

a. rectangle $l = 8$ m $w = 3$ m $A =$ _____ _____

b. square $s = 6$ ft. $A =$ _____ _____

c. circle $r = 10$ in. $A =$ _____ _____

d. triangle $b = 7$ cm $h = 4$ cm $A =$ _____ _____

e. parallelogram $b = 5$ yd. $h = 6$ yd. $A =$ _____ _____

11. Solve. (each answer, 1 point)

a. $(-2) + (-3) =$ _____

b. $(-5) + 6 =$ _____

c. $7 + 8 =$ _____

d. $12 + (-3) =$ _____

e. $0 + (-4) =$ _____

f. $(-8) + 6 =$ _____

12. Graph a function. (this question, 4 points)

   a. Complete a function table for add 2.

+ 2 (	0	2	4	6

   b. Write the coordinate numbers.

   (___,___) (___,___) (___,___) (___,___)

   c. Place the points on Graph 1.

   d. Connect and label.

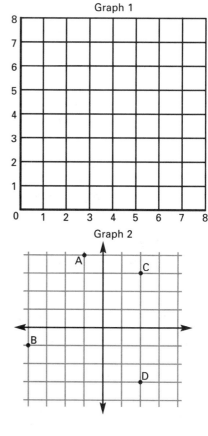

Graph 1

Graph 2

13. Label x-axis, y-axis, and point of origin (0) on Graph 2.
   (this question, 3 points)

14. Write (P) positive or (N) negative on the first line.
   Write the number of places on the second line.
   Name points (letters) on the coordinate graph.
   The coordinate points are ...
   (this question, 10 points)

   a. (2,-3) Begin at zero (0).
   2 is the first integer.   It is _____.   Move on the x-axis, to the right, _____ place(s).

   -3 is the second integer.   It is _____.   Move down _____ place(s).

   What is the point (letter) at (2,-3)?   _____

   b. (-1,4) Begin at zero (0).
   -1 is the first integer.   It is _____.   Move on the x-axis, to the left, _____ place(s).

   4 is the second integer.   It is _____.   Move up _____ place(s).

   What is the point (letter) at (-1,4)?   _____

15. Circle the positive integers. Underline the negative integers.
   Solve the problems. Circle or underline the answer for positive or negative.
   (each lettered question, 4 points)

   a. Kevin had 35 baseball cards. He sold 17.
   How many cards does Kevin have now?   _____

   b. The temperature was 8°F. During the night it fell 13 degrees.
   What was the temperature the next morning?   _____

16. Write the ... (each answer, 1 point)

   a. square of each number.   3 _____   6 _____

   b. square root of each number.   64 _____   25 _____

77

17. Answer the questions about time zones. (each answer, 1 point)

    a. How many time zones is the world divided into?   _____

    b. What is the name of the meridian at 180° longitude? _____

    c. How many time zones are there in the United States?   _____

    d. Is the United States the only country that
                        observes daylight-savings time?   _____

    e. If it is 4:00 P.M. CST, it is...   _____ EST.

    f. If it is 3:00 A.M. PST, it is ...   _____ AST.

18. If the area of a square is 49 in²., what is the measure of its side?
(this question, 1 point)   _____

19. Solve. Simplify. (each answer, 1 point)

    a. $7\frac{1}{8}$ b. $3\frac{3}{4} \div 5 =$ c.   42.9

          $-2\frac{3}{4}$ -15.78

    d. $.8\overline{)3.68}$ e.   3 lb.   7 oz.
                                               + 5 lb. 15 oz.

MATHEMATICS 608: Alternate LIFEPAC TEST

Name _____

Date _____

Score _____

80 / 100

1. Write numbers in words. (each answer, 1 point)

a. $\frac{5}{7}$ _____

b. .009 _____

c. -6 _____

d. $24\frac{1}{3}\%$ _____

2. Solve each of the problems using ... (this question, 4 points)

a. repeated addition and multiplication. *Show all work.*

three 39's

b. repeated subtraction and division. *Show all work.*

how many 67's in 201

3. Write the missing numbers in the function table. Write the inverse operation. (this question, 4 points)

add 4		5	
	6		12

4. Write the square root. (each answer, 1 point)   a. 49 _____   b. 16 _____

5. Match. (each answer, 1 point)

_____ a. problem   1. question to be answered by interpretation of data

_____ b. graph   2. the possibility that something will or will not happen

_____ c. norm   3. arrangement of data in logical order

_____ d. predict   4. facts from which a conclusion may be drawn

_____ e. ratio   5. a relation of one number to another

_____ f. data   6. without deliberate choice

_____ g. random selection   7. standard of a particular group

_____ h. probability   8. small picture of a large group

_____ i. random sample 9. to tell in advance

6. Answer questions about random selection. (this question, 10 points)
    Jason has decided to sell some of the coins from his coin collection.

    The collection includes: Lincoln pennies 8   Jefferson nickels 2
                    Roosevelt dimes 4   Washington quarters 4   Kennedy half-dollars 2

    Jason wants to make a random selection of the coins to be sold.

    a. Write the proportions of each coin to the total number of coins.
        Reduce the proportions to a denominator of 10.

        pennies _____ = _____   nickels _____ = _____   dimes _____ = _____

                quarters _____ = _____   half-dollars _____ = _____

    b. What is the probability that Jason's first selection will be a dime?   _____

    c. (this question 1 point of total)
        Arrange the coins in order of the
            greatest probability of being
            drawn to the least probability. _____ _____ _____ _____ _____

    d. Suppose one Lincoln penny is drawn but not returned to the collection.

                    Does that change the ratio for the random selection?   _____

                    What would be the new ratio for the Lincoln Penny?   _____

        If the random selection is repeated several times, will the results always be the same? _____

7. Use the reduced ratios from 6.a to complete a *circle graph*. (this question, 4 points)
    The name of the graph is,

        "The Probability of One Coin Being Selected from a Set of Coins."

    a. How many equal parts should this
        circle graph be divided into?   _____

    b. The best way to display data is in
        color. How many colors are needed?   _____

    c. A *legend* describes the colors.
        Draw a set of boxes.
        Label each box with the name of one of the letters.

    d. Complete the graph.

8. Answer questions about a random sample. (this question, 10 points)
    The club leaders were planning a way to raise money for their organization.
    The club had 100 members. At the club meeting every tenth member was asked,

        "What is the best way to raise money for the club?"

    The votes were: sell candy – 2   car wash – 2   increase pledges – 1
                sponsor a marathon race – 3   sponsor a festival – 2

    a. Write the ratios of votes for each program to the total number of votes.

        candy _____ car wash _____ pledges _____ race _____ festival _____

    b. If a vote were held for all 100 people attending camp, how many would vote for:

        candy _____ car wash _____ pledges _____ race _____ festival _____

9. Answer questions about the metric system (SI).   (this question, 4 points)

   a. What number is the metric system based on?   _____

   b. Name the three basic units of the metric system.   _____   _____   _____

10. Express each number in terms of metric units. If *the number is expressed in grams, then the number in ones' place is grams.* Identify the other units by working to the right or left of ones' place. Write how many ... (this question, 6 points)

   kilograms   hectograms   decagrams   grams   decigrams   centigrams   milligrams

   a. 43.1 grams   _____

   b. 6.17 decigrams   _____

11. Write ... (each answer, 1 point)

   a. (M) multiply or (D) divide to change from ...

   m to dm   _____   kL to L   _____   mg to g   _____

   b. the multiplier or divisor (10,100, 1,000).

   m to km   _____   L to dL   _____   mg to cg   _____

12. Convert standard measurements and metric units.   (each answer, 1 point)
   The conversion chart (p.18) and a calculator may be used to complete this problem.

   a. 7 ounces = _____ grams   8 inches = _____ centimeters

   b. 5 kilograms = _____ pounds   9 liters = _____ quarts

13. Answer the questions.   (each answer, 1 point)

   a. 24 cookies are on the table. 8 of the cookies are chocolate.
      Write the number of chocolate cookies as a ...

      ratio _____   fraction _____   simplified fraction _____

   b. There are 27 animals at the pet store. $\frac{1}{3}$ of the animals are dogs.
      How many of the animals are dogs?   _____

   c. Jason had 12 cans of soda for the party. His friends drank $\frac{7}{8}$ of the cans.

      How many whole cans did they drink?   _____

      What part of a can did they drink?   _____

14. Solve for the missing number. (each answer, 1 point)

a. $\frac{3}{5}$ of a number is equal to 9.
What is the number? _____

Prove: $\frac{3}{5}$ of _____ = 9

b. $\frac{5}{6}$ of a number is equal to 15.
What is the number? _____

Prove: $\frac{5}{6}$ of _____ = 15

c. 12 is equal to $\frac{3}{4}$ of a number.
What is the number? _____

Prove: $12 = \frac{3}{4}$ of _____

d. 6 is equal to $\frac{2}{3}$ of a number.
What is the number? _____

Prove: $6 = \frac{2}{3}$ of _____

15. Solve. (each answer, 1 point)

3:9 of 27 = _____   .125 of 24 = _____   .15 of 22 = _____

16. Write fraction equivalents. (each answer, 1 point)

	ratio	decimal	percent		ratio	decimal	percent
$\frac{1}{3}$ =	_____	_____	_____	$\frac{3}{5}$ =	_____	_____	_____
$\frac{5}{8}$ =	_____	_____	_____	$\frac{1}{6}$ =	_____	_____	_____

17. Round to ... (each answer, 1 point)

a. the largest period.   593,271,895,140 _____

b. hundred billions' place.   185,072,321,954 _____

c. thousandths' place.   58.6745 _____

d. the nearest decimal place. $83.147\frac{2}{3}$ _____

82

MATHEMATICS 609: Alternate LIFEPAC TEST

Name _____

Date _____

Score _____

80 / 100

1. Write the missing words. (each answer, 1 point)

   a. Whole numbers are all of the numbers equal to or greater than _____.

   b. Fractions, decimals, ratios, and percent
      represent all of the numbers between _____ and _____.

2. Find the prime factors of 20 using the factor box.
   The prime factors written
      in exponential notation are _____, _____
   (this question, 3 points)

	20

3. Fill in the blanks for each set of prime factors. (this question, 4 points)

Base Factor(s)	Exponent(s)	Exponential Notation	Product

   $2 \times 3 \times 5 \times 5$ _____   _____   _____   _____

4. Round to ... (each answer, 1 point)

   a. billions' period.   605,192,883,406   _____

   b. ten billions' place.   974,026,382,785   _____

5. Write the missing numbers. (each answer, 1 point)

	ratio	fraction	decimal	percent		ratio	fraction	decimal	percent
a.	1:3	$\frac{1}{3}$	_____	_____	b.	_____	_____	.75	75%

6. Circle the whole numbers.
   (this question, 2 points)

   a. 29.45   b. 239%

7. Write in number order.
   (this question, 2 points)

   $\frac{2}{3}$ $\frac{11}{12}$ $\frac{1}{2}$ $\frac{7}{12}$ $\frac{3}{4}$ $\frac{5}{6}$

   _____ _____ _____ _____ _____ _____

8. Use a calculator to complete this problem. (each answer, 1 point)

   a. $15\% + 2.8 + \frac{1}{2} =$ _____

   b. $12 \times 3\frac{7}{8} =$ _____

9. Write the probability as a simplified ratio. (this question, 1 point)

   There were 4 chocolate, 8 lemon, 5 cherry, and
   7 mint candies in the bag.
   The first candy Aaron drew out of the bag was chocolate. _____

10. Find the pattern. Write the solution. (each answer, 1 point)

    On Monday, 3 of the 5 vehicles on the used car lot were vans.
    On Tuesday, 5 of 10 were vans, and on Wednesday, 7 of 15 were vans.
    If the pattern continues, how many vehicles will be on the lot on Thursday? _____

    How many will be vans? _____

11. Match words to definitions. (each answer, 1 point)

    1. scalene   2. square   3. circumference   4. isosceles   5. diameter   6. rectangle

    _____   a. distance around the outside of a circle

    _____   b. triangle with no equal sides

    _____   c. quadrilateral having opposite sides parallel and equal with 4 right angles

    _____   d. triangle having two equal sides

    _____   e. quadrilateral having opposite sides parallel, four sides equal, with 4 right angles

    _____   f. distance across a circle straight through the center

12. Match pictures to definitions. (each answer, 1 point)

    1. rectangular prism   2. triangular pyramid   3. rectangular pyramid

    a. _____   b. _____   c. _____

13. Express geometric symbols in words. (each answer, 1 point)

    a. $\overleftrightarrow{GH}$ _____   b. $\parallel$ _____   c. $\sim$ _____

14. Circle the correct symbol. (each answer, 1 point)

    a. $\frac{14}{10}$ (> , = , <) 1.04   b. $\frac{2}{6}$ (> , = , <) $\frac{3}{10}$ c. 2^4 (> , = , <) 3^3

15. Write an equation. Solve using inverse operations. (this question, 2 points)

    There were 127 books on the library shelf. 24 were about history,
    29 were about plants and animals, 34 were science fiction, and 12 were
    biographies. The rest of the books were mysteries.
    How many mystery books were there?
    Let x represent the number of mystery books. $x =$ _____

84

16. Write a proportion. Solve using cross multiplication.
   $\triangle RST \sim \triangle XYZ$
   The ratio of $\triangle RST$ to $\triangle XYZ$ is 3:5.
   (this question, 2 points)

   Find the length of $\overline{XY}$ if $\overline{RS}$ is 6 in. long. $\overline{XY} =$ _____

17. Write the standard measurements. (each answer, 1 point)

   _____ days = 1 year   _____ years = 1 decade   _____ feet = 1 mile

   _____ ounces = 1 pound   _____ sq. feet = 1 sq. yard   _____ pints = 1 quart

18. Write the formula on the lines. Solve the problem. (this question, 8 points)

   a. The distance is 174 miles. The time is 3 hours.   _____ = _____
      What is the rate of travel?

   b. The length is 8 ft. The width is 3 ft.   _____ = _____
      What is the perimeter?

   c. The diameter of a circle is 10 inches.   _____ = _____
      What is its circumference?

   d. The area of a square is 36 sq. in.   _____ = _____
      What is the measure of its side?

19. Solve the problem with two variables. (each answer, 1 point)

   There were 4 times as many boys in the room as there were girls.
   Altogether, there were 25 students.

   How many girls were there?   _____

                 boys?   _____

20. Complete the function tables. Graph the functions.
    (this question, 8 points)

add −2	6	4	2	0	-2	-4

   (___,___) (___,___) (___,___) (___,___) (___,___) (___,___)

85

21. The gallons of milk sold by the store in the first five days of November ...
    (this question, 4 points)

            Mon. – 73   Tues. – 96   Wed. – 128   Thurs. – 121   Fri. – 92

    Establish a norm by finding the average sales for the five days.   _____
    During the week, what *percent* of the time was the sales ...

    normal? _____   above normal? _____   below normal? _____

22. Write the ... (each answer, 1 point)

    a. square of each number.   3 _____   5 _____   8 _____

    b. square root of each number. 4 _____   36 _____   121 _____

23. What is ...
    (each answer, 1 point)   a. 18% of 50? _____   b. 16% of 25? _____

24. Circle the correct symbol. (each answer, 1 point)

    a.   9 meters (> , = , <) 90 decimeters   b.   8 millimeters (> , = , <) 80 centimeters

    c.   5 kilometers (> , = , <) 400 meters   d. 5.3 decimeters (> , = , <) 53 centimeters

25. Solve. (this question, 16 points)

    a.
    $$\begin{array}{r} 4.02 \\ .697 \\ +\ 3.8 \\ \hline \end{array} \qquad \begin{array}{r} 2,800 \\ -\ 376 \\ \hline \end{array} \qquad \begin{array}{r} .493 \\ \times\ .07 \\ \hline \end{array} \qquad .06\overline{)58.2}$$

    b.
    $$\begin{array}{r} 9\ \text{lb.}\ 3\ \text{oz.} \\ -\ 6\ \text{lb.}\ 5\ \text{oz.} \\ \hline \end{array} \qquad \begin{array}{r} 11\frac{1}{9} \\ -\ 5\frac{2}{3} \\ \hline \end{array} \qquad 7.63 \times 100 = \qquad 8\frac{1}{3} \div 5\frac{2}{5} =$$

86

MATHEMATICS 610: Alternate LIFEPAC TEST

Name _____

Date _____

Score _____

80 / 100

1. Solve. Simplify answers. (each answer, 2 points)

a.
$$\frac{5}{12}$$
$$\frac{2}{3}$$
$$+\frac{3}{4}$$
———

$$\frac{2}{7} \times 4\frac{3}{8} =$$

$$6\frac{2}{3} \div \frac{5}{9} =$$

$$7.38$$
$$-4.9$$
———

b.
12%
× 6
———

5 qt. 1 pt.
+ 3 qt. 1 pt.
———

7 wk 4 da.
− 2 wk 5 da.
———

$$7\overline{)1 \text{ yd. } 6 \text{ in.}}$$

2. Use "shortcut" to solve. (this question, 6 points)

                a.   b.   c.

a. 500 × 36 = _____

b. 2,000 × 59 = _____

c. 63,000 × 41 = _____

3. Think the answer. Write the answer. (each answer, 1 point)

$\frac{1}{3}$ of 900 = _____

$\frac{3}{4}$ of 8,000 = _____

$\frac{4}{5}$ of 15,000 = _____

4. Solve. Round to the ... (this question, 8 points)

a. nearest cent.

b. nearest dollar.

$$4\overline{)\$8.73}$$ $$2\overline{)\$9.67}$$ $$6\overline{)\$40.26}$$ $$3\overline{)\$57.63}$$

5. Solve. (each answer, 1 point)

a. 20% of 75 days is _____ days.

b. Fifteen ft. is $\frac{5}{8}$ of how many feet? _____

c. Ten oranges is $\frac{2}{3}$ of how many oranges? _____

6. Divide. (this question, 4 points)

a.

$$413)\overline{25,193}$$

b.

$$642)\overline{13,485}$$

7. Do not rewrite the problems vertically. Think the answer. Write the answer.
(each answer, 1 point)

a. $7 + 8 + 6 + 5 =$ _____ $31 - 7 =$ _____ $56 - 29 =$ _____

b. $26 + 31 + 59 =$ _____ $682 - 78 =$ _____ $6 \times 37 =$ _____

c. $4 \times 365 =$ _____ $70 \div 5 =$ _____ $376 \div 8 =$ _____

d. $6.04 + .562 =$ _____ $9.1 - .48 =$ _____ $.02 \times 9 =$ _____

e. $.027 \div 3 =$ _____ $\frac{3}{4} + \frac{1}{2} =$ _____ $\frac{5}{8} - \frac{1}{4} =$ _____

8. Write numbers as ratios and simplified fractions. Convert to decimals. Write as percent.
(each answer, 1 point)

a. Nine of the 12 bicycles were red.   _____ _____ _____ _____

b. Ten of the 16 books were mysteries.   _____ _____ _____ _____

9. Predict outcomes. (this question, 6 points

a. Describe in order of events.
Aaron (A) and his friends Brian (B) and Kevin (K) planned to meet at the park to play tennis. Show all the possible orders in which they could arrive at the park.

_____ _____ _____ _____ _____ _____

b. Describe as relating to mean, median, mode. Write the answer.
If the group was lined up in order by their height, who would be standing in the middle?

Lisa – 4 ft. 3 in.   Corey – 5 ft. 1 in.   Judi – 4 ft. 9 in.   David – 4 ft. 10 in.   Sherry – 5 ft. 3 in.

_____ _____

c. Describe as a ratio and in percent.
Jason threw the dart to the target twelve times.
He hit the bullseye 4 times. What is the probability
that Jason will hit the bullseye on the next throw?   _____ _____

10. Check for divisibility. (this question, 4 points)

÷	2	5	10	3	9	6
435						
270						

11. In the space provided, draw an outline of a rectangular prism.
    Label the sides using letters (A, B, C, ...)
    Show the dimensions as : l = 7 in. w = 3 in. h = 4 in.
    (this question, 4 points)

    Find the total surface area of the two bases.   _____

    Find the total surface area of one set of congruent sides.   _____

    Find the total surface area of the second set of congruent sides.   _____

    What is the total surface area of the rectangular prism?   _____

12. Draw. Label correctly.
    Draw line RG.
    Draw a line segment MN parallel to line RG.
    (this question, 3 points)

13. Draw a(n) ... (each answer, 1 point)
    a. right angle   b. scalene triangle   c. hexagon

14. Solve for x. (each answer, 1 point)
    a. $x + x + x + x + 3 = 31$ b. $\frac{x}{8} = \frac{3}{12}$

15. Solve. (each answer, 1 point)

   a. A rectangle measures width 4 in., perimeter 20 in.
      What is the measure of its length?   _____

   b. A square has an area of 36 sq. ft.
      What is the measure of its side?   _____

   c. Paul started the summer reading 2 books in 7 days.
      At that rate, how many books could he read in 14 days? _____

16. Use the variable b to represent the range of numbers. (this question, 2 points)
    Lisa could earn more than $7 a day baby-sitting, but less than $10.
    What range of money could Lisa have at the end of 2 days?   _____ $< b <$ _____

                                                    $b =$ _____ or _____

17. Write the integers in number order. (this question, 3 points)

           +5   0   -3   +6   +3   -7

    _____   _____   _____   _____   _____   _____

18. Answer questions about the graph. (this question, 7 points)

   a. What type of graph is this? _____   Morgan Family Grocery Bills

   b. Write the date of each amount spent.

           Date   Amount

        _____ $72.35

        _____ $79.68

        _____ $82.19

        _____ $93.02

        _____ $97.81

   c. What is the title of the graph? _____

90

ANSWER KEYS

Part One

1.1 a. 863,549   thousands
     235,871,629   millions
     21,471   thousands
   b. 506   units
     6,729,108   millions
     93,239,658   millions
   c. 571,324   thousands
     351   units
     2,804,572   millions

1.2 a. two hundred thirty-six thousand
     four hundred ninety-five million
   b. two hundred sixty-two
     one hundred ninety-four thousand
   c. seven hundred eighty-one million
     eight hundred forty-six

1.3 a. 526,248,795
   b. 81,061,232

1.4 a. ninth
     fourteenth
     fifty-sixth
   b. eleventh
     thirteenth
     twenty-ninth
   c. two hundred seventy-eighth
     six hundred forty-third

1.5 a. 8   26   974   850   42
   b. 5   3,881   19   926,337   83

1.6 a. 12   1   6   2   4   3
     ×1   ×12   ×2   ×6   ×3   ×4
   b. 6
   c. 1, 2, 3, 4, 6, 12

1.7 a. 1, 3 - P   1, 2, 4 - C   1, 3, 5, 15 - C
   b. 1, 2, 3, 6, 9, 18, - C
     1, 23 - P
     1, 3, 9, 27 - C
   c. 1, 7 - P
     1, 2, 3, 4, 6, 8, 12, 24 - C
     1, 2, 4, 8, 16 - C
   d. 1, 3, 9 - C
     1, 5 - P
     1, 2, 4, 8, 16, 32 - C

1.8 a. ones **18**   **30**   48   ones **17**   **14**   tens **18**   **15**   331
   b. 6,425   51,331   141,637
   c. 2,548   2,697   2,319

1.9 a. 806   415   3156   6645
   b. 6,593   23,216   47,527   156,654
   c. 149   2,462   28,544   223,118

1.10 a. 2,795   2,436   6,992   4,560   3,180   4,214
    b. 8,892   38,080   16,328   41,109   34,916
    c. 249,600   254,223   316,046   186,558   272,734
    d. 311,284   497,787   274,770   157,808   212,023

1.11 a. 3, 6, 9, 12, 15, 18, 21, 24, 27
    b. 3, 6, 9, 12, 15, 18, 21, 24, 27

1.12 a. 6, 12, 18, 24, 30, 36, 42, 48, 54
    b. 6, 12, 18, 24, 30, 36, 42, 48, 54

1.13 a. 50 R2   49   147 R3   108   78
    b. 169   60 R3   209   150 R4   437
    c. 120 R5   96 R3   102   73 R1   320

Part Two

2.1 a. =   ≠   ≠
   b. =   ≠   =
   c. =   =   ≠

2.2 a. <   <   >
   b. <   >   <
   c. >   >   <

2.3 a. +, ×   ÷, ×   +, ×
   b. ÷, ÷   −, ×   ×, ×
   c. ÷, ×   −, ×   ×, ×, ×, ×
   d. +, ×   −, ×   −, ×, ×

2.4 a. 48   45   30   28   15
   b. 4   5   6   6   2
   c. 49   8   28   7   35
   d. 4   13   0   64   6

2.5 a. 5, 7, 12 - 7, 5, 12   6, 8, 14 - 8, 6, 14
     12, 5, 7 - 12, 7, 5   14, 6, 8 - 14, 8, 6
   b. 4, 5, 20 - 5, 4, 20   8, 9, 72 - 9, 8, 72
     20, 4, 5 - 20, 5, 4   72, 8, 9 - 72, 9, 8

2.6 a. 674   11,457   146,189
   b. 7,364   809   5,086
   c. 8,604   2,759   21,096
   d. 7,396   1,706   35,561
   e. 6,460   5,415   22,388   62,416
   f. 1,827   4,704   19,008   21,306
   g. 121 R2   46 R4   230 R1   127 R4
   h. 206 R1   142 R3   58 R7   238 R1
   i. 3,509   11,757   3,452
   j. 360,052   509,378   196

2.7 a. a   c   a   b   b   c   c   a
    b. a   c   b   c   b   a   b   c

2.8 a. five-eighths
       nine-thirds
       six and three-fifths
   b. three and one-fourth
       seven-tenths
       eleven-ninths

2.9   a. $4\frac{1}{2}$ $\frac{6}{8}$ $\frac{12}{2}$
    b. $8\frac{5}{6}$ $\frac{7}{9}$ $\frac{4}{5}$
    c. $3\frac{8}{10}$ $\frac{14}{12}$ $\frac{8}{10}$
    d. $2\frac{3}{5}$ $\frac{9}{3}$ $\frac{5}{6}$

2.10 a. 3   5   4   2   5
     b. 2   4   2   3   9
     c. 9   5   2   6   11

2.11 a. 6   16   10   10   20   12
     b. 4   4   7   1   2   8
     c. 15   6   4   28   8   4

2.12 a. 3 $1\frac{6}{9}$ $(1\frac{2}{3})$ $3\frac{3}{8}$ $7\frac{5}{6}$ 6   1
     b. $5\frac{2}{7}$ $9\frac{2}{3}$ $7\frac{2}{7}$ 1 $3\frac{4}{5}$ $3\frac{3}{7}$

2.13 a. $\frac{1}{2}$ $\frac{1}{3}$ $\frac{3}{4}$ $\frac{1}{2}$ $\frac{1}{3}$ $\frac{3}{4}$
     b. $\frac{1}{2}$ $\frac{1}{2}$ $\frac{2}{3}$ $\frac{1}{5}$ $\frac{1}{3}$ $\frac{2}{3}$

2.14 a. 1, 2,④ 8   1, 2, 3,④ 6, 12
     b. 1, 2, 3,⑥ 9, 18   1, 2, 3, 4,⑥ 8, 12, 24
     c. 1, 3,⑨   1, 3,⑨ 27

2.15 a. $\frac{2}{3}$ $\frac{2}{5}$ $\frac{3}{4}$ $\frac{1}{3}$ $\frac{1}{3}$ $\frac{5}{6}$
     b. $\frac{1}{2}$ $\frac{3}{5}$ $\frac{5}{6}$ $\frac{3}{5}$ $\frac{2}{3}$ $\frac{3}{4}$

2.16 a. $1\frac{1}{4}$ 1 $\frac{1}{2}$ $\frac{9}{10}$ $1\frac{3}{16}$ $\frac{2}{3}$
     b. $\frac{1}{3}$ $\frac{5}{8}$ $\frac{7}{10}$ $\frac{4}{9}$ $\frac{2}{3}$ $\frac{1}{3}$

2.17 a. $\frac{4}{8}$, $\frac{5}{8}$, $\frac{6}{8}$, $\frac{7}{8}$ b. 16, 20, 24, 28
     c. 1,100; 1,101; 1,102; 1,103
     d. $\frac{10}{15}$, $\frac{12}{18}$, $\frac{14}{21}$, $\frac{16}{24}$ e. $\frac{5}{10}$, $\frac{4}{8}$, $\frac{3}{6}$, $\frac{2}{4}$
     f. $12 - 3 = 9$ $12 - 9 = 3$
     g. 999,999; 999,998; 999,997; 999,996
     h. $7 \times 8 = 56$ $8 \times 7 = 56$

i.
j.

k.

2.18 a. >   <   <
     b. >   <   <
     c. <   >   >

2.19 a. 3,685,942
       3,856,924
       3,865,924
       6,685,942
       6,835,492
     b. 1,397,102
       1,973,102
       2,379,103
       2,397,102
       2,973,102

Part Three

3.1 a. $\frac{13}{100}$ $\frac{6}{10}$ $\frac{48}{1,000}$ $\frac{7}{100}$ $\frac{345}{1,000}$ $\frac{87}{1,000}$
    b. $\frac{9}{10}$ $\frac{3}{100}$ $\frac{506}{1,000}$ $\frac{90}{1,000}$ $\frac{18}{100}$ $\frac{450}{1,000}$

3.2 a. three tenths   eighteen hundredths
    b. five hundredths   twenty-one thousandths
    c. one hundred forty-seven thousandths

3.3 a. .3   .19   .004   .08   .134   .063
    b. .047   .5   .83   .009   .040   .27

3.4 a. $3\frac{8}{10}$ $6\frac{3}{100}$ $9\frac{45}{1,000}$ $24\frac{3}{1,000}$ $12\frac{39}{100}$
    b. $7\frac{23}{1,000}$ $4\frac{50}{1,000}$ $3\frac{42}{100}$ $38\frac{3}{10}$ $7\frac{4}{1,000}$

3.5 a. five and four tenths
       eight and three hundredths
    b. two and sixty-three thousandths
    c. seven and one hundred forty-five
       thousandths

3.6   Ø6,308   ØØ,495,367   384,002,621
       Ø90,601,230   23,054,060

3.7   6.0   15.00   35.000

3.8 a. $\frac{6}{100}$ $\frac{30}{100}$ $\frac{270}{1,000}$ $\frac{90}{1,000}$ $\frac{45}{1,000}$ $\frac{80}{1,000}$
    b. $7\frac{5}{100}$ $18\frac{36}{1,000}$ $24\frac{180}{1,000}$ $52\frac{40}{1,000}$

3.9 a. .2   .4   .6   .8

      b. .07   .09   .25   .31

      c. .007   .014   .096   .238

      d. .1   .3   .5   .9

      e. .06   .13   .34   .59

      f. .050   .056   .506   .561

3.10 a. .70   .40   .80   .10   .30

      b. .500   .370   .060   .700   .600

3.11 a. .450, .320, .708, .800, .060, .431, .500, .870

        .06, .32, .431, .45, .5, .708, .80, .87

      b. .300, .460, .500, .874, .293, .340, .900, .532

        .293, .3, .34, .46, .5, .532, .874, .9

3.12 a. 2.756   19.12   125.2

      b. 1.358   .565   6.05

      c. 54.66   62.54   .435

3.13 a. 35,629,041,685   billions

        1,695,638   millions

      b. 92,537   thousands

        640,290,434   millions

      c. 89   units

        276,328,546,957   billions

3.14 a. five hundred thirty-six billion
        ninety-three thousand

      b. eight hundred five
        two hundred seventy-six billion

      c. five hundred ninety-two million
        six hundred fifty-five thousand

3.15 a. ten thousandths   millionths

      b. ten millionths   ten millionths

      c. hundred thousandths   ten thousandths

3.16 a. 1,731 1,538 1,880 50.63 43.086 10.09

        1,731 1,538 1,880 50.63 43.086 10.09

      b. 805 805 429 195 92.95 92.95 45.63 29.15

             -376 -234 -195   -47.32 -16.48 -29.15

             429 195   0   45.63 29.15   0

3.17 1,212 5,353 22,136 49.601 4.724 1.16

      3,849 8,306 37,423 52.641 7.300 3.70

3.18 a. $(9 - 5) \times (13 - 6) = 4 \times 7 = 28$

        $(3 \times 8) + (6 \times 4) = 24 + 24 = 48$

        $(24 + 6) \div (2 \times 3) = 30 \div 6 = 5$

      b. $(72 \div 9) \div (15 - 7) = 8 \div 8 = 1$

        $(27 \div 3) \times (5 \times 0) = 9 \times 0 = 0$

        $(10 \times 5) - (25 \times 2) = 50 - 50 = 0$

      c. $20 + (8 + 5) + (15 - 4) = 20 + 13 + 11 = 44$

        $(39 - 11) \div 7 = 28 \div 7 = 4$

        $73 - (6 + 3) - (14 + 6) = 73 - 9 - 20 = 44$

3.19 a. Nine plus five is not equal to two
        times eight.

      b. Thirty-six divided by four is less than
        five plus five.

3.20 a. $27 \div 3 = 3 \times 3$

      b. $45 - 3 > 8 \times 5$

3.21 $6 \times 0 = 5 \times 0$ $4 + 7 = (2 \times 5) + 1$

3.22 a.

$$N + 32 = 87$$
$$N + 32 \,(- 32) = 87 - 32$$
$$N = 55$$

Prove. $55 + 32 = 87$

$$N - 64 = 152$$
$$N - 64 \,(+ 64) = 152 + 64$$
$$N = 216$$

Prove. $216 - 64 = 152$

$$N + 375 = 518$$
$$N + 375 \,(- 375) = 518 - 375$$
$$N = 143$$

Prove. $143 + 375 = 518$

      b.

$$256 = N + 179$$
$$256 - 179 = N + 179 \,(- 179)$$
$$77 = N$$

Prove. $256 = 77 + 179$

$$431 = N - 246$$
$$431 + 246 = N - 246 \,(+ 246)$$
$$677 = N$$

Prove. $431 = 677 - 246$

$$N - 59 = 113$$
$$N - 59 \,(+ 59) = 113 + 59$$
$$N = 172$$

Prove. $172 - 59 = 113$

      c.

$$N + 349 = 627$$
$$N + 349 \,(- 349) = 627 - 349$$
$$N = 278$$

Prove. $278 + 349 = 627$

$$N - 74 = 158$$
$$N - 74 \,(+ 74) = 158 + 74$$
$$N = 232$$

Prove. $232 - 74 = 158$

$$132 = N + 68$$
$$132 - 68 = N + 68 \,(- 68)$$
$$64 = N$$

Prove. $132 = 64 + 68$

Part Four

4.1   40   50   60   100   50   10

4.2 a. 1,600   778,400   16,400
     b. 6,000   49,000   313,000
     c. 100,000   4,850,000   60,000

4.3 a. 550,000   20,000   1,329,000
     b. 30,000,000 9,000,000   550,000,000
     c. 50,000,000 990,000,000 29,370,000,000
     d. 570,000,000,000   30,000,000,000

4.4 a. 1,001 800   12,072 8,000   5,811 4,000
           +200   +4,000   2,000
          1,000   12,000   6,000

     b. 1,080 300   1,789 500   10,890 9,000
           +300   400   2,000
          +500   + 900   11,000
          1,100   1,800

4.5 a. 467 1,000   2,350 6,000   24,266 90,000
          - 500   - 4,000   - 70,000
          500   2,000   20,000
     b. 276 500   3,383 9,000   12,472 50,000
          - 200   6,000   - 40,000
          300   3,000   10,000

4.6 a. 50 + 20 + 20 + 40 = 130 pieces
     b. $20 − ($5 + $3 + $8) = $20 − $16 = $4

4.7 a. 78,540
         32,012
         15,696
         20,520
         16,800
     b. 249,508
         231,770
         240,648
         135,044
         288,960
     c. 4,929,750
         2,046,072
         2,787,372
         2,543,064
     d. 4,357,150
         1,648,206
         5,520,415
         2,389,378

4.8 a. 24   42   54   12   0
     b. 9   54   27   72   18
     c. 4   0   12   24   28

4.9 a. 20, 40, 60, 80, 100, 120, 140, 160, 180
     b. 30, 60, 90, 120, 150, 180, 210, 240, 270
     c. 50, 100, 150, 200, 250, 300, 350, 400, 450
     d. 70, 140, 210, 280, 350, 420, 490, 560, 630

4.10 a. 13 R22   13 R20   21 R12   20 R27   10 R3
      b. 20 R16   27   14 R14   10 R64   15 R3
      c. 13 R63   48 R5   23 R33   12 R22   10 R57

4.11 a.
$$512 \quad 8\overline{)512}^{\,64} \qquad 273 \quad 7\overline{)273}^{\,39} \qquad 460 \quad 5\overline{)460}^{\,92} \qquad 270 \quad 6\overline{)270}^{\,45}$$
      b.
$$1,161 \quad 27\overline{)1,161}^{\,43} \qquad\qquad 3,016 \quad 52\overline{)3,016}^{\,58}$$
$$2,592 \quad 32\overline{)2,592}^{\,81} \qquad\qquad 5,734 \quad 61\overline{)5,734}^{\,94}$$

4.12 a. 22 R1
$$\begin{array}{r} 22 \\ \times\,4 \\ \hline 88 \\ +\,1 \\ \hline 89 \end{array} \qquad 34 \;\begin{array}{r} 34 \\ \times\,7 \\ \hline 238 \end{array} \qquad 69\text{ R3}\;\begin{array}{r} 69 \\ \times\,5 \\ \hline 345 \\ +\,3 \\ \hline 348 \end{array}$$

      b. 34 R16
$$\begin{array}{r} 34 \\ \times\,28 \\ \hline 952 \\ +\,16 \\ \hline 968 \end{array} \qquad 15\;\begin{array}{r} 52 \\ \times\,15 \\ \hline 780 \end{array} \qquad 14\text{ R5}\;\begin{array}{r} 31 \\ \times\,14 \\ \hline 434 \\ +\,5 \\ \hline 439 \end{array}$$

      c. 54
$$\begin{array}{r} 54 \\ \times\,9 \\ \hline 486 \end{array} \qquad 39\text{ R13}\;\begin{array}{r} 39 \\ \times\,19 \\ \hline 741 \\ +\,13 \\ \hline 754 \end{array} \qquad 24\text{ R3}\;\begin{array}{r} 35 \\ \times\,24 \\ \hline 840 \\ +\,3 \\ \hline 843 \end{array}$$

4.13
$$3,816\;\begin{array}{r} 70 \\ \times\,50 \\ \hline 3,500 \end{array} \qquad 5,712\;\begin{array}{r} 70 \\ \times\,80 \\ \hline 5,600 \end{array} \qquad 2,352\;\begin{array}{r} 600 \\ \times\,4 \\ \hline 2,400 \end{array}$$

4.14
$$82 \quad 5\overline{)400}^{\,80} \qquad 54\text{ R1} \quad 6\overline{)300}^{\,50} \qquad 20\text{ R3} \quad 4\overline{)80}^{\,20}$$

4.15 a. 1,800 cans
      b. 10 boxes
      c. 250 min
      d. 50 dandelions

Part Five

5.1   Suggested answers a and b

     a. 1,234,567,890; 3,456,789,012; 2,345,678,901; 4,567,890,123
     b. 1,234,567,890; 2,345,678,901; 3,456,789,012; 4,567,890,123
     c. one billions
     d. place holder

5.2 a. ninth
     b. 6, 18, 54, 162   1, 3, 9, 27, 81
         1, 3   6, 18, 9, 54, 27, 162, 81

c. 1, 2, 3, 6,⑨ 18   1, 3,⑨ 27
d. 3, 6, 9, 12, 15, 18, 21, 24, 27
   9, 18, 27, 36, 45, 54, 63, 72, 81
e. 0
f. suggested answer. $3 + 6 = 9$ $6 + 3 = 9$
   $9 - 3 = 6$ $9 - 6 = 3$
g. suggested answer. $3 \times 6 = 18$ $6 \times 3 = 18$
   $18 \div 3 = 6$ $18 \div 6 = 3$
h. suggested answer. $18 + 9 + 54 = 81$
i. suggested answers. $\frac{3}{6}$, $\frac{6}{18}$, $\frac{3}{18}$, $\frac{3}{27}$
j. multiply by 6, divide by 2
   486   243   1,458   729

5.3 a. 12,481
     b. 3,478
     c. 1,898
     d. 20 R25
     e.(a)   12,481 (sum)
            − 7,642 (addend)
              4,839 (addend)

       (b)   2,395
            + 3,478
              5,873

       (c)   73
            26)1,898

       (d)   47
               × 20
                940
              + 25
                965

5.4 a. 86 lb. + 74 lb. > 91 lb. + 68 lb.
     b. $45 + (2 \times 55) + (45 + 12) + 60 = 272$ min.
     c. $16 \div (16 + 8) + (16 − 3) − 21$
     d. $15 + 8 < 12 + 14$
     e. $23 < 35$ $46 > 35$ $15 < 35$ $23 < 35$ $48 > 35$

5.5 96×8 $96 \cdot 8 =$ $96(8) =$
     7)28 $28 \div 7 =$ $\frac{28}{7} =$

5.6 a. 30.576   b. 4.564

5.7 a   b   a   c   c   b

5.8 a. $2\frac{1}{3}$
     b. $\frac{7}{12}$
     c. $\frac{9}{4}$

5.9 10   12   5   9   18
      5   36   2   4   3

5.10 $\frac{12}{24}$, $\frac{5}{24}$, $\frac{14}{24}$, $\frac{18}{24}$, $\frac{15}{24}$, $\frac{4}{24}$ $\frac{1}{6}$, $\frac{5}{24}$, $\frac{1}{2}$, $\frac{7}{12}$, $\frac{5}{8}$, $\frac{3}{4}$

5.11 a. $\frac{1}{4}$ b. $\frac{2}{5}$ c. $\frac{1}{6}$

5.12 .050 .237 .800 .040 .530 .761 .900 .735
      .040 .05   .237 .53   .735 .761 .8   .90

5.13 a. $\frac{2}{3}$ $1\frac{1}{3}$ 2
      b. .3   .6   .8   1.0
      c. $\frac{3}{4}$ $1\frac{1}{2}$ 2
      d. $\frac{2}{3}$ $1\frac{1}{6}$ $1\frac{1}{2}$
      e. .02   .05   .10
      f. $\frac{1}{6}$ $\frac{1}{3}$ $\frac{3}{4}$

5.14 a. 53,000 < 56,000
      b. 66,000 > 56,000
      c. 84,000 > 56,000
      d. 51,000 < 56,000
      e. 121,000 > 56,000
      f. 10,000 < 56,000

5.15 56   21   49   63   35   42   28   0

5.16 80   320   240   360   200   0   120

5.17 Suggested equations:
      a. N = 144 − 45
         N = 99 stamps
      b. N = 128 ÷ 4
         N = 32 bottle caps
      c. N = 25 − (6 + 6 + 5 + 4)
         N = 25 − 21
         N = 4 miles
      d. $N = \frac{8}{8} − (\frac{1}{8} + \frac{2}{8} + \frac{4}{8})$
         $N = \frac{8}{8} − \frac{7}{8}$
         $N = \frac{1}{8}$ box of cereal
      e. N = (20 + 35 + 10) − (27.15 + 18.32)
         N = 65 − 45.47
         N = $19.53
      f. N = 21 + (21 + 2) + (21 + 2 + 5) + (3 × 25)
         N = 21 + 23 + 28 + 75
         N = 147 popsicles
      g. N = (1,860 − 60) ÷ 60
         N = 1,800 ÷ 60
         N = 30 times
      h. N = 15 + (15 ÷ 3)
         N = 15 + 5
         N = 20 fish
      i. N = 215 − (49 − 38) − (28 − 23) − (54 − 48)
         N = 215 − (11) − (5) − (6)
         N = 215 − 22
         N = 193 passengers

Math 602 Answer Key

Part One

1.1 5. 341. 8,546. 439,561,370. 26,309,641,827.

1.2 a. four hundred thirty billion, eight hundred fifty-one million, seven hundred sixty-nine thousand, twenty-three

b. five hundred twenty-six billion, forty-three million, two hundred ninety-seven thousand, six hundred

1.3 a. $\frac{5}{10}$ $\frac{36}{100}$ $\frac{25}{1,000}$ $\frac{3,768}{10,000}$ $\frac{90,176}{100,000}$

b. $\frac{2}{10}$ $\frac{9}{100}$ $\frac{350}{1,000}$ $\frac{9,354}{10,000}$ $\frac{65,130}{100,000}$

1.4 a. .90   .60   .20   .30

b. .400   .730   .060   .900

c. .8000   .3210   .0230   .0800

1.5 a. 00,365,490   4,506,143   60,521

000,756   0,496,002

b. 4,003,250   0,527,061   90,020

403,271   000,369

1.6 a. .30   .030   .007   .0250   .00960

b. .076   .54000   .063   .0800   .367000

1.7 1, 1, yes   2, 2, yes

1.8 a. 430   700   954,000

b. 80   4,200   60,000

c. 9,000   30,600   43,000

d. 510   2,400   700

1.9 4,545   1,603   1,107   4,346   13,215

1.10 a. .152   .664   .013   .36   .441

b. .3405   .2064   .469   .0308   .2822

1.11 1, 2, 3, 6, 9, 18

1.12 a. 1, 5 - P   1, 2, 4, 5, 10, 20 - C

b. 1, 2, 7, 14 - C   1, 23 - P

c. 1, 2, 3, 5, 6, 10, 15, 30 - C   1, 3, 5, 15 - C

d. 1, 3, 9, 27 - C   1, 29 - P

1.13 a. 20, 24, 28, 32, 36, 40, 44, 48

b. 45, 54, 63, 72, 81, 90 ,99, 108

c. 15, 30, 45, 60, 75, 90, 105, 120

1.14

18	1	9	2	6	3
×1	×18	×2	×9	×3	×6

1.15 a.

2, 2, 5   2, 3, 7   3, 5   3, 3, 3

b.

5, 5   2, 2, 3, 3   2, 2, 2, 7   2, 2, 2, 5

1.16 a. 210

b. 2, 2

c. 105, 105

d. 3, 3

e. 35, 35

f. 5, 5

g. 7, 7

h. 7, 7

i. 1, 1

j. 2, 3, 5, 7

1.17

2, 2, 3, 7   3, 3, 5, 5   2, 2, 3, 13

2, 3, 3, 7   2, 2, 2, 3, 3   2, 2, 3, 5, 7

Part Two

2.1 a. $\frac{1}{4}$ b. $\frac{1}{4}$

2.2 a. $1\frac{1}{6}$, 1 , $\frac{5}{6}$, $\frac{1}{8}$, $\frac{5}{6}$, $5\frac{1}{4}$

b. 7 , 9 , $\frac{2}{3}$, $\frac{9}{16}$, $\frac{5}{7}$, 3

c. 1 , 2 , $\frac{2}{5}$, $\frac{5}{7}$, 6 , $\frac{7}{9}$

2.3 a. 12, 6, 16, 9, 21, 25

b. 10, 9, 8, 21, 4, 8

c. 4, 9, 14, 4, 7, 10

2.4 a. 4, 8, 12, 16, 20, 24, 28, 32, 36, 40

b. 7, 14, 21, 28, 35, 42, 49, 56, 63, 70

2.5 a. 5, 10, 15, 20, 25
4, 8, 12, 16, 20
20
20

b. $\dfrac{3}{5} = \dfrac{12}{20}$

$+\dfrac{1}{4} = \dfrac{5}{20}$

$\dfrac{17}{20}$

2.6 $\dfrac{3}{6} = \dfrac{12}{24}$

$-\dfrac{3}{8} = \dfrac{9}{24}$

$\dfrac{3}{24} = \dfrac{1}{8}$

2.7 a. $1\dfrac{1}{9}$, $1\dfrac{1}{16}$, $\dfrac{19}{24}$, $\dfrac{13}{15}$, $1\dfrac{5}{24}$, $\dfrac{5}{6}$

b. $\dfrac{1}{3}$, $\dfrac{7}{15}$, $\dfrac{7}{16}$, $\dfrac{1}{12}$, $\dfrac{3}{10}$, $\dfrac{3}{10}$

c. $\dfrac{31}{36}$, $\dfrac{23}{24}$, $\dfrac{13}{14}$, $\dfrac{1}{4}$, $\dfrac{13}{30}$, $\dfrac{13}{18}$

2.8 a. $\dfrac{3}{4}$, 1, $1\dfrac{1}{4}$, $1\dfrac{1}{5}$, $\dfrac{7}{8}$, 1, $\dfrac{2}{3}$

b. $\dfrac{1}{3}$, $\dfrac{1}{3}$, $\dfrac{3}{4}$, $\dfrac{3}{5}$, $\dfrac{2}{5}$, $\dfrac{2}{9}$, $\dfrac{1}{2}$

c. $1\dfrac{1}{8}$, $\dfrac{13}{15}$, $1\dfrac{7}{24}$, $\dfrac{13}{20}$, $\dfrac{9}{20}$, $1\dfrac{4}{15}$

d. $\dfrac{1}{2}$, $\dfrac{1}{16}$, $\dfrac{8}{15}$, $\dfrac{5}{36}$, $\dfrac{11}{24}$, $\dfrac{1}{6}$

e. $\dfrac{41}{60}$, $1\dfrac{5}{12}$, $1\dfrac{5}{28}$, $\dfrac{25}{32}$, $\dfrac{31}{45}$, $1\dfrac{1}{15}$

f. $\dfrac{1}{24}$, $\dfrac{1}{4}$, $\dfrac{1}{12}$, $\dfrac{1}{3}$, $\dfrac{7}{24}$, $\dfrac{1}{15}$

2.9 a. 35 R7   22 R27   36 R15   29 R6   23 R24
b. 18 R41   58 R5   37 R3   49 R12   22 R9
c. 18 R18   33 R3   35   15 R26   58

2.10 a. 2   4 2^4 16
b. 5   3 5^3 125
c. 3   4 3^4 81
d. 7   3 7^3 343
e. 2   5 2^5 32

2.11 a. 2, 3   2, 2 $2^2 \times 3^2$ 36
b. 3, 5   2, 2 $3^2 \times 5^2$ 225
c. 2, 7   2, 2 $2^2 \times 7^2$ 196
d. 2, 5   2, 3 $2^2 \times 5^3$ 500
e. 2, 3   3, 3 $2^3 \times 3^3$ 216

2.12 a. five cubed
$5 \times 5 \times 5$ 125

b. two to the fifth power
$2 \times 2 \times 2 \times 2 \times 2$ 32

c. eleven squared
11×11 121

d. three to the fourth power
$3 \times 3 \times 3 \times 3$ 81

e. seven cubed
$7 \times 7 \times 7$ 343

f. three square
3×3 9

g. five to the fourth power
$5 \times 5 \times 5 \times 5$ 625

2.13 a. ten to the fourth power
$10 \times 10 \times 10 \times 10$ 10,000

b. ten to the fifth power
$10 \times 10 \times 10 \times 10 \times 10$ 100,000

c. ten to the first power
10   10

d. ten cubed
$10 \times 10 \times 10$ 1,000

e. ten to the ninth power
$10 \times 10 \times 10 \times 10 \times 10 \times 10 \times 10 \times 10 \times 10$

1,000,000,000

Part Three

3.1 a. 138   62   127   117
E E E   O O E   E O O   O E O
58   36   39   71
E E E   O O E   E O O   O E O
b. even   even   odd   odd
even   even   odd   odd
c. even   even   odd
d. ⑧③   ③⑥④   ②③⑧
①①②

3.2 a. 40   200   350   8,960
b. 7,200   60,300   4,900   800
c. 59,000   21,000   7,000   460,000

3.3 a. Ⓒ1, 2, 4, 8   Ⓒ1, 2, 5, 10
b. Ⓟ1, 13   Ⓒ1, 2, 4, 8, 16
c. Ⓒ1, 2, 3, 6, 9, 18   Ⓟ1, 7
d. Ⓒ1, 3, 7, 21   Ⓒ1, 3, 9, 27
e. Ⓟ1, 2   Ⓒ1, 2, 4, 5, 8, 10, 20, 40

3.4 a.

	32
2	16
2	8
2	4
2	2
2	1

2^5

	72
2	36
2	18
2	9
3	3
3	1

$2^3 \times 3^2$

	216
2	108
2	54
2	27
3	9
3	3
3	1

$2^3 \times 3^3$

	300
2	150
2	75
3	25
5	5
5	1

$2^2 \times 3 \times 5^2$

b.

	252
2	126
2	63
3	21
3	7
7	1

$2^2 \times 3^2 \times 7$

	180
2	90
2	45
3	15
3	5
5	1

$2^2 \times 3^2 \times 5$

	189
3	63
3	21
3	7
7	1

$3^3 \times 7$

	588
2	294
2	147
3	49
7	7
7	1

$2^2 \times 3 \times 7^2$

3.5 a. 350   490   140   210   560   70
b. 270   0   360   630   450   180
c. 120   540   240   60   0   360

3.6 23,715   18,067   16,974
180,540   314,484   162,099

3.7 $\frac{1}{15}, \frac{2}{15}, \frac{6}{15}, \frac{7}{15}, \frac{8}{15}, \frac{9}{15}, \frac{11}{15}, \frac{15}{15}$

3.8 a. 4   24   15   36
b. 30   24   14   30
c. 12   12   18   28
d. 20   24   30   24

3.9 a. $\frac{5}{18}$ $\frac{1}{3} = \frac{6}{18}$ $\frac{5}{9} = \frac{10}{18}$ $\frac{1}{2} = \frac{9}{18}$ $\frac{5}{6} = \frac{15}{18}$ $\frac{7}{9} = \frac{14}{18}$

$\frac{5}{18}, \frac{1}{3}, \frac{1}{2}, \frac{5}{9}, \frac{7}{9}, \frac{5}{6}$

b. $\frac{3}{4} = \frac{18}{24}$ $\frac{1}{6} = \frac{4}{24}$ $\frac{2}{3} = \frac{16}{24}$ $\frac{7}{12} = \frac{14}{24}$ $\frac{11}{24}$ $\frac{5}{8} = \frac{15}{24}$

$\frac{1}{6}, \frac{11}{24}, \frac{7}{12}, \frac{5}{8}, \frac{2}{3}, \frac{3}{4}$

3.10 a. $\neq$ $6 \times 3 = 18$ $2 \times 8 = 16$
    $\neq$ $7 \times 5 = 35$ $4 \times 8 = 32$
b. $=$ $2 \times 21 = 42$ $6 \times 7 = 42$
    $=$ $3 \times 12 = 36$ $4 \times 9 = 36$
c. $\neq$ $4 \times 15 = 60$ $8 \times 9 = 72$
    $\neq$ $2 \times 16 = 32$ $5 \times 8 = 40$
d. $=$ $5 \times 30 = 150$ $10 \times 15 = 150$
    $=$ $4 \times 15 = 60$ $6 \times 10 = 60$

3.11 a. $7\frac{1}{2}$ $25\frac{2}{3}$ $12\frac{1}{3}$ $5\frac{1}{6}$ $3\frac{4}{5}$ $6\frac{1}{2}$

3.12 a. $10\frac{2}{5}$ 16 $26\frac{3}{7}$ $56\frac{1}{2}$ $34\frac{1}{2}$ $35\frac{1}{2}$
b. $15\frac{1}{3}$ 13 $29\frac{1}{15}$ $86\frac{4}{7}$ $81\frac{1}{5}$ $31\frac{1}{2}$

3.13 a. $13\frac{1}{10}$ $14\frac{11}{12}$ $9\frac{1}{8}$ $18\frac{1}{4}$ $14\frac{3}{10}$ $30\frac{4}{45}$
b. $5\frac{3}{8}$ $5\frac{2}{9}$ $3\frac{5}{16}$ $9\frac{7}{15}$ $7\frac{5}{14}$ $7\frac{11}{36}$

3.14 a. $12\frac{1}{3}$ 31 $22\frac{1}{2}$ $12\frac{1}{2}$ $6\frac{2}{5}$ $5\frac{1}{3}$
b. $14\frac{2}{5}$ $18\frac{1}{2}$ $13\frac{1}{3}$ $58\frac{1}{5}$ $63\frac{1}{8}$ $66\frac{1}{12}$
c. $6\frac{3}{8}$ $14\frac{4}{15}$ $15\frac{1}{2}$ $12\frac{1}{4}$ $31\frac{5}{6}$ $39\frac{19}{24}$
d. $4\frac{4}{15}$ $6\frac{1}{30}$ $8\frac{1}{24}$ $4\frac{11}{21}$ $7\frac{7}{20}$ $19\frac{4}{45}$
e. 36 $24\frac{1}{2}$ $25\frac{13}{15}$ $3\frac{1}{5}$ $6\frac{1}{3}$ $11\frac{1}{4}$
f. $11\frac{23}{24}$ $12\frac{1}{2}$ $31\frac{5}{18}$ 14 $7\frac{1}{6}$ $12\frac{1}{6}$

3.15 a. 538   317   71   98   109   528
b. Thornville   Mason City   Alston
    Lewiston   Westport   Janisberg
c. 1,661
d. 467

3.16 a. 5,000,000   6,000,000   11
b. 94,000,000   78,000,000   172
c. 110,000,000   638,000,000   748
d. 422,000,000   53,000,000   475
e. 626,000,000   238,000,000   388
f. 71,000,000   55,000,000   16
g. 385,000,000   272,000,000   113
h. 863,000,000   59,000,000   804

3.17 a. 439,000,000,000   349,000,000,000
    438,000,000,000   385,000,000,000
    384,000,000,000   440,000,000,000
b. 349, 384, 385, 438, 439, 440

Part Four

4.1 a. 28.258   66.804   68.65
b. 86.631   .669   24.44
c. 36.72   53.63   .746
d. 5.85   7.52   6.44   2.51
e. 3.04   6.684   3.96   3.37
f. 7.4   14.1   .539   1.75

4.2 a. .2072   5.888   2.1252   1.0368   .038394
b. .3448   43.424   26.88   .8192   2.34

4.3 a. 9 (E), 10.4 (L), 27 (M), 3.6 (L), 28.8 (M), 27 (E)
    b. 18 (E), 6.4 (L), 16.8 (M), 21 (E), 3.2 (L), 6 (E)
    c. 8 (E)   25.2 (M)
       14.7 (M)   18 (E)

4.4 a. .02432 .002262 .000884 .001848 1.7654
    b. .002193 .03941 .01465 .24548 .36868

4.5 a. Forty-six plus seventeen equals
        sixty-three.
    b. Thirty-two is greater than twenty-seven.
    c. Eighty-two minus fifty-eight is not equal
        to thirty-five.
    d. Three plus six is less than fourteen
        minus three.

4.6 a. $69 < 93$
    b. $81 - 45 = 36$
    c. $24 + 39 \neq 61$
    d. $6 \times 5 > 3 \times 9$

4.7 a. $\neq$ N $=$ Y $=$ Y
    b. $=$ Y $\neq$ N $\neq$ N
    c. $=$ Y $\neq$ N $\neq$ N
    d. $\neq$ N $\neq$ N $=$ Y

4.8   9   4   8
        6   14   11

4.9 a.
$$236 + N = 529$$
$$236(-236) + N = 529 - 236$$
$$N = 293$$
$$236 + 293 = 529$$
$$N + 417 = 631$$
$$N + 417(-417) = 631 - 417$$
$$N = 214$$
$$214 + 417 = 631$$
$$518 + N = 874$$
$$518(-518) + N = 874 - 518$$
$$N = 356$$
$$518 + 356 = 874$$
$$N + 316 = 522$$
$$N + 316(-316) = 522 - 316$$
$$N = 206$$
$$206 + 316 = 522$$

    b.
$$207 = N + 95$$
$$207 - 95 = N + 95(-95)$$
$$112 = N$$
$$207 = 112 + 95$$

$$387 = 291 + N$$
$$387 - 291 = 291(-291) + N$$
$$96 = N$$
$$387 = 291 + 96$$
$$732 = N + 463$$
$$732 - 4635 = N + 463(-463)$$
$$269 = N$$
$$732 = 269 + 463$$
$$451 = 218 + N$$
$$451 - 218 = 218(-218) + N$$
$$233 = N$$
$$451 = 218 + 233$$

4.10 a.
$$N - 439 = 518$$
$$N - 439(+439) = 518 + 439$$
$$N = 957$$
$$957 - 439 = 518$$
$$N - 347 = 625$$
$$N - 347(+347) = 625 + 347$$
$$N = 972$$
$$972 - 347 = 625$$
$$N - 238 = 671$$
$$N - 238(+238) = 671 + 238$$
$$N = 909$$
$$909 - 238 = 671$$
$$N - 312 = 526$$
$$N - 312(+312) = 526 + 312$$
$$N = 838$$
$$838 - 312 = 526$$

    b.
$$319 = N - 45$$
$$319 + 45 = N - 45(+45)$$
$$364 = N$$
$$319 = 364 - 45$$
$$513 = N - 248$$
$$513 + 248 = N - 248(+248)$$
$$761 = N$$
$$513 = 761 - 248$$
$$281 = N - 163$$
$$281 + 163 = N - 163(+163)$$
$$444 = N$$
$$281 = 444 - 163$$
$$152 = N - 76$$
$$152 + 76 = N - 76(+76)$$
$$228 = N$$
$$152 = 228 - 76$$

4.11   210   420   350   560   140   0

4.12 $\frac{7}{7}$ $\frac{2}{2}$ $\frac{15}{15}$ $\frac{9}{9}$ $\frac{4}{4}$ $\frac{20}{20}$

4.13 $11\frac{1}{8}$ $9\frac{5}{6}$ $7\frac{1}{3}$ $9\frac{1}{2}$ $3\frac{3}{4}$ $5\frac{1}{9}$ $3\frac{5}{6}$

4.14 $6\frac{1}{3}$ $15\frac{5}{12}$ $13\frac{1}{5}$ $4\frac{7}{9}$ $5\frac{7}{10}$ $1\frac{2}{5}$ $10\frac{3}{8}$

4.15   a. $3\frac{7}{8}$ $13\frac{2}{3}$ $5\frac{3}{4}$ $20\frac{1}{2}$ $13\frac{3}{5}$ $19\frac{5}{7}$

    b. $14\frac{5}{9}$ $9\frac{4}{11}$ $17\frac{5}{12}$ $7\frac{3}{10}$ $6\frac{1}{4}$ $3\frac{7}{12}$

    c. $5\frac{2}{5}$ $4\frac{1}{2}$ $5\frac{1}{4}$ $4\frac{1}{3}$ $\frac{5}{6}$ $2\frac{3}{8}$

4.16   a. $2\frac{4}{5}$ $7\frac{2}{3}$ $2\frac{2}{3}$ $8\frac{1}{3}$ $11\frac{3}{4}$ $15\frac{7}{8}$

    b. $20\frac{3}{5}$ $10\frac{3}{5}$ $3\frac{6}{7}$ $7\frac{1}{2}$ $28\frac{1}{3}$ $2\frac{4}{5}$

    c. $5\frac{3}{4}$ $21\frac{2}{3}$ $3\frac{4}{5}$ $13\frac{1}{5}$ $16\frac{8}{9}$ $6\frac{5}{7}$

4.17   a.   54 R6   33 R5   209   70 R2   112
    b.   145 R2   95   30 R6   188   74 R4
    c.   91 R1   336   61 R4   115 R3   42

Part Five

5.1   a.   four tenths - .4 - $\frac{4}{10}$ - .40
    b.   four hundredths - .04 - $\frac{4}{100}$ - .040
    c.   four thousandths - .004 - $\frac{4}{1,000}$ - .0040
    d.   three-fifths - $\frac{3}{5}$ - $\frac{6}{10}$ - $\frac{15}{25}$
    e.   one-sixth - $\frac{1}{6}$ - $\frac{3}{18}$ - $\frac{5}{30}$
    f.   two-thirds - $\frac{2}{3}$ - $\frac{8}{12}$ - $\frac{14}{21}$
    g.   one-half - $\frac{1}{2}$ - $\frac{7}{14}$ - $\frac{9}{18}$
    h.   seven-eighths - $\frac{7}{8}$ - $\frac{14}{16}$ - $\frac{35}{40}$
    i.   three-fourths - $\frac{3}{4}$ - $\frac{15}{20}$ - $\frac{24}{32}$

5.2   a. $(3 \times 5) + 4 = 15 + 4 = 19$
       $9 + (8 - 3) = 9 + 5 = 14$
       $25 \div (6 - 1) = 25 \div 5 = 5$
       $(7 + 3) \times 45 = 10 \times 45 = 450$
    b. $8 + (54 \div 9) = 8 + 6 = 14$
       $43 - (2 \times 7) = 43 - 14 = 29$
       $(0 \times 5) + 12 = 0 + 12 = 12$
       $(5 \times 3) + (4 \times 6) = 15 + 24 = 39$

5.3   a.   4.4 miles
    b. $1\frac{5}{8}$ cups
    c.   12   24   36   48   60   72
    d.   1,855 miles
    e. $\frac{5}{8} = \frac{15}{24}$ $\frac{7}{12} = \frac{14}{24}$ Jodie was closer.
    f. $\frac{3}{8} = \frac{15}{40}$ $\frac{2}{5} = \frac{16}{40}$ Sister's friend received more.

5.4   60   60   24
    30-31   12   365
    10   20
    100   1,000

5.5   12   36   3   5,280
    144   9

5.6   16   2,000
    16   2
    2   4   12

5.7   a.   31   28   31   30   31   30
      31   31   30   31   30   31
    b.   6   20   160
      48   72   16
      4   2   16
      1   3   10
    c.   19 ft. 9 in.
      3 yr. 3 mo.
      21 pt. 14 oz.
      3 wk. 2 da.
    d.   2 qt.
    e.   linear units
    f.   12 boxes

5.8   a.   A.M.   P.M.
    b.   B.C.
    c.   A.D.
    d.   teacher check

5.9   a.   Julian Calendar 46 B.C.
    b.   366   46 B.C.
      It takes $365\frac{1}{4}$ days for the earth to revolve around the sun.
    c.   1752   11 days
      teacher check
    d.   2 millenniums
    e.   1776
    f.   teacher check

5.10   a.   769,000,000
    b.   687
    c.   1,500   83,200   40,000
    d.   4606

e. 36   45   54   63   72

f. 11, 13, 17, 19

g.

	294	
2	147	
3	49	
7	7	
7	1	$2 \times 3 \times 7^2$

	396	
2	198	
2	99	
3	33	
3	11	
11	1	$2^2 \times 3^2 \times 11$

h. $12\frac{1}{10}$ 9.127

i. 5.67 $5\frac{1}{2}$

j. 45

k. suggested answers (k and l)

    540,680   054,068

l. 4.057   4.570

m. 2

n. $\frac{2}{5} = \frac{8}{20}$ $\frac{1}{4} = \frac{5}{20}$ $\frac{7}{10} = \frac{14}{20}$ $\frac{9}{20}$ $\frac{4}{5} = \frac{16}{20}$ $\frac{3}{4} = \frac{15}{20}$

    $\frac{1}{4}$ $\frac{2}{5}$ $\frac{9}{20}$ $\frac{7}{10}$ $\frac{3}{4}$ $\frac{4}{5}$

5.11 a. $\frac{5}{6}$ $\frac{8}{9}$ $\frac{7}{16}$ $1\frac{1}{10}$ $11\frac{1}{2}$ $11\frac{1}{3}$

    b. 6 $9\frac{3}{4}$ $10\frac{11}{15}$ $13\frac{13}{24}$ $13\frac{3}{4}$ $7\frac{13}{16}$

    c. $\frac{3}{4}$ $\frac{1}{6}$ $\frac{1}{10}$ $\frac{1}{15}$ $5\frac{3}{5}$ $1\frac{15}{16}$

    d. $4\frac{1}{2}$ $2\frac{1}{8}$ $6\frac{1}{2}$ $8\frac{3}{10}$ $7\frac{5}{6}$ $3\frac{5}{18}$

    e. 4.884   19.826   23.607

    f. 9.6   38.38   36.2   22.77

    g. 2.55   .3016   .1363   .004473

5.12 a. O   E   E   O

    b. E   O   E   E

5.13 a. $37 - (2 \times 3) - 3 - 4 = \underline{\quad}$

       $37 - 6 - 3 - 4 = 24$ people

    b. $120 - (6 \times 8) - (5 \times 10) - (3 \times 4) = \underline{\quad}$

       $120 - 48 - 50 - 12 = 10$ favors

    c. Mark caught 12 fish.

       Kevin caught 9 fish.

       Bob caught 18 fish.

    d. $\$4.21 - (2 \times .25) - (4 \times .10) - (3 \times .05) =$

       $\$4.21 - .50 - .40 - .15 = \$3.16$

5.14 a.
$$285 = N + 46$$
$$285 - 46 = N + 46(-46)$$
$$239 = N$$

$$N - 38 = 127$$
$$N - 38(+38) = 127 + 38$$
$$N = 165$$

$$N + 85 = 154$$
$$N + 85(-85) = 154 - 85$$
$$N = 69$$

b.
$$69 + N = 153$$
$$69 + N(-69) = 153 - 69$$
$$N = 84$$

$$258 = N - 197$$
$$258 + 197 = N - 197(+197)$$
$$455 = N$$

$$N - 139 = 127$$
$$N - 139(+139) = 127 + 139$$
$$N = 266$$

Math 603 Answer Key

Part One

1.1 a. 41 R7 105 R3 48 R3 207 187 R1 92
   b. 15 R5 125 R4 54 R2 208 R2 72 433 R1
   c. 61 R3 116 R3 237 R2 65 R5 94 94

1.2 594,729 1,073,419 44,496 49,621

1.3 a. 60 2,760 38,410 582,680
   b. 3,600 79,300 580,500 1,873,300
   c. 5,000 83,000 170,000 2,360,000

1.4 a. 1,②,4 1,②,5, 10
   b. 1, 2, 3,⑥ 1, 2, 3, 4,⑥,8, 12, 24
   c. 1, 2,④,8 1, 2, 3,④,6, 12
   d. 1, 2,③,6 1,③,9
   e. 1, 2,④,8 1, 2,④,5, 10, 20
   f. 1,③,5, 15 1, 2,③,6, 9, 18

1.5 a. $\frac{10}{24} = \frac{5}{12}, \frac{4}{54} = \frac{2}{27}, \frac{6}{20} = \frac{3}{10}, \frac{2}{21}, \frac{3}{16}$

   b. $\frac{4}{27}, \frac{4}{40} = \frac{1}{10}, \frac{7}{18}, \frac{10}{18} = \frac{5}{9}, \frac{9}{16}$

   c. $\frac{4}{10} = \frac{2}{5}, \frac{10}{36} = \frac{5}{18}, \frac{15}{48} = \frac{5}{16}, \frac{7}{40}, \frac{3}{30} = \frac{1}{10}$

1.6 a. $\frac{1}{6}, \frac{2}{15}, \frac{8}{15}, \frac{9}{32}, \frac{1}{8}$

   b. $\frac{9}{20}, \frac{3}{20}, \frac{7}{16}, \frac{5}{18}, \frac{1}{6}$

   c. $\frac{5}{16}, \frac{8}{27}, \frac{4}{28} = \frac{1}{7}, \frac{2}{40} = \frac{1}{20}, \frac{6}{12} = \frac{1}{2}$

1.7 $\frac{5}{1}$ $\frac{13}{1}$ $\frac{9}{1}$ $\frac{42}{1}$ $\frac{28}{1}$ $\frac{15}{1}$ $\frac{36}{1}$

1.8 a. $\frac{42}{4} = 10\frac{2}{4} = 10\frac{1}{2}$ $\frac{80}{8} = 10$ $\frac{60}{9} = 6\frac{6}{9} = 6\frac{2}{3}$
   $\frac{6}{4} = 1\frac{2}{4} = 1\frac{1}{2}$ $\frac{14}{3} = 4\frac{2}{3}$
   b. $\frac{20}{5} = 4$ $\frac{25}{7} = 3\frac{4}{7}$ $\frac{48}{5} = 9\frac{3}{5}$
   $\frac{24}{5} = 4\frac{4}{5}$ $\frac{36}{8} = 4\frac{4}{8} = 4\frac{1}{2}$

1.9 a. 12 people 12 balls
   b. 21 coins 15 cars
   c. 24 pencils 10 peanuts

1.10 a. 6 cans 9 boxes
   b. 4 jars 4 pails
   c. 5 boxes 18 × 5 = 90 b-day cards

1.11 a. $\frac{1}{3}, \frac{8}{9}, \frac{3}{4}, \frac{3}{4}, \frac{5}{8}, \frac{7}{8}$

   b. $\frac{1}{2}, \frac{2}{3}, \frac{1}{2}, \frac{4}{5}, \frac{4}{5}, \frac{3}{7}$

1.12 a. $\frac{1}{6}$ $\frac{2}{3}$ $\frac{2}{3}$ $\frac{1}{4}$ $\frac{22}{27}$
   b. $\frac{7}{20}$ $\frac{27}{32}$ $\frac{1}{10}$ $\frac{10}{21}$ $\frac{28}{39}$
   c. $\frac{5}{9}$ $\frac{7}{10}$ $\frac{5}{21}$ $\frac{1}{4}$ $\frac{1}{4}$
   d. $\frac{5}{8}$ $\frac{1}{4}$ $\frac{2}{3}$ $\frac{3}{5}$ $\frac{3}{7}$

1.13 a. 16 47 30
   b. 22 48 27
   c. 465 261 422
   d. 17 23

1.14 a. 14 + 18 = 32 215 − 89 = 126
   b. 75 = 5 × 15 24 = 120 ÷ 5

1.15 a. subtract 19 + N = 45
   19(− 19) + N = 45 − 19
   N = 26
   divide N × 8 = 104
   N × 8(÷ 8) = 104 ÷ 8
   N = 13
   b. subtract N + 36 = 91
   N + 36(− 36) = 91 − 36
   N = 55
   add 143 = N − 265
   143 + 265 = N − 265(− 265)
   408 = N
   c. multiply 32 = N ÷ 7
   32 × 7 = N ÷ 7(× 7)
   224 = N
   add N − 481 = 253
   N − 481(+ 481) = 253 + 481
   N = 734
   d. divide 7 × N = 168
   7 × N(÷ 7) = 168 ÷ 7
   N = 24
   multiply N ÷ 5 = 120
   N ÷ 5(× 5) = 120 × 5
   N = 600
   e. add N − 83 = 27
   N − 83(+ 83) = 27 + 83
   N = 110
   subtract 138 = N + 91
   138 − 91 = N + 91(− 91)
   47 = N

1.16 80, 160, 240, 320, 400, 480, 560, 640, 720
   240, 560, 80, 320, 160, 400, 160

1.17 70 50 60 60 90 70

1.18 a. 315 35 R7 61 31 R12 36
   b. 204 R4 156 410 R11 169 R2 51
   c. 432 805 403 702 460

1.19 ten millions   hundred billions
hundred thousands   ten billions
hundreds   ten thousands
tens   hundred millions

Part Two

2.1 $\frac{7}{2}$ $\frac{23}{4}$ $\frac{49}{5}$ $\frac{20}{3}$ $\frac{77}{6}$ $\frac{59}{7}$ $\frac{37}{8}$

2.2
a.   4   3   40
b.   7 $5\frac{1}{4}$ 21
c. $2\frac{4}{7}$ $1\frac{1}{5}$ $58\frac{1}{2}$
d.   3 $3\frac{1}{4}$ 36
e.   4 $8\frac{3}{4}$ 90
f.   3 $1\frac{1}{3}$ $8\frac{1}{3}$

2.3
a.   24   63   8   8   9
b.   49   6   28   6   42
c.   4   27   5   10,000   40

2.4   56   14   35   21   42   49   63   0   28

2.5
a.   6 $10\frac{1}{2}$ $\frac{7}{12}$ 8
b. $\frac{16}{35}$ $4\frac{4}{5}$ $\frac{33}{40}$ 55
c. $9\frac{1}{3}$ $2\frac{2}{3}$ $9\frac{1}{3}$ $40\frac{1}{2}$
d. $\frac{2}{3}$ $\frac{15}{28}$ 21   32

2.6
a. $5 + 8 = 4 + 9$
b. $3 \times 5 > 2 \times 7$
c. $27 \div 3 < 12 - 2$
d. $15 - 2 \neq 4 \times 3$

2.7
a.   even   odd   odd
b.   odd   even   even

2.8
a.   seven-eighths
two-thirds
one-half
b.   two and five ninths
six and three-fourths
c.   fourteen and one-fifth
twelve and five-sixths

2.9
a.   2,730   21,717   51,595
599,417   124,992   237,150
b.   219,696   118,218   1,326,894
2,734,020   5,026,317

2.10
a. $>$ $=$ $<$ $>$
b. $=$ $<$ $>$ $=$
c. $<$ $=$ $=$ $<$
d. $<$ $=$ $>$ $>$

2.11
a. $<$ $>$
b. $>$ $=$
c. $<$ $<$
d. $=$ $=$

2.12
a. $\frac{7}{16}, \frac{10}{16}, \frac{8}{16}, \frac{12}{16}$ $\frac{7}{16}, \frac{1}{2}, \frac{5}{8}, \frac{3}{4}$
b. $\frac{21}{24}, \frac{18}{24}, \frac{20}{24}, \frac{16}{24}, \frac{19}{24}$ $\frac{2}{3}, \frac{3}{4}, \frac{19}{24}, \frac{5}{6}, \frac{7}{8}$
c. $\frac{13}{18}, \frac{9}{18}, \frac{14}{18}, \frac{12}{18}, \frac{15}{18}$ $\frac{1}{2}, \frac{2}{3}, \frac{13}{18}, \frac{7}{9}, \frac{5}{6}$
d. $\frac{16}{36}, \frac{24}{36}, \frac{21}{36}, \frac{30}{36}, \frac{25}{36}$ $\frac{4}{9}, \frac{7}{12}, \frac{2}{3}, \frac{25}{36}, \frac{5}{6}$
e. $\frac{2}{3} = \frac{8}{12}$ $\frac{3}{4} = \frac{9}{12}$ $\frac{5}{6} = \frac{10}{12}$ $\frac{7}{12}$

Mark, Jess, James, Karen

2.13   a. 9   b. 23   c. 129   d. 1,386

2.14   a. 13   b. 32   c. 369   d. 872
      13   32   369   872

2.15   a. 17   b. 219   c. 39
      17   219   39

2.16   a. 139   b. 43   c. 191
      139   43   191

      d. 1,720   e. 1,722
        1,720   1,722

2.17
a. $(18 + 52) + (34 + 16) = 70 + 50 = 120$
    $(27 + 33) + 15 = 60 + 15 = 75$
b. $(11 + 9) + (15 + 25) = 20 + 40 = 60$
    $(44 + 26) + (19 + 1) = 70 + 20 = 90$
c. $(75 + 25) + 41 = 100 + 41 = 141$
    $(68 + 22) + (10 + 9) = 90 + 19 = 109$
d. $(37 + 13) + 15 = 50 + 15 = 65$
    $(81 + 19) + (16 + 24) = 100 + 40 = 140$
e. $(56 + 34) + (12 + 8) = 90 + 20 = 110$
    $(5 + 25) + 17 = 30 + 17 = 47$

2.18 $\frac{5}{10} = \frac{50}{100}$ $\frac{5}{100} = \frac{50}{1,000}$ $\frac{75}{100} = \frac{750}{1,000}$ $\frac{75}{100} = \frac{7,500}{10,000}$

2.19 $.5 = .50$ $.5 = .500$ $.75 = .750$ $.75 = .7500$

2.20   a.   .4   .6   .7   .8   .9

      b.   .70   .60   .40   .80   .90

         .40   .60   .70   .80   .90

      c.   .700   .600   .400   .800   .900

         .400   .600   .700   .800   .900

2.21   a.   .450   .300   .070   .590   .060

         .060   .07   .3   .45   .59

      b.   .300   .320   .040   .541   .175

         .04   .175   .3   .32   .541

      c.   .600   .076   .138   .250   .270

         .076   .138   .25   .27   .6

      d.   .090   .910   .430   .351   .048

         .048   .09   .351   .43   .91

2.22   a.   .8   .4   .1   .9   .1   .3

      b.   .25   .63   .04   .10   .57

      c.   .386   .947   .144   .793

2.23   a.

Name: <u>Vehicle Sales</u>

      b.

Name: <u>Vehicle Sales</u>

2.24   a.   1.44   27.06   .5272   20.51   .01872   .368

      b.   114.66   .04648   .1862   46.177   .37582   69.496

Part Three

3.1   equal to one-half $\dfrac{8}{16}, \dfrac{\cdot 10}{20}$

      more than one-half $\dfrac{6}{8}, \dfrac{9}{12}, \dfrac{11}{18}, \dfrac{16}{25}$

3.2   8   4   10   14   17   23

      10   34   53   95   173   216

3.3   a. $252\frac{2}{3} = 253$ $80\frac{2}{6} = 80$ $156\frac{4}{5} = 157$ $168\frac{3}{4} = 169$

      b. $42\frac{6}{9} = 43$ $77\frac{3}{7} = 77$ $197\frac{1}{2} = 198$ $115\frac{1}{8} = 115$

      c. $15\frac{6}{38} = 15$ $7\frac{27}{52} = 8$ $45\frac{3}{21} = 45$ $8\frac{33}{63} = 9$

      d. $45\frac{1}{29} = 45$ $81\frac{3}{47} = 81$ $94\frac{3}{18} = 94$ $21\frac{4}{56} = 21$

3.4   a.   .34   .09   .002   4.3   4.02

      b.   21.8   .0688   69.4   .053   .391

3.5   a.   .418   .64   .9   .03   .508

      b.   .05   .30   2.2   7.4   3.65

3.6   a. $.81\frac{3}{4} = .82$ $7.9\frac{5}{8} = 8.0$ $.007\frac{1}{6} = .007$

         $.70\frac{2}{9} = .70$ $.315\frac{1}{3} = .315$

      b. $.033\frac{2}{5} = .033$ $.070\frac{3}{7} = .070$ $.125\frac{4}{6} = .126$

         $7.0\frac{3}{4} = 7.1$ $6.5\frac{5}{8} = 6.6$

      c. $.91\frac{2}{5} = .91$ $.082\frac{2}{3} = .083$ $.020\frac{1}{2} = .021$

         $1.02\frac{1}{3} = 1.02$ $8.1\frac{7}{9} = 8.2$

3.7   a.   .6   .625(.63)   .75   .333(.33)   .833(.83)

      b.   .5   .22(.22)   .166(.17)   .583(.58)   .375(.38)

3.8   a.   Four times nine is equal to six times six.

      b.   Seven plus six is greater than eighteen minus four.

      c.   Twenty-three minus zero is not equal to twenty-three times zero.

      d.   Forty-two divided by six is less than four times four.

3.9   a.   477,000   477

         567,360,000   567,360

      b.   382,000,000   382

         6,322,000,000   6,322

      c.   10,000,000,000   10

         477,000,000,000   477

3.10   a.

	10,423	8,000	80,805	24,000	634,810	258,000
		+ 2,000		+ 57,000		+ 376,000
		10,000		81,000		634,000

      b.

	2,441	5,000	33,035	69,000	376,425	814,000
		− 3,000		− 35,000		− 438,000
		2,000		34,000		376,000

3.11   141   1,245

3.12   a. $4 < 5$ $10 > 9$

      b. $6 > 2$ $7 < 11$

      c. $35 \div 7 = 15 \div 3$

      d. $14 - 2 \neq 8 + 5$

3.13   a. $3,957 < 4,558 < 6,492$

      b. $6,492 > 4,558 > 3,957$

3.14   a.   8, 9, 10

      b.   15, 14, 13

      c.   2, 4, 6, 8, 10

      d.   13, 11, 9, 7, 5

      e.   15, 20, 25, 30

      f.   180, 150, 120, 90

3.15 a. The set of numbers that are equal to or greater than twenty but less than twenty-three is twenty, twenty-one, and twenty-two.

 b. The set of numbers that are equal to or less then thirty-five but greater than thirty two is thirty-five, thirty-four, and thirty-three.

3.16   81   49   125   32   0

3.17 a. 2^4 $2^2 \times 5$ $2^3 \times 3$

 b. $2^2 \times 7^2$ $2^2 \times 3^2$ 2×5^2

3.18

6		8		9		12		20

2×3 2^3 3^2 $2^2 \times 3$ $2^2 \times 5$

3.19 a. 2×3 3^2
 $2 \quad 3^2$
 $2 \times 3^2 = 18$

 b. 2^3 $2^2 \times 3$
 $2^3 \quad 3$
 $2^3 \times 3 = 24$

3.20 $2, 3$ $2^2, 5$
 $2^2 \quad 3 \quad 5$
 $2^2 \times 3 \times 5 = 60$

3.21

4		12		15		18		27

2^2 $2^2, 3$ $3, 5$ $2, 3^2$ 3^3

3.22 a. $2^2, 3$ $3, 5$
 $2^2 \quad 3 \quad 5$
 $2^2 \times 3 \times 5 = 60$

 b. $3, 5$ $2, 3^2$
 $2 \quad 3^2 \quad 5$
 $2 \times 3^2 \times 5 = 90$

 c. $2, 3^2$ 3^3
 $2 \quad 3^3$
 $2 \times 3^3 = 54$

3.23 a. $1\frac{1}{18}$ $\frac{19}{24}$ $\frac{31}{60}$ $\frac{37}{45}$ $1\frac{7}{40}$ $\frac{29}{36}$

 b. $\frac{13}{36}$ $\frac{19}{40}$ $\frac{25}{36}$ $\frac{11}{30}$ $\frac{3}{20}$ $\frac{23}{54}$

Part Four

4.1   8.   257.   58,356.

4.2 a. 23.0.   230   5.60.   560
 b. 763.000.   763,000   9.040.   9,040
 c. 9,342.00.   934,200   6.8.72   68.72
 d. 23,548.0.   235,480   .325.   325

4.3 a. 5.6.   5.6   .09.5   .095
 b. .083.   .083   .006.24   .00624
 c. .007.   .007   .08.01   .0801
 d. .054.   .054   .7.18   .718

4.4 $100 \times \$.17 = .17. = \$17$

4.5 $1,560 \div 10 = 156.0. = 156$ paper clips

4.6 $\frac{5}{6}$ $1\frac{5}{8}$ $\frac{8}{9}$ $\frac{19}{24}$ $1\frac{1}{15}$ $\frac{37}{45}$

4.7   6   10   14   18

4.8 a. $\frac{4}{24} = \frac{1}{6}$ $\frac{12}{24} = \frac{1}{2}$ $\frac{8}{24} = \frac{1}{3}$

 b. 6   18   12

4.9 a. $7\frac{1}{2}$ $12\frac{2}{3}$ $14\frac{3}{5}$ $17\frac{7}{10}$ $26\frac{7}{30}$

 b. $5\frac{1}{3}$ $2\frac{3}{8}$ $3\frac{1}{2}$ $3\frac{3}{8}$ $14\frac{3}{7}$

 c. $2\frac{1}{12}$ $2\frac{2}{3}$ $8\frac{5}{12}$ $11\frac{3}{10}$ $7\frac{5}{16}$

 d. $1\frac{3}{4}$ $3\frac{7}{10}$ $\frac{5}{24}$ $4\frac{7}{16}$ $10\frac{1}{2}$

4.10 a. 8   b. 1   c. 5   d. 2   e. 3
 f. 6   g. 9   h. 4   i. 7

4.11 a. 1   b. 5   c. 4   d. 2   e. 3

4.12 a.

 b. R

 c.

 d.

4.13   oval, circle

4.14 a. 3   b. 2   c. 1   d. 4

4.15   Suggested Answers:

4.16 a. 4   b. 1   c. 3   d. 5   e. 2

4.17 $\overrightarrow{FG} \parallel \overleftrightarrow{MN}$ $\angle TSO \cong \angle BDS$
 $\overline{LM} \perp \overline{YZ}$ $\overleftrightarrow{XY} \cong \overrightarrow{RS}$

4.18 a. 18   b. 20   c. 45   d. 63

2×3^2 $2^2 \times 5$ $3^2 \times 5$ $3^2 \times 7$

 e. 2 3^2

4.19   Suggested Answers:
   a. 437,000,000,000   437 billions
   b. 276,000,000   276 million
   c. 8,000,000,000   8 billions
   d. 51,000,000   51 millions
   e. 370,000,000   370 millions
   f. 54,000,000,000   54 billions
   g. 93 million
   h. 36 million
   i. 141 million
   j. Mercury, Earth, Mars

4.20   Suggested Answers:
   a. 400,000,000,000 437×10^{11}
   b. 300,000,000 3×10^{8}
   c. 7,000,000,000 7×10^{9}
   d. 50,000,000 5×10^{7}
   e. 9,000 9×10^{3}
   f. 300,000 3×10^{5}
   g. 4×10^{9}
   h. 5×10^{8}
   i. 67×10^{6}
   j. Pluto, Jupiter, Venus

4.21 a. seven times ten to the twelfth power
   b. forty-two times ten to the eighth power
   c. thirty-five times ten to the second power
       (times ten squared)

4.22 a. 490   140   560   210   350
   b. 40   60   20   80   100

Part Five

5.1 a. 8,340
   b. 3.239
   c. $\frac{3}{10}$
   d. .233

5.2   6 + 9 = 15   9 + 6 = 15
       15 − 6 = 9   15 − 9 = 6
       5 × 7 = 35   7 × 5 = 35
       35 ÷ 5 = 7   35 ÷ 7 = 5

5.3   10,004   3.772 $\frac{5}{8}$ $12\frac{14}{15}$

       5,238   3.69 $\frac{3}{8}$ $8\frac{9}{15} = 8\frac{3}{5}$

5.4   4,052   5.27 $\frac{7}{18}$ $4\frac{4}{12} = 4\frac{1}{3}$

       6,931   8.79 $\frac{10}{18} = \frac{5}{9}$ $8\frac{9}{12} = 8\frac{3}{4}$

5.5   1 2 3 4 5 6 7 8 9
       10 20 30 40 50 60 70 80 90
       multiples of ten

5.6 a. cardinal
   b. ordinal

5.7 a. $2\frac{3}{4}$ $2\frac{2}{3}$ $\frac{3}{10}$ 18
   b. $\frac{7}{18}$ 4 $1\frac{3}{7}$ 14
   c. 4 $5\frac{1}{2}$ 12 $\frac{2}{3}$
   d. 56   22 $6\frac{2}{3}$ 5

5.8 a. 1,000   10,000   100,000
   b. 1,000,000   10,000,000

5.9 a. five and four-hundredths
       eight and five ten-thousandths
   b. three and nine-tenths
       two and six hundred-thousandths

5.10   b   f   c   g   e   d   a

5.11   .5380   .4200   .0800   6.5000   3.0410

5.12 a. 28.854   11.832   7.985
   b. 44.808   1.3863   51.982
   c. 3.8532   15.306   16.23
   d. 21.037   17.75   41.002

5.13 a. 20.705   34.535   65.109
   b. .015   3.479   33.878
   c. 3.093   17.459   .0313
   d. 1.48   .0171   4.8091

5.14 a. $(3 + 4) \times (15 \div 3) = N$
                       $7 \times 5 = N$
                           $35 = N$
              $8 + (2 \times 3) + 9 = N$
                   $8 + 6 + 9 = N$
                         $23 = N$
              $(9 − 2) \times (5 + 5) = N$
                    $7 \times 10 = N$
                         $70 = N$
   b. $14 + 16 + (4 \times 2) = N$
              $14 + 16 + 8 = N$
                    $38 = N$
         $(37 − 9) \div (2 + 2) = N$
                $28 \div 4 = N$
                     $7 = N$
         $(52 + 8) + (46 − 6) = N$
                $60 + 40 = N$
                   $100 = N$

c. $7 + (2 \times 6) + (2 \times 8) = N$
$7 + 12 + 16 = N$
$35 \text{ hits} = N$

5.15 a. $>$ $=$ $>$ $=$ $<$

b. $\frac{2}{5}$ $(>, =, <)$ $\frac{4}{10}$ $\qquad$ $\frac{1}{3}$ $(>, =, <)$ $\frac{2}{9}$
$\frac{3}{4}$ $(>, =, <)$ $\frac{12}{16}$ $\qquad$ $\frac{5}{9}$ $(>, =, <)$ $\frac{3}{8}$
$\frac{10}{16}$ $(>, =, <)$ $\frac{5}{8}$

5.16 a. $\frac{8}{12}$ $(>, =, <)$ $\frac{6}{10}$ $\qquad$ Jeremy

b. $\frac{13}{15}$ $(>, =, <)$ $\frac{17}{20}$ $\qquad$ Math

5.17 a. 2,372 $\qquad$ rounds to 2,000
$2,000 \div 5 = 400$ miles per day

b. $8 \times 12 = 96$
$\frac{1}{8} \times 96 = 12$ cookies
(first & second class each)
$\frac{1}{6} \times 96 = 16$ cookies (third class)
$\frac{1}{4} \times 96 = 24$ cookies (fourth class)
$\frac{1}{3} \times 96 = 32$ cookies (fifth class)

c. Corrie 5 ft. 2 in.
Jennifer 4 ft. 6 in.

d. $\frac{1}{4} \times 2,000 = 500$ lb.

e. 16 wks. ($\$124 \div 8 = 15\frac{1}{2}$)

f. 4 yd. ($140 \div 36 = 3\frac{26}{36}$)

g. 10

h. 128 cups $\div 2 = 64$ pt. $\div 2 = 32$ qt. $\div 4 = 8$ gal.

i. Before Christ, Anno Domini
(in the year of the Lord)

j. $5,280 \div 2 = 2,640$ ft.

k. $21 \times 9 = 189$ sq. ft.

5.18 a. 2,999,999,999

b. $.6591 \times 10,000 = 6,591$

c. 6×10^9

d. 10 (1,2,5,10) factors of composite numbers

e. (any 6-sided figure)

f. $\frac{4}{12}$

g.

h. $\frac{4}{32}$

i. $5 < 6 < 7$

j. $2^5 = 32$

k. $7 \geq 7, 6, 5 > 4$

l. $\overleftrightarrow{AB} \perp \overleftrightarrow{AC}$

m. $42.5 \div 10,000 = .00425$

n.

o. $\frac{12}{16}$

p. $56 \div 8 = 7$

q. 300, 18

109

Part One

1.1

$\frac{1}{6}$ $\frac{2}{12}$ $\frac{2}{15}$

1.2 $\frac{1}{3}$ $\frac{7}{10}$ $\frac{1}{4}$ $\frac{1}{3}$ $\frac{3}{4}$ $\frac{2}{3}$

1.3 $1\frac{1}{2}$ $3\frac{3}{4}$ 6 18 $14\frac{2}{3}$ $11\frac{2}{3}$

1.4 a. 2 56 $2\frac{2}{3}$ 22 3

   b. 5 3 20 5 24

1.5 $\frac{3}{2}$ $\frac{9}{4}$ $\frac{1}{8}$ $\frac{16}{15}$ $\frac{8}{1}$ $\frac{1}{24}$

1.6 a. 15 12 20 14 8

   b. 27 10 20 21 16

1.7 a. $8\frac{3}{4}$ $3\frac{3}{7}$ $10\frac{2}{3}$ $5\frac{5}{7}$ $13\frac{1}{2}$

   b. $7\frac{1}{5}$ $10\frac{4}{5}$ $16\frac{1}{2}$ $6\frac{2}{5}$ $13\frac{1}{3}$

1.8 a. $\frac{1}{32}$ $\frac{3}{35}$ $\frac{2}{25}$ $\frac{2}{27}$ $\frac{6}{49}$

   b. $\frac{5}{12}$ $\frac{7}{40}$ $\frac{2}{35}$ $\frac{1}{15}$ $\frac{3}{16}$

1.9 a. $1\frac{1}{5}$ $\frac{1}{2}$ $\frac{1}{2}$ $3\frac{1}{2}$ $1\frac{1}{3}$

   b. $2\frac{1}{4}$ $1\frac{1}{4}$ $\frac{7}{8}$ $\frac{2}{5}$ $1\frac{1}{5}$

1.10 a. $6 \div \frac{1}{3} = \frac{6}{1} \times \frac{3}{1} = 18$ friends

   b. $3 \div \frac{1}{8} = \frac{3}{1} \times \frac{8}{1} = 24$ friends

   c. $\frac{2}{3} \div 8 = \frac{\cancel{2}^{1}}{3} \times \frac{1}{\cancel{8}_{4}} = \frac{1}{12}$ of a box

   d. $\frac{4}{5} \div 12 = \frac{\cancel{4}^{1}}{5} \times \frac{1}{\cancel{12}_{3}} = \frac{1}{15}$ of a box

   e. $\frac{3}{4} \div \frac{1}{8} = \frac{3}{\cancel{4}_{1}} \times \frac{\cancel{8}^{2}}{1} = 6$ friends

1.11 a. — line segment – part of a line that begins and ends with end points

   b. ↔ line – a series of dots that has no beginning or end

   c. ∥ parallel – lines the same distance apart along their entire length

   d. ∠ angle – distance between two rays with a common end point

   e. ⊥ perpendicular – lines that form square corners where they meet

   f. ≅ congruent – identical in form and size

   g. → ray – line with one end point

1.12 a. Line segment AB is perpendicular to line segment CD

   b. Angle RST is congruent to angle XYZ

1.13 a. R b. A c. O d. O e. A f. R

1.14 a. 25° acute
   b. 90° right
   c. 165° obtuse
   d. 130° obtuse
   e. 105° obtuse
   f. 60° acute

1.15 a. O A R R A O
   b. S I E S I E

Part Two

2.1 a. $\frac{2}{3}$ $1\frac{1}{4}$ $\frac{3}{8}$ $1\frac{1}{3}$

   b. $7\frac{1}{2}$ $\frac{6}{25}$ 12 $\frac{7}{32}$

   c. $\frac{6}{7}$ $1\frac{3}{5}$ $1\frac{2}{11}$ $1\frac{9}{11}$

   d. $2\frac{2}{5}$ $1\frac{1}{2}$ $4\frac{2}{7}$ $2\frac{3}{4}$

2.2

   a.

   b.

   c.

2.3 a. P = 12 in. A = 4 sq. in.
   b. P = 10 in. A = 4 sq. in.
   c. P = 8 in. A = 4 sq. in.
   d. no, yes

2.4 a. P = 14 in. A = 6 sq. in.
   b. P = 10 in. A = 6 sq. in.
   c. P = 12 in. A = 6 sq. in.

2.5 P = 24 in. A = 35 sq. in.

2.6 yes

2.7 P = 2L × 2W   A = L W
   P = (2 · 9) + (2 · 4)   A = 9 · 4
   P = 18 + 8   A = 36 sq. in.
   P = 26 in.

2.8 a. P = 38 in.   A = 84 sq. in.
    b. P = 24 ft.   A = 27 sq. ft.
    c. P = 26 mi.   A = 40 sq. mi.
    d. P = 70 yd.   A = 300 sq. yd.

2.9 a. w = 7 in.
    b. l = 14 ft.
    c. w = 4 yd.
    d. l = 16 mi.

2.10 a. w = 8 in.
    b. l = 15 ft.
    c. w = 12 yd.
    d. l = 20 mi.

2.11 a. P = 48 ft.   A = 144 sq. ft.
    b. P = 12 mi.   A = 9 sq. mi.
    c. P = 60 yd.   A = 225 sq. yd.
    d. P = 96 in.   A = 576 sq. in.

2.12 a. 9 ft.   b. 39 in.
    c. 15 mi.   d. 32 yd.

2.13 a. a = 36 sq. ft.
    b. l = 12 in.
    c. w = 7 ft.
    d. p = 42 yd.
    e. a = 121 sq. ft.
    f. w = 5 ft.
    g. s = 16 ft.
    h. w = 12 mi.

2.14 a. eight hundredths   four and nine-tenths
    b. six and three hundred twelve-thousandths

2.15 $\frac{9}{10}$ $3\frac{28}{100}$ $\frac{6}{1,000}$ $5\frac{1}{100}$ $\frac{3,267}{10,000}$

2.16 hundredths   tenths   thousandths   ones

2.17 .63114   .368   .06076   2,553.6   387.66

2.18 a. $.0074\frac{7}{9} = .0075$
       $.099\frac{1}{6} = .099$
       $2.02\frac{1}{3} = 2.02$
       $9.1\frac{5}{7} = 9.2$
       $.011\frac{4}{5} = .012$

    b. $002\frac{12}{42} = .002$
       $1.4\frac{26}{37} = 1.5$
       $.045\frac{3}{21} = .045$
       $.0024\frac{12}{13} = .0025$
       $3.0\frac{16}{28} = 3.1$

2.19 a. .4   .6   .4   .5   .1
    b. .59   .49   .40   .85   .41

2.20 1.16 = 1.2   .37 = .4   1.28 = 1.3   .66 = .7   .83 = .8

2.21 .2   .25   .5   .75   .8

2.22 19.2   23.25   15.5   67.75   58.8

2.23 a. .625 $.\overline{33}$ .125   .4 $.\overline{833}$
    b. $.\overline{22}$ .375 $.\overline{77}$ .6   .875

2.24 a. 11 ÷ 9   9)$\overline{11}$ $1\frac{2}{9}$ $1.\overline{22}$ 1.22...
    b. 7 ÷ 6   6)$\overline{7}$ $1\frac{1}{6}$ $1.1\overline{66}$ 1.166...

2.25 a. 350   4.6   6,230   6.9
    b. 8.56   .4136   .0734   .021

Part Three

3.1 a. 1.3   16   490   820   9
    b. 3   5   .4   .06   3
    c. .06   8   200   1.4   18.6

3.2 a. 143   .32   23.7   8.7
    b. 91   54 *or* 54.07   2.8   1.2
    c. 18   .26   1.2   3.8

3.3 a. 2   b. 4   c. 5   d. 3   e. 6   f. 1

3.4 638,257,134 < 638,257,314 < 638,572,134
    < 683,257,314 < 683,275,134 < 683,527,134

3.5 98,448,362 > 98,362,484 > 94,362,484 >
    89,362,448 > 89,348,462 > 83,362,448

3.6 a. 9 + (2 × 8) − 5 = 9 + 16 − 5 = 20
       14 − (6 × 0) + 16 = 14 − 0 + 16 = 30

    b. (56 ÷ 7) − (4 × 2) = 8 − 8 = 0
       (84 + 16) ÷ (5 × 5) = 100 ÷ 25 = 4

    c. 63 − (2 · 5) + 9 = 63 − 10 + 9 = 62
       (27 − 8) + (4 · 2) = 19 + 8 = 27

3.7 360°

3.8 4 , 90° , 360°

3.9 3 , 60° + 80° + 40° , 180°

3.10 no   no
     The sum of the angles would be more
     than 180°

3.11 a. 180° ÷ 3 = 60°
    b. (180° − 30°) ÷ 2 = 150° ÷ 2 = 75°
    c. 180° − (53° + 69°) = 180° − 122° = 58°

3.12

a.
$P = S + S + S$
$P = 6 + 10 + 8$
$P = 24$ in.

$A = \frac{1}{2} B \times H$
$A = \frac{1}{2} (10 \times 5)$
$A = \frac{1}{2} \times 50$
$A = 25$ sq. in.

b.
$P = S + S + S$
$P = 7 + 7 + 7$
$P = 21$ in.

c.
$P = S + S + S$
$P = 5 + 11 + 11$
$P = 27$ ft.

d.
$A = \frac{1}{2} B \times H$
$A = \frac{1}{2} (3 \times 6)$
$A = \frac{1}{2} \times 18$
$A = 9$ sq. ft.

e.
$A = \frac{1}{2} B \times H$
$A = \frac{1}{2} (14 \times 7)$
$A = \frac{1}{2} \times 98$
$A = 49$ sq. ft.

f.
$P = S + S + S$
$23 = (9 + 7) + N$
$23 = 16 + N$
$23 - 16 = (16 - 16) + N$
7 in. $= N$ (side)

g.
$A = \frac{1}{2} B \times H$
$18 = \frac{1}{2} (N \times 4)$
$18 \times 2 = \frac{1}{2} \times 2(N \times 4)$
$36 = N \times 4$
$36 \div 4 = N \times (4 \div 4)$
9 in. $= N$ (height)

3.13   64, 81, 64, 625, 243

3.14 a. $2, 3^2$ 5^2 $2^2, 3^2$
b. $2^2, 3$ 3^3 2^5

3.15

15	20	21	30	42
3 5	2 10	3 7	2 15	2 21
5 1	2 5	7 1	3 5	3 7
	5 1		5 1	7 1

3, 5 $2^2, 5$ 3, 7   2, 3, 5   2, 3, 7

3.16 a. $2^2, 3$ 3, 7
3
3

b. 3^3 $2^2, 3^2$
3^2
9

3.17
$\frac{5}{9}$ $\frac{5}{8}$ $\frac{3}{8}$ $\frac{2}{3}$ $\frac{5}{14}$
$\frac{4}{9}$ $\frac{5}{7}$ $\frac{2}{3}$ $\frac{4}{5}$ $\frac{3}{5}$

3.18
$\frac{15}{36} = \frac{5}{12}$

$\frac{18}{42} = \frac{3}{7}$

$\frac{\overset{5}{\cancel{15}}}{\underset{8}{\cancel{16}}} \times \frac{\overset{5}{\cancel{10}}}{\underset{14}{\cancel{42}}} = \frac{25}{112}$

$\frac{9}{14} \div \frac{18}{21} = \frac{\overset{1}{\cancel{9}}}{\underset{2}{\cancel{14}}} \times \frac{\overset{3}{\cancel{21}}}{\underset{2}{\cancel{18}}} = \frac{3}{4}$

$\frac{\overset{4}{\cancel{32}}}{\underset{1}{\cancel{5}}} \times \frac{\overset{1}{\cancel{5}}}{\underset{3}{\cancel{24}}} = \frac{4}{3} = 1\frac{1}{3}$

$\frac{18}{25} \div 2\frac{6}{15} = \frac{\overset{1}{\cancel{18}}}{\underset{5}{\cancel{25}}} \times \frac{\overset{3}{\cancel{15}}}{\underset{2}{\cancel{36}}} = \frac{3}{10}$

3.19 a. 720   0   80   400   320
b. 630   270   540   810   180

3.20 $\frac{3}{4} = \frac{15}{20}$ $\frac{4}{5} = \frac{16}{20}$ $\frac{3}{10} = \frac{6}{20}$ $\frac{7}{20} = \frac{7}{20}$ $\frac{2}{5} = \frac{8}{20}$ $\frac{1}{2} = \frac{10}{20}$
$\frac{3}{10} < \frac{7}{20} < \frac{2}{5} < \frac{1}{2} < \frac{3}{4} < \frac{4}{5}$

3.21 $.45 = .450$ $.376 = .376$ $.21 = .210$ $.7 = .700$
$.453 = .453$ $.5 = .500$
$.21 < .376 < .45 < .453 < .5 < .7$

3.22 a. $\frac{7}{8} > \frac{4}{5}$ $\frac{4}{6} = \frac{12}{18}$ $\frac{9}{12} > \frac{7}{10}$ $\frac{2}{3} > \frac{5}{9}$
$35 > 32$ $72 = 72$ $90 > 84$ $18 > 15$

b. $\frac{3}{8} < \frac{6}{15}$ $\frac{8}{12} = \frac{10}{15}$ $\frac{13}{14} > \frac{9}{10}$ $\frac{6}{7} < \frac{14}{15}$
$45 < 48$ $120 = 120$ $130 > 126$ $90 < 98$

3.23 a. $18 \leq 18, 19, 20, 21 < 22$
b. $24 \geq 24, 20, 16, 12 > 8$

3.24 a. $1\frac{7}{36}$ $1\frac{1}{24}$ $1\frac{3}{10}$ $12\frac{13}{14}$ $10\frac{5}{6}$
b. $\frac{3}{10}$ $\frac{13}{20}$ $\frac{23}{42}$ $3\frac{1}{15}$ $2\frac{3}{4}$

Part Four

4.1 a. 8 gal. 2 qt.   3 hr. 33 min.
b. 4 pt 5 oz.   19 yd. 2 ft.
c. 16 da. 12 hr.   10 ft. 5 in.

4.2   8 gal. 3 qt.   4 da. 2 hr   4 lb. 3 oz.

4.3 a. 30 ft. 16 in. = 31 ft. 4 in.
6 yr. 432 da. = 7 yr. 67 da.
15 mi. 7,375 ft. = 16 mi. 2,095 ft.
48 lb. 72 oz. = 52 lb. 8 oz.

b. 9 pt. 20 oz. = 10 pt. 4 oz.
    13 gal. 5 qt. = 14 gal. 1 qt.
    16 yd. 72 in. = 18 yd.
    72 min. 96 sec. = 73 min. 36 sec.

4.4 a. 2 ft. 11 in.
         5 bu. 2 pk.
         4 lb. 12 oz.
         3 da. 8 hr.

     b. $$\frac{1 \text{ yd } 2\frac{2}{3} \text{ ft.}}{3\overline{)3 \text{ yd } 8 \text{ ft.}}}$$

         $$\frac{2 \text{ yd. } 20 \text{ in.}}{2\overline{)4 \text{ yd. } 40 \text{ in.}}}$$

         $$\frac{1 \text{ wk. } 4\frac{4}{5} \text{ da.}}{5\overline{)5 \text{ wk. } 24 \text{ da.}}}$$

         $$\frac{1 \text{ qt. } 1\frac{3}{4} \text{ pt.}}{4\overline{)4 \text{ qt. } 7 \text{ pt.}}}$$

4.5 a. $\begin{array}{r} 45 \\ \times\ 20 \\ \hline 900 \end{array}$ $\begin{array}{r} 15 \text{ hours} \\ 60\overline{)900} \end{array}$

     b. $\begin{array}{r} 24 \\ \times\ 5 \\ \hline 120 \end{array}$ $\begin{array}{r} 20 \text{ balls} \\ 6\overline{)120} \end{array}$

     c. 93 + 124 + 140 = 357
         357 ÷ 3 ft. = 119 yd.

     d. $\dfrac{}{2\overline{)3 \text{ pt. } 1 \text{ cup}}}$ = $\dfrac{1 \text{ pt. } 1\frac{1}{2} \text{ cup}}{2\overline{)2 \text{ pt. } 3 \text{ cup}}}$

     e. $\begin{array}{r} 16 \text{ oz.} \\ \times\ 5 \text{ oz.} \\ \hline 80 \text{ oz.} \end{array}$ $\begin{array}{r} 11\frac{3}{7} \text{ da.} \\ 7\overline{)80} \end{array}$

     f. $\dfrac{}{8\overline{)9 \text{ ft. } 4 \text{ in.}}}$ = $\dfrac{1 \text{ ft. } 2 \text{ in.}}{8\overline{)8 \text{ ft. } 16 \text{ in.}}}$ = 14 in.

4.6 a. 108 mi.   378 mi.
     b. 144 items   156 items

4.7 a. 6 hr.   40 mph
     b. 7 hr.   62 iph
     c. 45 mph
     d. 5 min.
     e. .5 hr. or $\frac{1}{2}$ hr. or 30 min.
     f. 6 hr.
     g. 220 mi.
     h. 11 per day

4.8 a. 5 hundred billions
         3 ten millions

b. 9 billions
    9 hundred millions

4.9 a. 4×10^{11} 3×10^{7}
     b. 9×10^{10} 5×10^{6}

4.10 a. 1,575   300 + 300 + 1,000 = 1,600
     b. 30,768   50,000 − 20,000 = 30,000
     c. 124,798   5,000 × 20 = 100,000
     d. 1,607   6,000 ÷ 4 = 1,500
     e. 7,858 mi. 2,000 + 2,000 + 1,000 +
                        2,000 + 700 = 7,700mi.
     f. 387,823 sq. mi.   700,000 − 300,000 =
                               400,000 sq. mi.
     g. $215.10   12 × 20 = $240.00
     h. $93   3,000 ÷ 30 = $100

4.11 a. 5   10   11
     b. 17   23.5 or 23 1/2   27.8 or 27 4/5

4.12 a. 8 + (27 ÷ 3) − (5 × 3) = 8 + 9 − 15 = 2
         (6 × 7) − (4 × 5) + 9 = 42 − 20 + 9 = 31
     b. 14 + (3 × 2) − 10 = 14 + 6 − 10 = 10
         17 − (5 × 3) + (4 × 4) = 17 − 15 + 16 = 18
     c. (7 × 6) + (32 ÷ 4) − 16 = 42 + 8 − 16 = 34
         (2 × 0) × (5 × 7) = 0 × 35 = 0

4.13 a. 3 × [(2 × 6) − 5] = 3 × (12 − 5) =
            3 × 7 = 21

         [7 + (3 × 6)] ÷ 5 = (7 + 18) ÷ 5 =
            25 ÷ 5 = 5

         8 + [5 × (4 + 3)] = 8 + (5 × 7) =
            8 + 35 = 43

     b. [2 × (9 − 5)] − 6= (2 × 4) − 6 =
            8 − 6 = 2

         36 ÷ [13 − (2 × 2)] = 36 ÷ (13 − 4) =
            36 ÷ 9= 4

         [3 + (4 × 6)] ÷ 9 = (3 + 24) ÷ 9 =
            27 ÷ 9 = 3

     c. [(54 − 12) ÷ 6] × 3 = (42 ÷ 6) × 3 =
            7 × 3 = 21

         4 × [9 + (3 × 4)] = 4 × (9 + 12) =
            4 × 21 = 84

         64 ÷ [4 + (28 ÷ 7)] = 64 ÷ (4 + 4) =
            64 ÷ 8 = 8

4.14 a. $18 \div 2 + 3 \times 4 = 9 + 12 = 21$
$4 \times 5 - 3 \times 2 = 20 - 6 = 14$
$35 \div 7 + 28 \div 4 = 5 + 7 = 12$

b. $2 \times 5 - 6 \div 2 = 10 - 3 = 7$
$9 - 8 \div 2 + 17 = 9 - 4 + 17 = 22$
$7 \times 3 + 48 \div 6 = 21 + 8 = 29$

c. $25 + 6 \times 5 - 11 = 25 + 30 - 11 = 44$
$56 \div 7 - 42 \div 6 = 8 - 7 = 1$
$2 + 3 \times 4 - 7 = 2 + 12 - 7 = 7$

4.15 a. $<$ $<$ $=$ $=$
b. $>$ $=$ $<$ $=$

4.16 a.
$$\frac{2}{4} = \frac{N}{10}$$
$$20 = N \cdot 4$$
$$20 \div 4 = N \cdot (4 \div 4)$$
$$5 = N$$
$$\frac{2}{4} = \frac{1}{2} = \quad \frac{5}{10} = \frac{1}{2}$$

$$\frac{2}{6} = \frac{N}{9}$$
$$18 = N \cdot 6$$
$$18 \div 6 = N \cdot (6 \div 6)$$
$$3 = N$$
$$\frac{2}{6} = \frac{1}{3} = \quad \frac{3}{9} = \frac{1}{3}$$

$$\frac{6}{8} = \frac{N}{16}$$
$$96 = N \cdot 8$$
$$96 \div 8 = N \cdot (8 \div 8)$$
$$12 = N$$
$$\frac{6}{8} = \frac{3}{4} = \quad \frac{12}{16} = \frac{3}{4}$$

$$\frac{2}{10} = \frac{N}{15}$$
$$30 = N \cdot 10$$
$$30 \div 10 = N \cdot (10 \div 10)$$
$$3 = N$$
$$\frac{2}{10} = \frac{1}{5} = \quad \frac{3}{15} = \frac{1}{5}$$

b.
$$\frac{4}{6} = \frac{N}{9}$$
$$36 = N \cdot 6$$
$$36 \div 6 = N \cdot (6 \div 6)$$
$$6 = N$$
$$\frac{4}{6} = \frac{2}{3} = \quad \frac{6}{9} = \frac{2}{3}$$

$$\frac{2}{8} = \frac{N}{12}$$
$$24 = N \cdot 8$$
$$24 \div 8 = N \cdot (8 \div 8)$$
$$3 = N$$
$$\frac{2}{8} = \frac{1}{4} = \quad \frac{3}{12} = \frac{1}{4}$$

$$\frac{9}{15} = \frac{N}{10}$$
$$90 = N \cdot 15$$
$$90 \div 15 = N \cdot (15 \div 15)$$
$$6 = N$$
$$\frac{9}{15} = \frac{3}{5} = \quad \frac{6}{10} = \frac{3}{5}$$

$$\frac{2}{12} = \frac{N}{18}$$
$$36 = N \cdot 12$$
$$36 \div 12 = N \cdot (12 \div 12)$$
$$3 = N$$
$$\frac{2}{12} = \frac{1}{6} = \quad \frac{3}{18} = \frac{1}{6}$$

c.
$$\frac{8}{12} = \frac{N}{18}$$
$$144 = N \cdot 12$$
$$144 \div 12 = N \cdot (12 \div 12)$$
$$12 = N$$
$$\frac{8}{12} = \frac{2}{3} = \quad \frac{12}{18} = \frac{2}{3}$$

$$\frac{15}{25} = \frac{N}{10}$$
$$150 = N \cdot 25$$
$$150 \div 25 = N \cdot (25 \div 25)$$
$$6 = N$$
$$\frac{15}{25} = \frac{3}{5} = \quad \frac{6}{10} = \frac{3}{5}$$

$$\frac{3}{24} = \frac{N}{16}$$
$$48 = N \cdot 24$$
$$48 \div 24 = N \cdot (24 \div 24)$$
$$2 = N$$
$$\frac{3}{24} = \frac{1}{8} = \quad \frac{2}{16} = \frac{1}{8}$$

$$\frac{5}{20} = \frac{N}{24}$$
$$120 = N \cdot 20$$
$$120 \div 20 = N \cdot (20 \div 20)$$
$$6 = N$$
$$\frac{5}{20} = \frac{1}{4} = \quad \frac{6}{24} = \frac{1}{4}$$

4.17 a. $\frac{4}{5} = \frac{n}{40}$ $n = 32$ peanuts
b. $\frac{7}{8} = \frac{n}{32}$ $n = 28$ boys
c. $\frac{2}{3} = \frac{12}{n}$ $n = 18$ cats
d. $\frac{1}{3} = \frac{6}{n}$ $n = 18$ days

Part Five

5.1 a. $\underline{9}$ $\frac{63}{7}$ 3^2 $3(3\,)$

b. $\underline{8}$ 2^3 $\frac{\overset{4\times 6}{18}}{1}$ $2\cdot 4$

c. $\underline{18}$ $2(3^2)$ $\frac{\overset{2}{18}}{1}$ $3\cdot 6$

d. $\underline{15}$ $3\cdot 5$ $5(3)$ $\frac{45}{3}$

e. $\frac{1}{4}$ $\frac{8}{32}$ $.25$ $4\overline{)1}$

f. $1\frac{1}{2}$ $4\overline{)6}$ $\frac{6}{4}$ 1.5

g. $\frac{5}{8}$ $.625$ $.6\frac{1}{4}$ $\frac{10}{16}$

h. $\underline{27}$ 3^3 $\frac{54}{2}$ $9(3)$

5.2 Suggested answers:

a. $\frac{5}{1}$ 5.0 $\frac{\overset{2\times 10}{}}{4}$ $5\overline{)25}$

b. $3(2^2)$ $2(6)$ $\frac{24}{2}$ $3\cdot 4$

c. $2\cdot 8$ 2^4 $\frac{32}{2}$ 4^2

d. $\frac{2}{4}$ $.5$ $2\overline{)1}$ $\frac{8}{16}$

5.3 a. $85{,}000{,}000 = 85 \times 10^6$

b. $\frac{1}{4}$ of $24 = 6$

c. $9 \div \frac{3}{5} = 15$

d. $\overline{AB} \perp \overline{CD}$

e. $\overleftrightarrow{MN} \parallel \overleftrightarrow{OP}$

f. $\triangle XYZ \cong \triangle RST$

g. $\angle PST + \angle STP + \angle TPS = 180°$

h. $A = L\,W$

i. $A = S^2$

j. $A = \frac{1}{2}BH$

k. $36 \geq 36,\ 30,\ 24,\ 18 > 12$

l. $3 \leq 3,\ 5,\ 7,\ 11,\ 13 < 17$

5.4 a. $\frac{5}{14}$ $\frac{5}{14} \div \frac{5}{8} = \frac{5}{14} \times \frac{8}{5} = \frac{4}{7}$

    15 $\frac{15}{1} \times \frac{4}{25} = \frac{12}{5} = 2\frac{2}{5}$

b. 2 $2 \div \frac{5}{9} = \frac{2}{1} \times \frac{9}{5} = \frac{18}{5} = 3\frac{3}{5}$

    64 $3\frac{5}{9}$

    $18\overline{)64}$ or $\frac{\overset{32}{64}}{1} \times \frac{1}{18} = \frac{32}{9} = 3\frac{5}{9}$

c. $6\frac{3}{5}$ $6\frac{3}{5} \div 7\frac{1}{3} = \frac{33}{5} \times \frac{3}{22} = \frac{9}{10}$

    3 $3 \div 2\frac{3}{5} = \frac{3}{1} \times \frac{5}{13} = \frac{15}{13} = 1\frac{2}{13}$

5.5 a. 12 $\frac{12}{1} \times \frac{7}{9} = \frac{28}{3} = 9\frac{1}{3}$

    $1\frac{1}{7}$ $1\frac{1}{7} \times 5\frac{5}{6} = \frac{8}{7} \times \frac{35}{6} = \frac{20}{3} = 6\frac{2}{3}$

b. $\frac{1}{4}$ $\frac{1}{4} \times 3\frac{2}{3} = \frac{1}{4} \times \frac{11}{3} = \frac{11}{12}$

    4 $4 \times 7\frac{1}{2} = \frac{4}{1} \times \frac{15}{2} = 30$

c. $1\frac{1}{3}$ $1\frac{1}{3} \times 5 = \frac{4}{3} \times \frac{5}{1} = \frac{20}{3} = 6\frac{2}{3}$

    4 $\frac{4}{1} \times \frac{7}{8} = \frac{7}{2} = 3\frac{1}{2}$

5.6 a. 6 eggs   6 eggs

b. 7 mi.   7 mi.

c. 24 pages   24 pages

d. 24 students   24 students

e. 14 doughnuts   14 doughnuts

f. 27 mints   27 mints

g. 21 oranges   21 oranges

5.7 a.
$$\frac{3}{N} = \frac{6}{14}$$
$$42 = 6 \cdot N$$
$$42 \div 6 = (6 \div 6) \cdot N$$
$$7 = N$$
$$\frac{3}{7} = \frac{6}{14} = \frac{3}{7}$$

$$\frac{6}{9} = \frac{4}{N}$$
$$6 \cdot N = 36$$
$$(6 \div 6) \cdot N = 36 \div 6$$
$$6 = N$$
$$\frac{6}{9} = \frac{2}{3} = \frac{4}{6} = \frac{2}{3}$$

$$\frac{N}{10} = \frac{6}{20}$$
$$N \cdot 20 = 60$$
$$N \cdot (20 \div 20) = 60 \div 20$$
$$N = 3$$
$$\frac{3}{10} = \frac{6}{20} = \frac{3}{10}$$

$$\frac{8}{10} = \frac{N}{15}$$
$$120 = N \cdot 10$$
$$120 \div 10 = N \cdot (10 \div 10)$$
$$12 = N$$
$$\frac{8}{10} = \frac{4}{5} = \frac{12}{15} = \frac{4}{5}$$

b.
$$\frac{2}{N} = \frac{3}{24}$$
$$48 = 3 \cdot N$$
$$48 \div 3 = (3 \div 3) \cdot N$$
$$16 = N$$
$$\frac{2}{16} = \frac{1}{8} = \frac{3}{24} = \frac{1}{8}$$

$$\frac{5}{15} = \frac{10}{N}$$
$$5 \cdot N = 150$$
$$(5 \div 5) \cdot N = 150 \div 5$$
$$N = 30$$
$$\frac{5}{15} = \frac{1}{3} = \frac{10}{30} = \frac{1}{3}$$

$$\frac{N}{8} = \frac{18}{24}$$
$$N \cdot 24 = 144$$
$$N \cdot (24 \div 24) = 144 \div 24$$
$$N = 6$$
$$\frac{6}{8} = \frac{3}{4} = \frac{18}{24} = \frac{3}{4}$$

$$\frac{10}{12} = \frac{N}{30}$$
$$300 = N \cdot 12$$
$$300 \div 12 = N \cdot (12 \div 12)$$
$$25 = N$$
$$\frac{10}{12} = \frac{5}{6} = \frac{25}{30} = \frac{5}{6}$$

5.8

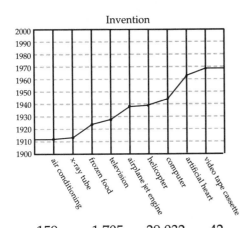

Invention

5.10 a.

b. ray, horizontal
c. line segment, vertical
d. perpendicular
e.

f. parallel
g. 5 ft.
h. rectangle

P = 2L + 2W	A = L W
P = (2 · 7) + (2 · 5)	A = 7 · 5
P = 14 + 10	A = 35 sq. ft.
P = 24 ft.	

i.

j. equilateral triangle
60°

P = S + S + S	A = $\frac{1}{2}$ BH
P = 10 + 10 + 10	A = $\frac{1}{2}$ (10 × 4)
P = 30 ft.	A = $\frac{1}{2}$ · 40
	A = 20 sq. ft.

k. red - <u>30 ft.</u>   blue - <u>10 ft.</u>   green - <u>24 ft.</u>

5.9
a.	159	1,705	29,032	42	8.194
b.	15,700	2.8	286,961	57	28
c.	15	70	12	3.24	135
d.	6.72	34.15	28	4	8.53
e.	$11\frac{5}{6}$	$6\frac{1}{10}$	$14\frac{3}{16}$	$6\frac{13}{15}$	$60\frac{4}{5}$
f.	$\frac{1}{21}$	.006	55	$9.2\frac{4}{7}$	8,700
g.	$11\frac{1}{45}$	$4\frac{2}{7}$	$42\frac{2}{3}$	$13\frac{13}{60}$	$6\frac{2}{5}$
h.	31.5	3.27	63	.593	4

Part One

1.1 a.   964,000,000,000,000,000,000
   b.   742,000,000,000,000,000,000,000,000,000
   c.   35,000,000,000,000,000,000,000
   d.   4,000,000,000,000,000

1.2 a. 485×10^9
   b. 372×10^{12}
   c. 863×10^{21}

1.3 a.   269 billions
   b.   573 quadrillions
   c.   428 septillions

1.4 a.   375 thousand (3 zeros) $\times$ 1 trillion (12 zeros) =
       375 quadrillion (15 zeros)
   b.   263 million (6 zeros) $\times$ 1 billion (9 zeros) =
       263 quadrillion (15 zeros)

1.5 a.   .5   .25   .75
   b.   .2   .4   .6   .8
   c.   .125   .375   .625   .875

1.6   They are equivalent to $\frac{1}{2}, \frac{1}{4}, \frac{1}{2},$ and $\frac{3}{4}$.

1.7 a.   3.75   7.625   9.5   2.6
   b.   5.2   1.375   7.25   4.875
   c.   27.4   6.125   109.375   8.8

1.8 $.\overline{33}$ $.\overline{66}$ $.1\overline{66}$ $.8\overline{33}$

1.9   They are equivalent to $\frac{1}{3}, \frac{1}{2},$ and $\frac{2}{3}$.

1.10 a. $5.\overline{33}$ $9.8\overline{33}$ $7.\overline{66}$ $8.1\overline{66}$
   b. $29.8\overline{33}$ $37.\overline{66}$ $158.1\overline{66}$ $300.\overline{33}$

1.11 a. $.\overline{33}$ $\frac{3}{5}$ $\frac{1}{2}$ .125   .4
   b. $\frac{1}{8}$ .875 $.\overline{66}$ $\frac{5}{8}$ $\frac{1}{5}$
   c. $8.1\overline{66}$ $7\frac{1}{2}$ $9\frac{1}{3}$ 2.6 $4\frac{4}{5}$

1.12 $.\overline{33} = .\overline{333}$ $.125 = .125$ $.2 = .200$
     $.625 = .625$ $.\overline{66} = .\overline{666}$ $.6 = .600$
     .125   .2 $.\overline{33}$ .6   .625 $.\overline{66}$

1.13 $.1\overline{66} = .1\overline{66}$ $.625 = .625$ $.\overline{33} = .\overline{333}$
     .4 = .400   .75 = .750
     $\frac{1}{6}$ $\frac{1}{3}$ $\frac{2}{5}$ $\frac{5}{8}$ $\frac{3}{4}$

1.14 a. $.\overline{33} \times 84 =$ $.875 + .25 =$
   b. $64 \div .4 =$ $.5 \times 126 =$
   c. $.625 - .6 =$ $.8\overline{33} - .\overline{33} =$
   d. $.375 + .2 =$ $48 \div .75 =$

1.15 $\frac{3}{4}$ $\frac{5}{9}$ $\frac{1}{2}$ $\frac{7}{8}$ $\frac{8}{15}$

1.16
$$\frac{6}{N} = \frac{3}{4}$$
$$24 = 3 \cdot N$$
$$24 \div 3 = (3 \div 3) \cdot N$$
$$8 = N$$

$$\frac{7}{N} = \frac{5}{6}$$
$$42 = 5 \cdot N$$
$$42 \div 5 = (5 \div 5) \cdot N$$
$$8\frac{2}{5} \ (8.4) = N$$

$$\frac{4}{N} = \frac{2}{3}$$
$$12 = 2 \cdot N$$
$$12 \div 2 = (2 \div 2) \cdot N$$
$$6 = N$$

$$\frac{8}{N} = \frac{4}{5}$$
$$40 = 4N$$
$$40 \div 4 = (4 \div 4) \cdot N$$
$$10 = N$$

$$\frac{2}{N} = \frac{5}{8}$$
$$16 = 5 \cdot N$$
$$16 \div 5 = (5 \div 5) \cdot N$$
$$3\frac{1}{5} \ (3.2) = N$$

1.17 a.
$$\frac{ST}{NO} = \frac{2}{3}$$
$$\frac{6}{NO} = \frac{2}{3}$$
$$18 = 2 \cdot \overline{NO}$$
$$18 \div 2 = (2 \div 2) \cdot \overline{NO}$$
$$9 = \overline{NO}$$

   b.
$$\frac{RT}{MO} = \frac{2}{3}$$
$$\frac{7}{MO} = \frac{2}{3}$$
$$21 = 2 \cdot \overline{MO}$$
$$21 \div 2 = (2 \div 2) \cdot \overline{MO}$$
$$10\frac{1}{2} \ (10.5) = \overline{MO}$$

1.18 a. $\dfrac{EF}{JK} = \dfrac{1}{3}$ $\dfrac{FG}{KL} = \dfrac{1}{3}$ $\dfrac{EG}{JL} = \dfrac{1}{3}$
        $\dfrac{6}{JK} = \dfrac{1}{3}$ $\dfrac{12}{KL} = \dfrac{1}{3}$ $\dfrac{9}{JL} = \dfrac{1}{3}$
        $18 = \overline{JK}$ $36 = \overline{KL}$ $27 = \overline{JL}$

117

b.

$$\frac{AB}{XY} = \frac{2}{5}$$

$$\frac{4}{XY} = \frac{2}{5}$$

$$20 = 2 \cdot \overline{XY}$$

$$20 \div 2 = (2 \div 2) \cdot \overline{XY}$$

$$10 = \overline{XY}$$

$$\frac{BC}{YZ} = \frac{2}{5}$$

$$\frac{7}{YZ} = \frac{2}{5}$$

$$35 = 2 \cdot \overline{YZ}$$

$$35 \div 2 = (2 \div 2) \cdot \overline{YZ}$$

$$17\tfrac{1}{2}(17.5) = \overline{YZ}$$

$$\frac{AC}{XZ} = \frac{2}{5}$$

$$\frac{6}{XZ} = \frac{2}{5}$$

$$30 = 2 \cdot \overline{XZ}$$

$$30 \div 2 = (2 \div 2) \cdot \overline{XZ}$$

$$15 = \overline{XZ}$$

1.19

$$\frac{AC}{XZ} = \frac{2}{5}$$

$$\frac{5}{XZ} = \frac{2}{5}$$

$$25 = 2 \cdot \overline{XZ}$$

$$25 \div 2 = (2 \div 2) \cdot \overline{XZ}$$

$$12\tfrac{1}{2}(12.5) = \overline{XZ}$$

1.20 $\overline{EF} : \overline{RS} = 8:10 = \frac{8}{10}$ simplifies $\frac{4}{5}$

a.

$$\frac{FG}{ST} = \frac{4}{5}$$

$$\frac{14}{ST} = \frac{4}{5}$$

$$70 = 4 \cdot \overline{ST}$$

$$70 \div 4 = (4 \div 4) \cdot \overline{ST}$$

$$17\tfrac{1}{2}(17.5) = \overline{ST}$$

$$\frac{EG}{RT} = \frac{4}{5}$$

$$\frac{12}{RT} = \frac{4}{5}$$

$$60 = 4 \cdot \overline{RT}$$

$$60 \div 4 = (4 \div 4) \cdot \overline{RT}$$

$$15 = \overline{RT}$$

b.

$$\frac{FJ}{LM} = 6:8 = \frac{6}{8} = \frac{3}{4}$$

$$\frac{FK}{MN} = \frac{3}{4}$$

$$\frac{9}{MN} = \frac{3}{4}$$

$$36 = 3 \cdot \overline{MN}$$

$$36 \div 3 = (3 \div 3) \cdot \overline{MN}$$

$$12 = \overline{MN}$$

$$\frac{JK}{LN} = \frac{3}{4}$$

$$\frac{7}{LN} = \frac{3}{4}$$

$$28 = 3 \cdot \overline{LN}$$

$$28 \div 3 = (3 \div 3) \cdot \overline{LN}$$

$$9\tfrac{1}{3}(9.\overline{33}) = \overline{LN}$$

1.21   3   4   5   6   8

1.22   pentagon

1.23   hexagon   octagon

Part Two

2.1 a. base 10
10
 b. meter, liter, gram
 c. milli   kilo
 d. decimeter   centimeters   millimeter
 e. 4 in., 25 mm, $2\tfrac{1}{2}(2.5)$ cm
 f. 9 dm, 10dm, yard

2.2 a. quart, ounce
 b. 1. liter/gram   2. gram
3. meter   4. gram
5. liter/gram   6. meter
 c. 10, 100, 1,000
 d. 10, 100, 1,000
 e. milli centi deci deca hecto kilo
 f. Suggested answers:
2.8 dm   1.5 dm

2.3	0	0	3	9
2.4	32	42	45	96
	32	42	45	96
2.5	64	140	72	126
	64	140	72	126

2.6 22   99   70
      22   99   70

2.7 $P = 2L + 2W$ $P = 2(L + W)$
   $P = (2 \cdot 14) + (2 \cdot 9)$ $P = 2(14 + 9)$
   $P = 28 + 18$ $P = 2 \cdot 23$
   $P = 46$ ft. $P = 46$ ft.

2.8 a. $16 \times 12 = 192$ $8 \times 24 = 192$
       $7 \times 0 \times 8 = 0$ $56 \times 0 = 0$
       $15 + 24 = 39$ $3 \times 13 = 39$
   b. $7 \times 8 = 56$ $1 \times 56 = 56$
       $20 + 40 = 60$ $5 \times 12 = 60$
       $27 \times 0 = 0$ $0 \times 18 = 0$

2.9 a.
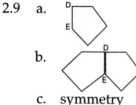
   b.
   c. symmetry

2.10
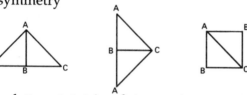
   triangle(isosceles) triangle(isosceles) square

2.11 a. $\triangle ABC \sim \triangle RST$
   b. $\overrightarrow{OF} \perp \overleftrightarrow{GH}$
   c. $\angle RST \cong \angle MNO$
   d. $\overline{EF} \parallel \overline{CD}$

2.12 a. $P = $ sum of sides
       $P = 4 + 6 + 4 + 5 + 8 + 11$
       $P = 38$ ft.
   b. $A = LW$ $A = LW$
       $A = 6 \cdot 4$ $A = 8 \cdot 5$
       $A = 24$ sq. ft. $A = 40$ sq. ft.
       $A = 24$ sq. ft. $+ 40$ sq. ft.
       $A = 64$ sq. ft.

2.13 a. $P = $ sum of sides
       $P = 6 + 12 + 6 + 8 + 3 + 4 + 3$
       $P = 42$ ft.
   b. $A = LW$ $A = LW$
       $A = 4 \cdot 3$ $A = 12 \cdot 6$
       $A = 12$ sq. ft. $A = 72$ sq. ft.
       $A = 12$ sq. ft. $+ 72$ sq. ft.
       $A = 84$ sq. ft.

2.14 a. $>$ $<$ $<$
   b. $=$ $<$ $=$
   c. $=$ $>$ $>$

2.15 15 million $<$ 19 million $<$ 20 million
       $<$ 12 billion $<$ 13 billion $<$ 18 billion
   15 million $< 19 \times 10^6 < (4 \times 5) \times 10^6$
       $< \frac{24}{2}$ billion $< 13 \times 10^9 <$ 18 billion

2.16 $21 \le 21, 22, 23, 24, 25 < 26$
   $13 \le 13, 17, 19 < 23$
   $240 \ge 240, 210, 180 > 150$

2.17 a. $6 \times [27 - (4 + 3)] = 6 \times (27 - 7) =$
       $6 \times 20 = \$120$
   b. $[(3 \times 18) + 26] \div 4 = (54 + 26) \div 4 =$
       $80 \div 4 = \$20$
   c. $4\{[5(35 + 15)] + 15\} = 4\{[5 \times 50] + 15\} =$
       $4\{250 + 15\} = 4\{265 \text{ min.}\} = 1060$ min. or
       17 hr. 40 min.

2.18 a. 246   2,009
   b. 814   1,776
   c. 461   1,314

2.19 a. DCCXXXIX   MMIII
   b. CDXCIII   MDCCCLXI
   c. CCXLV   MMXLVII

2.20 a. $36\frac{6}{8} = 37$ $145\frac{2}{6} = 145$ $75\frac{1}{5} = 75$ $254\frac{2}{3} = 255$
   b. $29\frac{8}{23} = 29$ $18\frac{11}{49} = 18$ $11\frac{57}{62} = 12$ $17\frac{45}{55} = 18$
   c. $35\frac{63}{78} = 36$ $41\frac{7}{83} = 41$ $166\frac{19}{38} = 167$ $68\frac{26}{27} = 69$

Part Three

3.1 a. 4   b. 2   c. 1   d. 3   e. 5
   triangle square circle rectangle circle

3.2 a.   square pyramid
   b.   rectangular prism
   c.   triangular pyramid
   d.   triangular prism

3.3 Teacher Check

3.4

3.5 a. 32 cu. in.
    b. L = 8 W = 4   L $\times$ W = 32 cu. in.
    c. 6
    d. 6 $\times$ 32 = 192 cu. in.

3.6 a. V = LWH
      V = 8 $\cdot$ 6 $\cdot$ 3
      V = 144 cu. ft.
    b. V = LWH
      V = 5 $\cdot$ 2 $\cdot$ 7
      V = 70 cu. yd.
    c. V = LWH
      V = 15 $\cdot$ 4 $\cdot$ 8
      V = 480 cu. in.

3.7 a. V = S³
      V = 9³
      V = 729 cu. yd.
    b. V = S³
      V = 10³
      V = 1,000 cu. in.
    c. V = S³
      V = 14³
      V = 2,744 cu. ft.

3.8 2, 3, 1, 1, 3, 2, 3, 2, 1

3.9 a. 4   6   8   25   10   7   8
    b. $\frac{2}{3}$ $\frac{3}{4}$ $\frac{2}{5}$ $\frac{2}{3}$ $\frac{2}{3}$ $\frac{4}{5}$ $\frac{7}{9}$

3.10 $2\frac{1}{2}$ $2\frac{2}{5}$ $10\frac{1}{2}$ $6\frac{2}{9}$ 7 $4\frac{1}{3}$

3.11 a.

	90
2	45
3	15
3	5
5	1

	315
3	105
3	35
5	7
7	1

    b. 2, 3², 5   3², 5, 7
              3², 5
              45
    c. $\frac{2}{7}$ 2, 7

3.12

	63
3	21
3	7
7	1

	180
2	90
2	45
3	15
3	5
5	1

    a. 3², 7   2², 3², 5
    b.   3² = 9
    c. $\frac{63}{180} = \frac{7}{20}$ or 7:20

3.13 $\frac{11}{16}$ $\frac{19}{24}$ $10\frac{11}{15}$ $9\frac{13}{18}$ $15\frac{19}{30}$ $10\frac{15}{28}$

3.14 $\frac{7}{15}$ $\frac{5}{18}$ $7\frac{11}{21}$ $8\frac{1}{12}$ $6\frac{5}{8}$ $5\frac{5}{12}$

3.15 a. $\frac{7}{16}$ $\frac{1}{3}$ $\frac{1}{3}$ 6   1 $4\frac{4}{5}$
    b. $2\frac{3}{5}$ $\frac{13}{28}$ 30   63   2
    c. $7\frac{1}{2}$ $1\frac{1}{2}$ 14   51 $9\frac{1}{3}$

3.16 a. $\frac{5}{6}$ $\frac{1}{21}$ 30   1   63 $\frac{2}{3}$
    b. 10 $\frac{3}{20}$ $1\frac{1}{3}$ $\frac{9}{10}$ $13\frac{1}{3}$
    c. $2\frac{1}{2}$ $\frac{1}{32}$ $25\frac{3}{5}$ $6\frac{2}{9}$ $\frac{13}{14}$

3.17 a. 7.497   b. 26.368 8.742 56.107
      18.091
      674.85   c. 92.05 .954   15.871
      6.214

3.18 a. 6.086   b. 22.75 5.56   .467
      .592
      9.144   c. 18.79 2.79   22.16
      2.742

3.19 .2516 .7434 2.976 4.32   5.561 46.636

3.20 a. $.4\frac{7}{8} = .5$ $9.1\frac{2}{7} = 9.1$ $.16\frac{1}{4} = .16$
      $.73\frac{2}{5} = .73$ $15\frac{2}{3} = 16$ $866\frac{4}{6} = 867$
    b. $1.8\frac{28}{37} = 1.9$ $.20\frac{8}{23} = .20$ $.014\frac{52}{56} = .015$
      $.23\frac{47}{48} = .24$ $.008\frac{1}{61} = .008$ $.48\frac{1}{56} = .48$

3.21 a. no   yes
    b. 360°   360°   360°
    c. - g.

    f. 90°, 90°
    g. Arc MN < Arc RS < Arc XY
      Chord MN < Chord RS < Chord XY
      Angle MEN = Angle RES = Angle XEY
    h. same, increased

3.22 a. $C = \pi d$
      $C = 3.14 \cdot 9$
      $C = 28.26$ m

    b. $C = \pi d$
      $C = 3.14 \cdot 5$
      $C = 15.7$ ft.

    c. $C = \pi d$
      $C = 3.14 \cdot 18$
      $C = 56.52$ in.

    d. $C = \pi d$
      $C = 3.14 \cdot 23$
      $C = 72.22$ in.

Part Four

4.1 a. 7
    b. 3 5 5 ⑥ 8 9 13
    c. 3 ⑤ ⑤ 6 8 9 13

4.2 a. 50%, 60%, 67%, 71%, 72%, 75%, 90%, 95%, 95%
    b. 75%   72%   95%
    c. received passing grade
    d. 9, 4
    e. median
       The mean score gives the appearance that half the class passed the test. The median score shows that more than half the class failed.
    f. The mode score of 95% raised the average.

4.3 a. 9   3, 6, 7 ⑧ 9, 15, 15   15
    b. 13   3, 11, 11, ⑭ 15, 16, 21   11
    c. 14   5, 10, 11, ⑬ 13, 17, 29   13
    d. 50   28, 34, 43, 59, 68, 68   68
                   \51/

4.4 a. 17   28   28   30   45   50
    b. #2
    c. 33, #2, #3
    d. mode 28   #1, #5
    e. #6, #1, #5
       They received the fewest number of rates

4.5 a. 5 ft. 3 in.
         5 ft. 4 in.
      + 4 ft. 8 in.
      14 ft. 15 in. = 15 ft. 3 in. ÷ 3 = 5 ft. 1 in.
    b. 70202   to find the most popular shoe; to restock his inventory
    c. 70 73 75 ⑦⑥ 82 85 85
    d. mode 8
    e. $134,000
    f. $11.95
    g. 38 min.

4.6 a. 14.54   1,241   925
    b. 5.84   952.72   18.6
    c. 33.052   851.63   52.08   36.14   11.152
    d. 18,784   12.167   45.83   165,711   47.09

4.7 a. 172.62   36   343,516
    b. 186,615   233   1.55
    c. 1.3185 $3.\overline{03}$ 304,128 $40.\overline{88}$
    d. 4,128,331 $88.0\overline{45}$ .003658   8.25

4.8 a. $2.25 + 7.5 = 9.75$ $10.6 - 7.75 = 2.85$
    b. $4.5 \times 3.8 = 17.1$ $12.5 \div 6.25 = 2$
    c. $6.875 + 11.6 = 18.475$ $24.2 - 14.5 = 9.7$
    d. $16.75 \times 9.5 = 159.125$ $10.8 \div 2.4 = 4.5$

4.9 $2 \times 12 \div 3 = 8$ $5 \times 8 \div 9 = 4.\overline{44}$

4.10 a. 10, 10
     b. 2, 3, 4, 1
     c. men $= \frac{2}{10} = \frac{1}{5}$
        women $= \frac{3}{10}$
        boys $= \frac{4}{10} = \frac{2}{5}$
        girl $= \frac{1}{10}$

4.11 a. $\frac{50}{500} = \frac{1}{10} = \frac{1}{10}$ $\frac{200}{500} = \frac{2}{5} = \frac{4}{10}$ $\frac{50}{500} = \frac{1}{10} = \frac{1}{10}$
        $\frac{100}{500} = \frac{1}{5} = \frac{2}{10}$ $\frac{100}{500} = \frac{1}{5} = \frac{2}{10}$
     b. 10
     c. - d.
       expenses $= 1$
       trip $= \frac{2}{5} = 4$
       gift $= 1$
       equipment $= \frac{1}{5} = 2$
       improvements $= \frac{1}{5} = 2$

     d. Suggested answer:
       title: Distribution of Earnings from Fair

4.12 a. $6 \times [28 - (3 \times 5)] = 6 \times (28 - 15) =$
         $6 \times 13 = 78$
      $[(32 - 5) \div 3] \times 6 = (27 \div 3) \times 6 =$
         $9 \times 6 = 54$
      $[(20 \div 4) + (18 \div 2)] - 7 = (5 + 9) - 7 =$
         $14 - 7 = 7$
     b. $42 - [(2 \times 3) + (5 \times 6)] = 42 - (6 + 30) =$
         $42 - 36 = 6$
      $16 + [(5 \times 8) - 12] = 16 + (40 - 12) =$
         $16 + 28 = 44$
      $[37 + (9 \times 3)] \div 8 = (37 + 27) \div 8 =$
         $64 \div 8 = 8$

c. $72 \div [(17 - 12) + 3] = 72 \div (5 + 3) =$
$\quad 72 \div 8 = 9$
$\quad [3 \times (6 + 3)] + 15 = (3 \times 9) + 15 =$
$\quad 27 + 15 = 42$
$\quad 54 - [(9 \times 2) + 15] = 54 - (18 + 15) =$
$\quad 54 - 33 = 21$

4.13 a. $7 \times 3 + 6 \times 2 - 11 = 21 + 12 - 11 = 22$
$\quad 42 \div 7 + 8 \times 3 - 15 = 6 + 24 - 15 = 15$
$\quad 2 + 5 \times 6 + 12 \div 4 = 2 + 30 + 3 = 35$

b. $35 - 3 \times 7 + 56 \div 7 = 35 - 21 + 8 = 22$
$\quad 81 \div 9 + 2 - 5 \times 2 = 9 + 2 - 10 = 1$
$\quad 75 - 6 \times 4 - 15 \div 3 = 75 - 24 - 5 = 46$

c. $63 \div 9 + 48 \div 6 = 7 + 8 = 15$
$\quad 14 + 5 \times 7 + 12 = 14 + 35 + 12 = 61$
$\quad 5 \times 8 + 7 \times 6 = 40 + 42 = 82$

4.14 a. 5   17   23   84   47
b. 68   80   51   93   33

Part Five

5.1 a. 9
b. 9, 7   plus 3 minus 2
c. 133
d. 1.95
e. $1\frac{1}{2}$
f. .625
g. 290
h. third, second, first, fifth, fourth
i. six and four-thousandths, 9.0056
j. seven and eight-fifteenths, $14\frac{11}{16}$
k. 2.   58.   365.
l. .500   .670   9.400   8.320   .700   .030
$\quad$ .03   .5   .67   .70   8.32   9.4
m. $46 + 28 + 32 = 106$ 106
$\qquad\qquad\qquad\qquad\qquad\qquad - 46$
$\qquad\qquad\qquad\qquad\qquad\qquad\quad 60$
$\qquad\qquad\qquad\qquad\qquad\qquad - 28$
$\qquad\qquad\qquad\qquad\qquad\qquad\quad 32$
$\qquad\qquad\qquad\qquad\qquad\qquad - 32$
$\qquad\qquad\qquad\qquad\qquad\qquad\quad\quad 0$

$\quad 6.4 - 2.31 = 4.09$ 6.40
$\qquad\qquad\qquad\qquad\qquad\quad - 2.31$
$\qquad\qquad\qquad\qquad\qquad + 4.09$
$\qquad\qquad\qquad\qquad\qquad\quad 6.40$

$3\frac{1}{3} \times 18 = \frac{10}{3} \times 18 = 60$
$60 \div 3\frac{1}{3} = 60 \div \frac{10}{3} = 60 \times \frac{3}{10} = 18$
$15 \div 5\frac{1}{4} = 15 \div \frac{21}{4} = 15 \times \frac{4}{21} = \frac{20}{7} = 2\frac{6}{7}$
$2\frac{6}{7} \times 5\frac{1}{4} = \frac{20}{7} \times \frac{21}{4} = 15$

5.2 a. $2{,}000 + 600 + 2{,}000 + 1{,}000 = 5{,}600$ mi.
b. $5{,}000 - (1{,}000 + 2{,}000) =$
$\quad 5{,}000 - 3{,}000 = 2{,}000$ cars
c. $500 \times 10 = 6{,}000$ cans
d. $8{,}000 \div 20 = 400$ sheets

5.3 a. $13 \leq 13, 17, 19, 23 < 29$
b. $30 \geq 30, 28, 27, 26 > 25$
c. $30 \leq 30, 32, 34, 36, 38 < 40$
d. $49 \geq 49, 47, 45, 43 > 41$
e. 6   1, 2, 3, 6
$\quad$ 8   1, 2, 4, 8
$\quad$ 12   1, 2, 3, 4, 6, 12
$\quad$ 15   1, 3, 5, 15
$\quad$ 18   1, 2, 3, 6, 9, 18
f.

12		15		18		27	
2	6	3	5	2	9	3	9
2	3	5	1	3	3	3	3
3	1			3	1	3	1

$\quad 2^2, 3$ 3, 5 $2, 3^2$ 3^3

g. $\frac{2}{3} \times 12 = 8$ $\frac{1}{5} \times 60 = 12$ min.
h. $\frac{3}{4} - \frac{1}{4} = \frac{1}{2}$ $\frac{1}{2} - \frac{1}{3} = \frac{1}{6}$ bag
i. $2{,}640$ ft. $= \frac{1}{2}$ mi. Ben was $\frac{1}{4}$ mi. from home
$\quad \frac{1}{4} \times 2{,}640 = 660$ ft.

j. 4:5
$\quad \frac{8}{8}$
$\quad \frac{12}{18}$
$\quad \frac{7}{8}$
$\quad \frac{1}{9}$
$\quad \frac{1}{4}$

5.4 a. horizontal or parallel
b. intersecting or perpendicular
c. $P = 4S$ $A = S^2$
$\quad P = 4 \cdot 45$ $A = 45^2$
$\quad P = 180$ in. $A = 2{,}025$ sq. in.
d. similar

e. right triangle
f. five
g. C = πd d = 2 × 4 ft.
C = 3.14 × 8 d = 8 ft.
C = 25.12 ft
25.12 ft. × 8 = 200.96 ft.
h. V = L × W × H
V = 6 × 4 × 3
V = 72 cu. in.
i. 3, 4, 6, 8

5.5 a. D = R × T
D = 56 × 7
D = 392 mi.

b. D = R × T
330 = R × 5.5
330 ÷ 5.5 = R × (5.5 ÷ 5.5)
60 mph = R

c. 24 $\frac{1}{2}$ hr = 30 min.
× 12
288 berries

A = R × T
288 = R × 30 min.
288 ÷ 30 = R × (30 ÷ 30)
9.6 bpm = R

d. A = R × T
A = 64 × 8
A = 512 times

5.6 a. 3 ft. 7 in.
9 ft. 8 in.
+ 6 ft. 5 in.
18ft. 20 in. = 19 ft. 8 in.

b. 5 da. 8 hr.
× 5
25 da. 40 hr.
− 14 hr.
25 da. 26 hr. = 26 da. 2 hr.

c. 1 doz. 1$\frac{1}{2}$ cookies
8)9 doz.
8 doz.
1 doz. = 12 cookies

or 9 × 12 = 108 cookies

13$\frac{1}{2}$ cookies
8)108

d. 32 oz.
× 6 qt.
192 oz.

16 glasses
12)192

5.7 a. 2,421, 259
b. MCCCLXVIII, DCCXXXIV

5.8 a. Milky Way
b. yes
c. light year
d. 186,282 miles per second
e. 24,901 miles, days, $\frac{1}{7}$ of a second
f. 93 million miles
g. 8 minutes
h. light travelling six trillion miles in one year
i. 105 × 6 trillion miles
100 × 6,000,000,000,000 =
600,000,000,000,000 =
600 trillion miles

5.9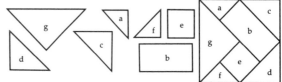

5.10 a.

×	6	8.1	.54	$\frac{1}{2}$	$9.01	$\frac{3}{4}$	72	.008	3.5
10	60	81	5.4	5	$90.10	7.5	720	.08	35
100	600	810	54	50	$901.	75	7,200	.8	350
1,000	6,000	8,100	540	500	$9,010.	750	72,000	8	3,500

b.

÷	876	2.4	2,978	$\frac{3}{4}$	.04	$150	$\frac{3}{5}$	.2	60.7
10	87.6	.24	297.8	.075	.004	$15	.06	.02	6.07
100	8.76	.024	29.78	.0075	.0004	$1.50	.006	.002	.607
1,000	.876	.0024	2.978	.00075	.00004	$.15	.0006	.0002	.0607

5.11 a.

13	8	9
6	10	14
11	12	7

b.

9	4	5
2	6	10
7	8	3

c.

15	10	11
8	12	16
13	14	9

d.

7	2	3
0	4	8
5	6	1

a. Sum is 30. b. Sum is 18.
c. Sum is 36. d. Sum is 12.

Part One

1.1 a. 2.6   42.1   .3   9.0   .4
    b. 3.09   .28   52.61   .03   8.47

1.2 a. 64   24   138   73   50
    b. 9   18   127   30   28

1.3 a. 2.7   47.1   .3   5.0   .9
    b. 6.09   95.38   15.27   .03   .55

1.4 $125\frac{1}{7} = 125$ $72\frac{2}{5} = 72$ $228\frac{3}{4} = 229$

    $86\frac{3}{6} = 87$ $191\frac{1}{3} = 191$

1.5 a. $59\frac{41}{63} = 60$ $67\frac{59}{94} = 68$ $307\frac{1}{26} = 307$ $174\frac{50}{51} = 175$
    b. $67\frac{33}{38} = 68$ $116\frac{28}{73} = 116$ $165\frac{41}{42} = 166$ $55\frac{75}{84} = 56$
    c. $107\frac{11}{26} = 107$ $300\frac{7}{18} = 300$ $59\frac{3}{31} = 59$ $18\frac{46}{74} = 19$

1.6
```
   59        67        307        174
 × 63      × 94      ×  26      ×  51
3,717     6,298      7,982      8,874
+  41     +  59      +   1      +  50
3,758     6,357      7,983      8,924
```

1.7   177,165   512,028   2,516,850
    4,800,240   3,858,372

1.8 a. fifteen-hundredths
     nine and five-tenths
     forty-three thousandths
     two and eight-hundredths
    b. .006   4.16
      .78   5.030

1.9 a. hundredths   tens   tenths
    b. ones   hundreds   hundred thousandths

1.10 a. 100   10   1,000   100
     b. 10   100   1,000   10

1.11 a. 7.168   306.38   1.253
       .389   2.27   6.62
     b. 51.97   364.33   .705
       .237   3.53   2.56

1.12 4.28   1.7262   .40004
     .188468   95.985

1.13 a. $2.24\frac{2}{3} = 2.25$ $.072\frac{3}{8} = .072$ $2.6\frac{1}{23} = 2.6$
      $.88\frac{2}{67} = .88$ $4.23\frac{2}{15} = 4.23$
     b. $4.2\frac{7}{9} = 4.3$ $.023\frac{1}{4} = .023$ $2.3\frac{1}{34} = 2.3$
      $.020\frac{34}{46} = .021$ $.004\frac{17}{82} = .004$

1.14 a. $8.1\frac{2}{7} = 8.1$ .56   160.
     $1.49\frac{33}{45} = 1.50$ .02
    b. $.8\frac{2}{62} = .8$ $6.5\frac{8}{9} = 6.6$ $2.8\frac{24}{34} = 2.9$
     832. $21\frac{28}{43} = 22$

1.15

	2	5	10	3	9	6
459				✓	✓	
76	✓					
500	✓	✓	✓			
84	✓			✓		✓
321				✓		
210	✓	✓	✓	✓		✓
585		✓		✓	✓	
143						
68	✓					
305		✓				
264	✓			✓		✓
462	✓			✓		✓
954	✓			✓	✓	✓

1.16

Prime numbers: 2, 3, 5, 7, 11, 13, 17, 19, 23, 29, 31, 37, 41, 43, 47, 53, 59, 61, 67, 71, 73, 79, 83, 89, 97

Part Two

2.1 a. 24, 48, 72, 84, 108, 132
    b. 36, 72, 108, 126, 162, 198

2.2   1, 2, 3, 4, 6, 12   1, 2, 3, 6, 9, 18

2.3   Circled numbers - 23, 61
    2, 3   Ø   3, 5   2   2   3   Ø   2   2   3

2.4   2, 3

2.5

2, 5 2^2, 3   3, 5   2, 3^2 2^3, 3 2^5

2.6 a. 2^3 2^2, 3

  2^3, 3

  24

  b. 2^3 2^2, 3

  2^2

  4

2.7

	PF	PF		LCM		GCF
10/12	2, 5	2^2, 3	$(2^2 \cdot 3 \cdot 5)$	60	(2)	2
15/18	3, 5	2, 3^2	$(2 \cdot 3^2 \cdot 5)$	90	(3)	3
24/32	2^3, 3	2^5	$(2^5 \cdot 3)$	96	(2^3)	8
12/15	2^2, 3	3, 5	$(2^2, 3, 5)$	60	(3)	3
18/24	2, 3^2	2^3, 3	$(2^3 \cdot 3^2)$	72	(2, 3)	6

2.8 a. $\frac{23}{40}$ $\frac{43}{60}$ $1\frac{7}{24}$ $1\frac{17}{30}$ $\frac{67}{90}$

  b. $1\frac{5}{42}$ $\frac{53}{72}$ $\frac{11}{20}$ $\frac{41}{72}$ $1\frac{23}{45}$

  c. $1\frac{1}{120}$ $1\frac{21}{40}$ $\frac{49}{50}$ $1\frac{11}{60}$ $1\frac{11}{30}$

2.9 a. $\frac{17}{36}$ $\frac{2}{70} = \frac{1}{35}$ $\frac{31}{48}$ $\frac{23}{40}$ $\frac{2}{18} = \frac{1}{9}$

  b. $\frac{1}{30}$ $\frac{16}{63}$ $\frac{3}{15} = \frac{1}{5}$ $\frac{37}{80}$ $\frac{59}{96}$

  c. $\frac{19}{40}$ $\frac{13}{36}$ $\frac{3}{14}$ $\frac{22}{30} = \frac{11}{15}$ $\frac{4}{12} = \frac{1}{3}$

2.10 a. $\frac{1}{4}$ 12   10 $1\frac{4}{5}$ 30

  b.   20 $2\frac{1}{10}$ $9\frac{3}{8}$ 20 $6\frac{3}{4}$

  c. $\frac{27}{50}$ 2 $\frac{11}{36}$ $7\frac{1}{2}$ $16\frac{1}{2}$

  d. $\frac{7}{40}$ $\frac{1}{12}$ 12   14 $26\frac{2}{3}$

2.11 $\frac{8}{7}$ $\frac{1}{9}$ $\frac{2}{9}$

2.12 Circled divisors: $\frac{4}{7}$, 6, $2\frac{3}{5}$

2.13 a. $\frac{1}{16}$ 28 $1\frac{1}{2}$ $4\frac{1}{2}$ $\frac{7}{16}$

  b. $\frac{5}{12}$ $\frac{4}{5}$ $1\frac{1}{20}$ 18 $1\frac{1}{5}$

  c.   32 $\frac{1}{9}$ 28 $1\frac{1}{4}$ 40

  d. $1\frac{3}{5}$ $\frac{3}{4}$ $\frac{1}{3}$ $\frac{1}{16}$ 6

2.14 a.   .5   .25   .75

  b.   .2   .4   .6   .8

  c.   .125   .375   .625   .875

2.15 $.\overline{33}$ $.\overline{66}$ $.1\overline{66}$ $.8\overline{33}$

2.16   7.5   6.6 $15.\overline{66}$ 24.375   32.75   40.6

2.17 a. $\frac{1}{8}$ $\frac{2}{3}$ $\frac{1}{2}$ $\frac{3}{4}$ $\frac{1}{3}$ $1\frac{1}{6}$

  b. $9\frac{1}{2}$ $6\frac{1}{4}$ $27\frac{1}{5}$ $14\frac{3}{5}$ $27\frac{7}{8}$ $30\frac{2}{5}$

2.18 a. $.5 \times 7.625 =$ $.6 + .25 =$ $.4 \times 1.875 =$

  b. $9.2 - 6.\overline{33} =$ $8.8 \div .75 =$ $5.25 - 2.375 =$

2.19 a.   1.475   .125   .30 $.0\overline{55}$

  b.   2.3   1.05   1.09375   3.12

  c.   7.375   6.1   3.12 $27.\overline{33}$

  d.   12.25   6   .72 $.097\overline{22}$

2.20 a.   .40   6.70   .80   29.00   1.50

  b.   .800   9.320   .700   5.900   3.020

2.21 a.   83.5   246   94.2   80   50.3

  b.   6,720   12,030   7,200   973   2,000

2.22 a.   .470, 3.620, 5.560, .048, 5.730, 3.060, 4.112

  .048, .47, 3.06, 3.62, 4.112, 5.56, 5.73

  b.   2.500, 3.160, .035, .370, 3.820, .071, .800

  .035, .071, .37, .8, 2.5, 3.16, 3.82

2.23 $\frac{3}{8} = \frac{9}{24}$ $\frac{2}{3} = \frac{16}{24}$ $\frac{1}{6} = \frac{4}{24}$ $\frac{1}{2} = \frac{12}{24}$

  $\frac{5}{6} = \frac{20}{24}$ $\frac{3}{4} = \frac{18}{24}$ $\frac{7}{8} = \frac{21}{24}$

  $\frac{1}{6}$ $\frac{3}{8}$ $\frac{1}{2}$ $\frac{2}{3}$ $\frac{3}{4}$ $\frac{5}{6}$ $\frac{7}{8}$

2.24 $\frac{3}{8} = .375$ $\frac{2}{3} = .\overline{666}$ $\frac{1}{6} = .1\overline{66}$ $\frac{1}{2} = .500$

  $\frac{5}{6} = .8\overline{33}$ $\frac{3}{4} = .750$ $\frac{7}{8} = .875$

  $.1\overline{66}$ .375   .500 $.\overline{666}$ .750 $.8\overline{33}$ .875

Part Three

3.1   32%   7%   94%   52%   5%   11%

3.2 a. $\frac{68}{100}$ .68   68% $\frac{4}{100}$ .04   4%

  b. $\frac{15}{100}$ .15   15% $\frac{70}{100}$ .70   70%

3.3 a.   46%   3%   51%   82%   27%

  b.   2%   61%   14%   91%   3%

3.4 a.   53:100 $\frac{53}{100}$ .53   16:100 $\frac{16}{100}$ .16

  b.   9:100 $\frac{9}{100}$ .09   74:100 $\frac{74}{100}$ .74

3.5 a.   .47   47% ,   .30   30% ,   .54   54%

  b.   .07   7% ,   .10   10% ,   .80   80%

3.6 a.   .50   50% ,   .25   25% ,   .75   75%

  b.   .20   20% ,   .40   40% ,   .60   60% ,   .80   80%

  c.   .13   13% ,   .38   38% ,   .63   63% ,   .88   .88%

  d.   .33   33% ,   .67   67% ,   .17   17% ,   .83   83%

125

3.7 a. $.43 = 43\%$ $.56 = 56\%$ $.27 = 27\%$ $.92 = 92\%$

    b. $.22 = 22\%$ $.86 = 86\%$ $.27 = 27\%$ $.69 = 69\%$

3.8 a. $\frac{4}{7} = .571 = 57\%$ $\frac{8}{15} = .533 = 53\%$

        $\frac{6}{11} = .545 = 55\%$ $\frac{4}{14} = .285 = 29\%$

    b. $\frac{4}{9} = .444 = 44\%$ $\frac{5}{12} = .416 = 42\%$

        $\frac{1}{7} = .142 = 14\%$ $\frac{2}{15} = .133 = 13\%$

3.9 a.
$$a + 32 = 118$$
$$a + 32(-32) = 118 - 32$$
$$a = 86$$
$$86 + 32 = 118$$

$$b - 47 = 138$$
$$b - 47(+47) = 138 + 47$$
$$b = 185$$
$$185 - 47 = 138$$

$$x \cdot 16 = 64$$
$$x \cdot 16(\div 16) = 64 \div 16$$
$$x = 4$$
$$4 \cdot 16 = 64$$

$$z \div 22 = 13$$
$$z \div 22(\cdot 22) = 13 \cdot 22$$
$$z = 286$$
$$286 \div 22 = 13$$

    b.
$$x + 63 = 215$$
$$x + 63(-63) = 215 - 63$$
$$x = 152$$
$$152 + 63 = 215$$

$$b - 115 = 312$$
$$b - 115(+115) = 312 + 115$$
$$b = 427$$
$$427 - 115 = 312$$

$$a \cdot 29 = 145$$
$$a \cdot 29(\div 29) = 145 \div 29$$
$$a = 5$$
$$5 \cdot 29 = 145$$

$$z \div 12 = 15$$
$$z \div 12(\cdot 12) = 15 \cdot 12$$
$$z = 180$$
$$180 \div 12 = 15$$

3.10 a.
$$\frac{a}{5} = \frac{14}{35}$$
$$a \cdot 35 = 70$$
$$a \cdot 35(\div 35) = 70 \div 35$$
$$a = 2$$
$$\frac{2}{5} = \frac{14}{35}$$

$$\frac{9}{10} = \frac{x}{20}$$
$$180 = x \cdot 10$$
$$180 \div 10 = x \cdot 10(\div 10)$$
$$18 = x$$
$$\frac{9}{10} = \frac{18}{20}$$

$$\frac{6}{9} = \frac{30}{b}$$
$$6 \cdot b = 270$$
$$6 \cdot b(\div 6) = 270 \div 6$$
$$b = 45$$
$$\frac{6}{9} = \frac{30}{45}$$

$$\frac{4}{y} = \frac{20}{25}$$
$$100 = 20y$$
$$100 \div 20 = 20 \cdot y(\div 20)$$
$$5 = y$$
$$\frac{4}{5} = \frac{20}{25}$$

$$\frac{3}{6} = \frac{n}{14}$$
$$42 = 6 \cdot n$$
$$42 \div 6 = 6 \cdot n(\div 6)$$
$$7 = n$$
$$\frac{3}{6} = \frac{7}{14} \left(\frac{1}{2}\right)$$

    b.
$$\frac{z}{16} = \frac{3}{24}$$
$$z \cdot 24 = 48$$
$$z \cdot 24(\div 24) = 48 \div 24$$
$$z = 2$$
$$\frac{2}{16} = \frac{3}{24} \left(\frac{1}{8}\right)$$

$$\frac{10}{15} = \frac{4}{r}$$
$$10 \cdot r = 60$$
$$10 \cdot r(\div 10) = 60 \div 10$$
$$r = 6$$
$$\frac{10}{15} = \frac{4}{6} \left(\frac{2}{3}\right)$$

$$\frac{c}{8} = \frac{10}{16}$$
$$c \cdot 16 = 80$$
$$c \cdot 16(\div 16) = 80 \div 16$$
$$c = 5$$
$$\frac{5}{8} = \frac{10}{16}$$

$$\frac{3}{9} = \frac{12}{s}$$
$$3 \cdot s = 108$$
$$3 \cdot s(\div 3) = 108 \div 3$$
$$s = 36$$
$$\frac{3}{9} = \frac{12}{36}$$

$$\frac{m}{18} = \frac{4}{6}$$
$$m \cdot 6 = 72$$
$$m \cdot 6(\div 6) = 72 \div 6$$
$$m = 12$$
$$\frac{12}{18} = \frac{4}{6} \left(\frac{2}{3}\right)$$

3.11   15, 24, 30   3, 8, 15   12, 20, 26

3.12   add 5   multiply by 6

3.13   11, 5, 17, 12   12, 7, 24, 9

3.14 $a = 7$ $x = 9$ $c = 6$

3.15   3, 4, 5, 6, 7   0, 6, 12, 18, 24

3.16   a.   15, 24, 19, 30, 27   b.   5, 14, 10, 22, 2
       c.   36, 63, 27, 81, 99   d.   7, 3, 4, 1, 0

3.17   a.   4
       b.   6
       c.   3
       d.   5
       e.   2
       f.   1

3.18   a.   perimeter - length - width -
            perimeter of rectangle
       b.   area - length - width - area of rectangle
       c.   perimeter - side - perimeter of square
       d.   area - side - area of a square
       e.   perimeter - side - perimeter of triangle
       f.   area - base - height - area of triangle
       g.   circumference - π (3.14) - diameter
            circumference of circle
       h.   volume - length - width - height -
            volume of rectangular prism
       i   volume - side - volume of square prism
       j.   distance - rate - time - distance
       k.   amount - rate - time - amount

3.19   a. $D = rt$
            $D = 53 \cdot 9$
            $D = 477$ mi.

       b. $P = 4s$
            $P = 4 \cdot 5$
            $P = 20$ ft.

c. $V = lwh$
     $V = 12 \cdot 9 \cdot 7$
     $V = 756$ cu. in.

d. $A = lw$
     $A = 29 \cdot 15$
     $A = 435$ sq. yd.

e. $A = \frac{1}{2} bh$
     $A = \frac{1}{2} (14 \cdot 8)$
     $A = \frac{14 \cdot 8}{2}$
     $A = \frac{112}{2}$
     $A = 56$ sq. in.

f. $A = lw$
          $576 = 32 \cdot w$
     $576 \div 32 = 32 \cdot w(\div 32)$
     18 in. $= w$

g. $A = s^2$
     $A = 23^2$
     $A = 529$ sq. ft.

h. $A = rt$
          $280 = 35 \cdot t$
     $280 \div 35 = 35 \cdot t(\div 35)$
     8 hr. $= t$

i. $P = 2l + 2w$
          $94 = (2 \cdot l) + (2 \cdot w)$
          $94 = (2 \cdot l) + 36$
     $94 - 36 = (2 \cdot l) + 36(- 36)$
          $58 = 2 \cdot l$
     $58 \div 2 = 2 \cdot l (\div 2)$
     29 ft. $= 1$

j. $C = \pi d$
     $C = 3.14 \cdot 8$
     $C = 25.12$ in.

k. $P = s + s + s$
          $27 = 9 + 12 + s$
          $27 = 21 + s$
     $27 - 21 = 21 + s(- 21)$
     6 ft. $= s$

l. $P = 4s$
          $48 = 4s$
     $48 \div 4 = 4s(\div 4)$
     12 yd. $= s$

m.
$$D = rt$$
$$576 = r \cdot 8$$
$$576 \div 8 = r \cdot 8(\div 8)$$
$$72 \text{ mph} = r$$

n. $V = s^3$
$V = 5^3$
$V = 125$ cu. in.

o.
$$A = \tfrac{1}{2}bh$$
$$42 = \tfrac{1}{2}(12 \cdot h)$$
$$42 = \frac{(12 \cdot h)}{2}$$
$$42 \cdot 2 = \frac{\overset{1}{\cancel{2}}(12 \cdot h)}{\underset{1}{\cancel{2}}}$$
$$84 = 12 \cdot h$$
$$84 \div 12 = 12 \cdot h(\div 12)$$
$$7 \text{ in.} = h$$

p.
$$A = \tfrac{1}{2}bh$$
$$18 = \tfrac{1}{2}(bh)$$
$$18 = \frac{(b \cdot 9)}{2}$$
$$18 \cdot 2 = \frac{\overset{1}{\cancel{2}}(b \cdot 9)}{\underset{1}{\cancel{2}}}$$
$$36 = b \cdot 9$$
$$36 \div 9 = b \cdot 9(\div 9)$$
$$4 \text{ ft.} = b$$

Part Four

4.1   circle A ~ circle F

4.2   c

4.3

4.4 $\frac{1}{4}$ in. , 1 mi.

4.5   C
$$\frac{.25}{1 \text{ mi.}} = \frac{.75}{x \text{ mi.}}$$
$$.25 \cdot x = .75$$
$$.25 \cdot x(\div .25) = .75 \div .25$$
$$x = 3 \text{ mi.}$$

D
$$\frac{.25}{1 \text{ mi.}} = \frac{1.25}{x}$$
$$.25x = 1.25$$
$$.25 \cdot x(\div .25) = 1.25 \div .25$$
$$x = 5 \text{ mi.}$$

E
$$\frac{.25}{1 \text{ mi.}} = \frac{1.75}{x \text{ mi.}}$$
$$.25 \cdot x = 1.75$$
$$.25 \cdot x(\div .25) = 1.75 \div .25$$
$$x = 7 \text{ mi.}$$

F
$$\frac{.25}{1 \text{ mi.}} = \frac{2.00}{x}$$
$$.25 \cdot x = 2.00$$
$$.25 \cdot x(\div .25) = 2.00 \div .25$$
$$x = 8 \text{ mi.}$$

4.6
a.	northwest	7 mi.	40°
b.	north	5 mi.	85°
c.	northeast	8 mi.	125°
d.	east	3 mi.	170°
e.	west	2 mi.	25°
f.	southeast	5 mi.	70°
g.	south	8 mi.	95°
h.	southwest	7 mi.	140°
i.	west	3 mi.	165°

4.7   a.   black   pink
            purple   blue   orange
       b. $2\frac{7}{8}$ in. , $5\frac{3}{16}$ in.

4.8 $1\frac{1}{16}$ in. $1\frac{9}{16}$ in. $\frac{7}{16}$ in.
       $2\frac{3}{16}$ in. $1\frac{15}{16}$ in.

4.9 $1\frac{1}{4}$ in., 1.25 in. $1\frac{3}{4}$ in., 1.75 in.
       $1\frac{3}{8}$ in., 1.375 in. $1\frac{7}{8}$ in., 1.875 in.

4.10   surface
       what it holds, or the space it displaces

4.11 $A = lw$ $V = lwh$

4.12   a. 5   2
       b. 720   9,680
       c. 5,184   4
       d. 1,600   56.25

4.13 $C = \pi d$ $C = 2\pi r$
       $C = 3.14 \cdot 9$ $C = 2 \cdot (3.14 \cdot 7)$
       $C = 28.26$ in. $C = 2 \cdot 21.98$
                              $C = 43.96$ in.

4.14   a. $A = \pi r^2$
           $A = 3.14 \cdot 8^2$
           $A = 3.14 \cdot 64$
           $A = 200.96$ sq. in. or 201 sq. in.
       b. $A = \pi r^2$
           $A = 3.14 \cdot 4^2$
           $A = 3.14 \cdot 16$
           $A = 50.24$ sq. ft. or 50 sq. ft.

c. $A = \pi r^2$
$A = 3.14 \cdot 3^2$
$A = 3.14 \cdot 9$
$A = 28.26$ sq. yd. or 28 sq. yd.

d. $A = \pi r^2$
$A = 3.14 \cdot 6^2$
$A = 3.14 \cdot 36$
$A = 113.04$ sq. mi. or 113 sq. mi.

4.15

3	14	a.
7	19	b.
1	12	c.
6	17	d.
10	15	e.
2	11	f.
5	20	g.
4	13	h.
8	16	i.
9	18	j.

4.16   yard   quart   ounce

4.17 a. M   M   D
b. D   M   M
c. M   M   D

4.18 a. 10   1,000   10
b. 100   10   100
c. 1,000   10   1,000

4.19 a. 80   .43   5,000   43.8
b. 7,200   .009   6,300   .75
c. 23.0   .003   7   .00459

4.20 a. $3 \times 10 = 30$
$18 \times 1,000 = 18,000$
$73 \times 10 = 730$

b. $5,000 \div 1,000 = 5$
$23 \div 10 = 2.3$
$14 \times 1,000 = 14,000$

c. $2 \times 1,000 = 2,000$
$1,346 \div 1,000 = 1.346$
$90 \div 10 = 9$

4.21 a. 10 , $\frac{1}{10}$, .1 , 1
b. 100 , $\frac{1}{100}$, .01 , 1
c. 10 , $\frac{1}{10}$, .1 , 1
d. $\frac{5}{10}$, .5 , 5

4.22 a. 3 L 5 dL   4 cm 3mm   2 dm 7 cm
b. 9 m 45 cm   6 dL 23 mL   3 g 4 dg
c. 8 km 6 m   2kg 5 g   7 kL 9 L
d. 2 dm 7mm   2 L 1 dL   3 kg 6 g

Part Five

5.1 a. 16, 4, 2, 8   15, 9, 11, 3
b. 2, 11, 3   16, 4, 15, 9, 8
Suggested answers - c., d., e., f., g., l., m.
c. $3 + 8 = 11, 8 + 3 = 11, 11 - 3 = 8, 11 - 8 = 3$
d. $2 \times 4 = 8, 4 \times 2 = 8, 8 \div 2 = 4, 8 \div 4 = 2$
e. 2, 4, 8, 16 … multiply by 2
f. fourth
g. $\frac{2}{4}$, 3:15
h. $2 \le 2, 3, 4, 8 < 9$
i. $16 \ge 16, 15, 11, 9 > 8$
j. XVI , IV , XV , IX
k. $16 = 2^4$ $4 = 2^2$ $15 = 3, 5$ $9 = 3^2$
l. $19 + 15 + 16 = 50$
m. $3 \times 4 \times 16 = 192$

5.2   10
4
15
8
10
3

5.3 a. 5:30 A.M.   2:02 P.M.   12:24 P.M.   6:45 P.M.
b. 5:00 P.M.   12:54 A.M.   9:13 A.M.   10:18 P.M.

5.4 a. 07.04   15.00   23.32   10.14
b. 08.30   21.14   00.04   19.45

5.5 a. twenty-five degrees, twelve minutes
sixteen degrees, five minutes
b. one hundred forty-six degrees,
fourteen minutes
one hundred twenty-one degrees,
twenty-seven minutes

5.6   the earth is tilted toward the sun.
the earth is tilted away from the sun.

5.7 a. $20:25 = \frac{20}{25} = \frac{4}{5} = .80 = 80\%$

b. $8:20 = \frac{8}{20} = \frac{2}{5} = .40 = 40\%$

$\frac{12}{20} = \frac{3}{5} = .60 = 60\%$

c. $27:90 = \frac{27}{90} = \frac{3}{10} = .30 = 30\%$

$18:90 = \frac{18}{90} = \frac{1}{5} = .20 = 20\%$

$45:90 = \frac{45}{90} = \frac{1}{2} = .50 = \underline{50\%}$

$\phantom{45:90 = \frac{45}{90} = \frac{1}{2} = .50 = } 100\% \qquad$ yes

d. $\frac{45}{50} = \frac{9}{10} = .90 = 90\%$

e. $\frac{14}{56} = \frac{1}{4} = .25 = 25\%$

f. $\frac{3.50}{5.00} = \frac{70}{100} = .70 = 70\%$

5.8 a. $\$100 - [\$22.55 + (3 \cdot \$22.55)] = n$
$\$100 - (\$22.55 + \$67.55) = n$
$\$100 - \$90.20 = n$
$\$9.80$ change $= n$

b. $450 - (20 \times 15) = n$
$450 - 300 = n$
150 - enough paint to cover 150 sq. ft. $= n$

c. $5(2 \times \frac{2}{5}) = n$
$5(2 \times \frac{4}{5}) = n$
4 mi. $= n$

d. $120 - [(\frac{1}{5} \cdot 120) + (\frac{1}{3} \cdot 120)] = n$
$120 - (24 + 40) = n$
$120 - 64 = n$
56 pages $= n$

e. $\frac{87 + 85 + 81 + 79 + n}{5} = 85$

$\frac{332 + n}{5} = 85$
$5(\frac{332 + n}{5}) = 85 \times 5$
$332 + n = 425$
$n = 93$

f. $(144 \div 12) \div 4 = n$
$12 \div 4 = n$
3 cookies $= n$

g. $(8 + 6 + 4) \div (21 + 18 + 15) = n$
$18 \div 54 = n$
$\frac{18}{54}$ reduces to $\frac{1}{3}$
$\frac{1}{3} = n$
$.33 = n$
$33\% = n$

5.9 a. $a = $ Casey $a + \$4.15 = $ Joseph
$a + a + 4.15 = 15.37$
$2a + 4.15 = 15.37$
$2a + 4.15(-4.15) = 15.37 - 4.15$
$2a = 11.22$
$a = \$5.61$
$a + \$4.15 = \$9.76$

b. $a = $ first box $a - 8$ lb. $= $ second box
$a + a - 8 = 46$
$2a - 8 = 46$
$2a - 8(+8) = 46 + 8$
$2a = 54$
$a = 27$ lb.
$a - 8 = 19$ lb.

c. $a = $ Bethany $a + 37 = $ Jordan
$a + a + 37 = 165$
$2a + 37 = 165$
$2a + 37(-37) = 165 - 37$
$2a = 128$
$a = 64$ mi.
$a + 37 = 101$ mi.

d. $a = $ Sam $3a = $ Sam's dad
$a + 3a = 260$
$4a = 260$
$a = 65$ lbs.
$3a = 195$ lbs.

e. $a = $ second grade $6a = $ fifth grade
$a + 6a = 420$
$7a = 420$
$a = 60$ books
$6a = 360$ books

f. $a = $ Joseph, $a + 4 = $ Beth, $a + 3 = $ Jenny
$a + a + 4 + a + 3 = 19$
$3a + 7 = 19$
$3a + 7(-7) = 19 - 7$
$3a = 12$
$a = 4$
$a + 4 = 8$
$a + 3 = 7$

5.10 a. 1,007 $\frac{13}{18}$ $4\frac{5}{8}$ 16.58

b. 4,018 $\frac{7}{24}$ $8\frac{2}{5}$ 5.99

c. 2,378   3,734 $1\frac{1}{6}$ $1\frac{11}{12}$ 2.58
38,523   1.84

d. 17,616   25 $\frac{5}{21}$ $32\frac{1}{2}$ .02636
15   $1\frac{5}{8}$ 9

e. $31\frac{5}{9}$ 10 $\frac{5}{48}$ 6 $6.2\frac{3}{6}$ $(6.2\frac{1}{2})$

f. 159 $2\frac{3}{10}$ $2\frac{2}{9}$ 3   .91

g. $21\frac{3}{32}$ $114\frac{14}{41}$ 800 $.02\frac{3}{41}$ 950

h. 99,202   .44874   90   5   54

Part One

1.1   0, 1, 2, 3, 4, 5, 6, 7, 8, 9

1.2   a. three hundred eighty-five million
     b. six hundred four billion
     c. eight hundred thirty-two trillion

1.3   a. thousands   8,000
     b. billions   3,000,000,000
     c. trillions   2,000,000,000,0000

1.4   a. $(3 \times 10,000) + (9 \times 1,000) + (4 \times 100) +$
       $(2 \times 10) + (6 \times 1)$
     b. $(6 \times 100,000) + (4 \times 10,000) + (3 \times 1,000)$
       $+ (2 \times 100) + (8 \times 10) + (7 \times 1)$
     c. $(1 \times 1,000,000) + (7 \times 100,000) + (1 \times 10,000)$
       $+ (5 \times 1,000) + (9 \times 100) + (0 \times 10)$
       $+ (8 \times 1)$

1.5   a. $(3 \times 10,000) + (6 \times 1,000) + (5 \times 100) +$
       $(4 \times 10) + (2 \times 1)$
       $(3 \times 10^4) + (6 \times 10^3) + (5 \times 10^2) +$
       $(4 \times 10^1) + (2 \times 10^0)$
     b. $(6 \times 1,000,000) + (1 \times 100,000) +$
       $(5 \times 10,000) + (8 \times 1,000) + (9 \times 100) +$
       $(2 \times 10) + (7 \times 1)$
       $(6 \times 10^6) + (1 \times 10^5) + (5 \times 10^4) +$
       $(8 \times 10^3) + (9 \times 10^2) + (2 \times 10^1) +$
       (7×10^0)
     c. $(4 \times 1,000,000,000) + (2 \times 100,000,000) +$
       $(9 \times 10,000,000) + (5 \times 1,000,000) +$
       $(5 \times 100,000) + (8 \times 10,000) +$
       $(6 \times 1,000) + (2 \times 100) + (0 \times 10) + (3 \times 1)$
       $(4 \times 10^9) + (2 \times 10^8) + (9 \times 10^7) + (5 \times 10^6) +$
       $(5 \times 10^5) + (8 \times 10^4) + (6 \times 10^3) + (2 \times 10^2) +$
       $(0 \times 10^1) + (3 \times 10^0)$

1.6   45   (+1)   45
      45   (+2) $\times 5$
      45   (+3)   225 minutes
      45   (+4)
      45   (+5)
   225 minutes

1.7   140
    $- 35 = 105$ (-1)   4 days
        $- 35 = 70$ (-2) $35\overline{)140}$
           $- 35 = 35$ (-3)
             $- 35 = 0$ (-4)   4 days

1.8   a. 5, 7, 10, 8 - subtract 3
       14, 0, 6, 16 - divide by 2
     b. 5, 1, 2, 8 - add 4
       3, 6, 2, 5 - multiply by 9
     c. 10, 0, 14, 5 - subtract 7
       36, 2, 24, 0 - divide by 6

1.9   15, 11, 14, 8   3, 5, 1, 8

1.10 $a = 2$ $b = 4$

1.11   a. 2, 3   b. 3, 1   c. 4, 5

1.12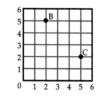

1.13   2, 3, 4, 5, 6, 7, 8

1.14   a. 0, 1, 2, 3, 4, 5
       (3,0) (4,1) (5,2) (6,3) (7,4) (8,5)

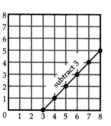

     b. 0, 2, 4, 6, 8
       (0,0) (1,2) (2,4) (3,6) (4,8)

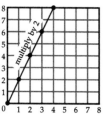

1.15 a. 9, 18, 27, 36, 45, 54, 63, 72, 81, 90, 99, 108
     b. 10, 20, 30, 40, 50, 60, 70, 80, 90, 100, 110, 120
     c. 11, 22, 33, 44, 55, 66, 77, 88, 99, 110, 121, 132
     d. 12, 24, 36, 48, 60, 72, 84, 96, 108, 120, 132, 144

1.16   9, 16, 25, 36, 49, 64, 81, 100, 121, 144

1.17   12, 11, 10, 9, 8, 7, 6, 5, 4, 3

1.18 a. side equals   8 in   11 ft.   7 yd.
     b. side equals   5 mi.   9 in. 3 m^2

1.19   a.   A   60   b.   C   12
      c.   D   40   d.   A   12
      e.   D   56   f.   C   17
      g.   A   160   h.   C   13

1.20   a. $8(7 + 5) = 96$ b. $9(4 + 3) = 63$
      c. $6(9 + 8) = 102$ d. $12(3 + 5) = 96$
      e. $4(3 + 10) = 52$ f. $7(8 + 6) = 98$

1.21   a.   30, 60, 90, 120, 150, 180, 210, 240, 270
      b.   70, 140, 210, 280, 350, 420, 490, 560, 630

1.22   a. $470\frac{5}{8} = 471$ $484\frac{6}{9} = 485$ $1{,}973\frac{2}{3} = 1{,}974$

            $1{,}455\frac{4}{6} = 1{,}456$ $538\frac{3}{5} = 539$

      b. $15\frac{11}{25} = 15$ $6\frac{16}{47} = 6$ $60\frac{18}{61} = 60$

            $102\frac{14}{74} = 102$ $163\frac{29}{35} = 164$

Part Two

2.1   a. $+4$ -3
    b. -4 $+2$
    c. $+5$ -2
    d. -6 -3

2.2   a.   ($24) $15   ($9)
    b.   (124 lb.)   8 lb.   (116 lb.)
    c.   (12 pieces)   5 pieces   (7 pieces)
    d.   ($7) $2   ($5)
    e.   (85°F)   12°F   (73°F)
    f.   (5 eggs)   3   (2 eggs)

2.3   a. $+4$ -4
    b. -2 $+3$
    c. $+5$ -4
    d. -4 -2

2.4   a.   5 -5 2
    b.   5 -5 -1
    c.   7 -4 -3
    d.   7 -9 1

2.5   a.   positive
    b.   negative
    c.   positive or negative

2.6

2.7   a.   P   3
        P   2
        A
    b.   N   3
        P   2
        D
    c.   P   3
        N   2
        B
    d.   N   3
        N   2
        C

2.8   a.   3
    b.   1
    c.   4
    d.   2

2.9   a.   (14)   6   (8 blocks)
    b.   (4)   6   ($2)
    c.   (3)   7   4 ft.
    d.   (32)   3   (29 oz.)
    e.   (24)   5   (19 crayons)
    f.   (8)   10   -2°F

2.10   a. $2 \times 4 \times 6 \times 5 = (2 \times 5) \times (4 \times 6) =$
         $10 \times 24 = 240$
         $9 + 3 + 7 + 1 = (9 + 1) + (3 + 7) =$
         $10 + 10 = 20$
         $(8 \times 4) \times 5 = (4 \times 5) \times 8 = 20 \times 8 = 160$

     b. $13 + 8 + 7 + 2 = (13 + 7) + (8 + 2) =$
         $20 + 10 = 30$
         $3 \times (2 \times 8) = (3 \times 2) \times 8 = 6 \times 8 = 48$
         $8 + 9 + 7 + 8 = (8 + 8) + (9 + 7) =$
         $16 + 16 = 32$

     c. $6 + 2 + 6 + 3 + 8 + 6 + 7 + 6 =$
         $(4 \times 6) + (2 + 8) + (3 + 7) =$
         $24 + 10 + 10 = 44$
         $3 \times 3 \times 5 \times 2 \times 9 = [9(3 \times 3) \times (5 \times 2)] =$
         $9(9) \times 10 = 81 \times 10 = 810$

2.11 a. 2,916   5,992   8,722   32,536   58,432
      b. 202,910 438,820 302,080 2,072,565 2,289,608

2.12 a. 3   5   three-fifths
      b. 4   9   four-ninths or
                         four out of nine
      c. 72   1,000   seventy-two thousandths
      d. 45   100   forty-five percent or
                         forty five hundredths

2.13 a. $\frac{7}{8}$ .875   88%

      b. $\frac{3}{5}$ .6   60%

      c. $\frac{1}{4}$ .25   25%

      d. $\frac{3}{10}$ .3   30%

2.14 a. $\frac{3}{5} = .6$ $\frac{2}{3} = .\overline{66}$ $\frac{7}{8} = .875$ $\frac{1}{2} = .5$

      b. $\frac{1}{5} = .2$ $\frac{3}{4} = .75$ $\frac{2}{3} = .\overline{66}$ $\frac{1}{2} = .5$

2.15 a. 1:2   .5   50%   1:4   .25   25%
      b. 3:4   .75   75%   1:5   .2   20%
      c. 2:5   .4   40%   3:5   .6   60%
      d. 4:5   .8   80%   1:8   .125   13%
      e. 3:8   .375   38%   5:8   .625   63%
      f. 7:8   .875   88%   1:3   .$\overline{33}$ 33%
      g. 2:3   .$\overline{66}$ 67%   1:6   .1$\overline{66}$ 17%
      h. 5:6   .8$\overline{33}$ 83%

2.16 a. 40%
      b. $\frac{1}{4}$ of the book
      c. 75:100 passed
      d. .375 of the money

2.17 a. 24% + 27% = 51%
      b. 100% − (46% + 33%) = 100% − 79% =
              21% had a grade between 80% and 90%
      c. 20% × 3 = 60%
      d. 84% ÷ 6 = 14%
      e. (80% + 76% + 92% + 88%) ÷ 4 = 84%

Part Three

3.1 a. 2:5   b. 3:5
     c. 2:3   d. 3:2

3.2 a. $\frac{3}{5} = \frac{x}{25}$ $\begin{smallmatrix}\text{(green)}\\\text{(total)}\end{smallmatrix}$
             75 = 5x
         75 ÷ 5 = 5x (÷ 5)
             15 = x
             15 = green   25 − 15 = 10 ripe

     b. $\frac{2}{3} = \frac{x}{9}$ $\begin{smallmatrix}\text{(ripe)}\\\text{(green)}\end{smallmatrix}$
             18 = 3x
         18 ÷ 3 = 3x (÷ 3)
              6 = x
              6 = ripe   6 + 9 = 15 bananas

     c. $\frac{3}{2} = \frac{x}{14}$ $\begin{smallmatrix}\text{(green)}\\\text{(ripe)}\end{smallmatrix}$
             2x = 42
         2x (÷ 2) = 42 ÷ 2
              x = 21
             21 = green   21 + 14 = 35 bananas

3.3 a. $\frac{2}{3} = \frac{x}{42}$ $\begin{smallmatrix}\text{(men)}\\\text{(boys)}\end{smallmatrix}$
             84 = 3x
         84 ÷ 3 = 3x (÷ 3)
             28 = x   28 men

     b. $\frac{3}{8} = \frac{x}{72}$ $\begin{smallmatrix}\text{(mystery)}\\\text{(total)}\end{smallmatrix}$
            216 = 8x
        216 ÷ 8 = 8x (÷ 8)
             27 = x   27 mystery books

     c. $\frac{5}{8} = \frac{x}{32}$ $\begin{smallmatrix}\text{(baskets)}\\\text{(tries)}\end{smallmatrix}$
             8x = 160
        8x (÷ 8) = 160 ÷ 8
              x = 20   20 baskets

3.4 a. 10
     b. 2:10 = $\frac{2}{10}$ = $\frac{1}{5}$ 3:10 = $\frac{3}{10}$ 5:10 = $\frac{5}{10}$ = $\frac{1}{2}$
     c. 50 ÷ 5 = 5x (÷ 5)
             10 = x (lemon)
     d. $\frac{3}{10} = \frac{x}{50}$ $\begin{smallmatrix}\text{(cherry)}\\\text{(total)}\end{smallmatrix}$
            150 = 10x
        150 ÷ 10 = 10x (÷ 10)
             15 = x (cherry)
     e. $\frac{1}{2} = \frac{x}{50}$ $\begin{smallmatrix}\text{(orange)}\\\text{(total)}\end{smallmatrix}$
             50 = 2x
         50 ÷ 2 = 2x (÷ 2)
             25 = x (orange)
     f. 10 + 15 + 25 = 50   yes

3.5 a. 6
     b. 2:6 = $\frac{2}{6}$ = $\frac{1}{3}$ 3:6 = $\frac{3}{6}$ = $\frac{1}{2}$ 1:6 = $\frac{1}{6}$
     c. $\frac{1}{3} = \frac{x}{24}$ $\begin{smallmatrix}\text{(red)}\\\text{(total)}\end{smallmatrix}$
             24 = 3x
         24 ÷ 3 = 3x (÷ 3)
              8 = x (red)

d. $\frac{1}{2} = \frac{x}{24}$ (blue) (total)

$24 = 2x$

$24 \div 2 = 2x \, (\div 2)$

$12 = x$ (blue)

e. $\frac{1}{6} = \frac{x}{24}$ (green) (total)

$24 = 6x$

$24 \div 6 = 6x \, (\div 6)$

$4 = x$ (green)

f. $8 + 12 + 4 = 24$ yes

3.6 a. $\frac{4}{5} = \frac{8}{x}$ (AB) (XY)

$4x = 40$

$4x \, (\div 4) = 40 \div 4$

$x = 10$ ft.

b. $\frac{4}{5} = \frac{7}{x}$ (BC) (YZ)

$4x = 35$

$4x \, (\div 4) = 35 \div 4$

$x = 8\frac{3}{4}$ (8.75) ft.

c. $\frac{4}{5} = \frac{5}{x}$ (AC) (XY)

$4x = 25$

$4x \, (\div 4) = 25 \div 4$

$x = 6\frac{1}{4}$ (6.25) ft

3.7 a. $6{:}15 = \frac{6}{15} = \frac{2}{5}$

b. $\frac{2}{5} = \frac{4}{x}$ (RS) (DE)

$2x = 20$

$2x \, (\div 2) = 20 \div 2$

$x = 10$ m

3.8

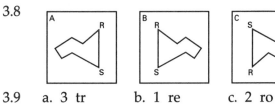

3.9 a. 3 tr   b. 1 re   c. 2 ro

3.10

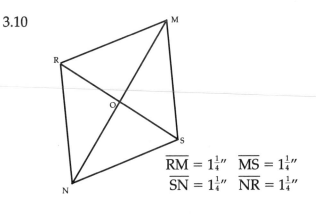

$\overline{RM} = 1\frac{1}{4}''$ $\overline{MS} = 1\frac{1}{4}''$

$\overline{SN} = 1\frac{1}{4}''$ $\overline{NR} = 1\frac{1}{4}''$

3.11 a. 15 sq. in. or 15 in.^{2}

b. 9 sq. in. or 9 in.^{2}

c. 8 sq. in. or 8 in.^{2}

3.12 a. $A = lw$ b. $A = s^2$

c. $A = \pi r^2$ d. $A = \frac{1}{2}bh$

3.13 a. $A = lw$ b. $A = s^2$

$A = 5 \cdot 3$ $A = 8^2$

$A = 15$ m^2 $A = 64$ cm^2

c. $A = \pi r^2$ d. $A = \frac{1}{2}bh$

$A = 3.14 \cdot 4^2$ $A = \frac{1}{2}(6 \cdot 9)$

$A = 3.14 \cdot 16$ $A = \frac{(6 \cdot 9)}{2}$

$A = 50.24$ in.^{2} $A = \frac{54}{2}$

$A = 27$ ft.^{2}

3.14 a. $A = bh$

$A = 7 \cdot 3$

$A = 21$ in.^{2}

b. $A = bh$

$A = 9 \cdot 8$

$A = 72$ m^2

c. $A = bh$

$A = 12 \cdot 11$

$A = 132$ ft^2

3.15 a. PY, T   b. PR, R   c. PY, S   d. PR, T

3.16 a. $V = lwh$

$V = 4 \cdot 3 \cdot 5$

$V = 60$ in.^{3}

b. $V = l \cdot w \cdot h$

$V = 7 \cdot 3 \cdot 4$

$V = 84$ cm^3

3.17

	2	5	10	3	9	6
459				✓	✓	
326	✓					
1,035		✓		✓	✓	
801				✓	✓	
107						
313						
420	✓	✓	✓	✓		✓
693				✓	✓	
84	✓			✓		✓
530	✓	✓	✓			
214	✓					

3.18 a.

	18				27
2	9		3	9	
3	3		3	3	
3	1		3	1	

b. $2, 3^2 \searrow$ 3^3
   $3, 3^2$
   9

c. $2, 3^2 \qquad 3^3$
   $2, 3^3 \swarrow$
   54

3.19 a. $\frac{61}{60} = 1\frac{1}{60}$ $1\frac{1}{18}$ $\frac{55}{36} = 1\frac{19}{36}$

   $15\frac{5}{30} = 15\frac{1}{6}$ $31\frac{49}{90}$ $35\frac{1}{33}$

b. $\frac{2}{24} = \frac{1}{12}$ $\frac{21}{56} = \frac{3}{8}$ $\frac{3}{72} = \frac{1}{24}$

   $6\frac{7}{36}$ $4\frac{14}{30} = 4\frac{7}{15}$ $39\frac{1}{70}$

c. $\frac{41}{48}$ $\frac{37}{40}$ $87\frac{11}{30}$

   $\frac{2}{54} = \frac{1}{27}$ $\frac{27}{42} = \frac{9}{14}$ $7\frac{23}{72}$

3.20 a. $\frac{5}{24}$ 18   9 $\frac{6}{7}$ $6\frac{3}{4}$

b. 1 $\frac{1}{30}$ $7\frac{1}{2}$ $\frac{11}{14}$ $1\frac{1}{2}$

c. $2\frac{1}{5}$ 6   26 $4\frac{1}{8}$ 39

d. 30 $1\frac{1}{2}$ $\frac{3}{5}$ 8   36

Part Four

4.1 a. 14   9 14 ⑭ 15 18   14
   b. 78   70 70 70 ⑦⑦ 81 86 92   70
   c. 35   25 30 33 ㉝ 37 42 45   33
   d. 6   2 2 4 ⑥ 7 8 9 10   2
       ⑥⑤
   e. 20   13 17 19 ㉒ 22 22 25   22

4.2 Suggested Answers:
a. mode
b. mean
c. median
d. mode - Because he reached that number (23) the greatest number of times it is probably the most accurate of what he is able to do

4.3 a. .45 $\frac{45}{100}$ .25 $\frac{25}{100}$ .64 $\frac{64}{100}$ .50 $\frac{50}{100}$
   b. .90 $\frac{90}{100}$ .75 $\frac{75}{100}$ .40 $\frac{40}{100}$ .34 $\frac{34}{100}$

4.4 a. 2.45 $2\frac{45}{100}$ 3.25 $3\frac{25}{100}$ 8.64 $8\frac{64}{100}$ 7.50 $7\frac{50}{100}$
   b. 4.90 $4\frac{90}{100}$ 9.75 $9\frac{75}{100}$ 3.40 $3\frac{40}{100}$ 1.34 $1\frac{34}{100}$

4.5 a. $1\frac{9}{36} = 1\frac{1}{4}$ 1.25   125%
   b. $3\frac{18}{24} = 3\frac{3}{4}$ 3.75   375%
   c. $6\frac{4}{20} = 6\frac{1}{5}$ 6.20   620%
   d. $1\frac{14}{28} = 1\frac{1}{2}$ 1.50   150%

4.6 .125   .375   .625   .875
   $.\overline{333}$ $.\overline{666}$ $.\overline{166}$ $.\overline{833}$

4.7 a. 13%   38%   63%   88%
       33%   67%   17%   83%
   b. 12.5% $12\frac{1}{2}\%$, 37.5% $37\frac{1}{2}$,
       62.5% $62\frac{1}{2}\%$, 87.5% $87\frac{1}{2}$
       $33.\overline{3}\%$ $33\frac{1}{3}\%$, $66.\overline{6}\%$ $66\frac{2}{3}$,
       $16.\overline{6}\%$ $16\frac{2}{3}\%$, $83.\overline{3}\%$ $83\frac{1}{3}$

4.8 a. 10.8   14.4   41.4
   b. 8.32   12.96   17.55
   c. 21.17   24   27

4.9 a. $\frac{1}{5} \times \frac{\overset{9}{\cancel{45}}}{1} = 9$ $\frac{3}{4} \times \frac{\overset{8}{\cancel{32}}}{1} = 24$ $\frac{7}{8} \times \frac{\overset{8}{\cancel{64}}}{1} = 56$
   b. $\frac{3}{5} \times \frac{\overset{11}{\cancel{55}}}{1} = 33$ $\frac{1}{4} \times \frac{\overset{4}{\cancel{16}}}{1} = 4$ $\frac{1}{3} \times \frac{\overset{6}{\cancel{18}}}{1} = 6$
   c. $\frac{1}{2} \times \frac{\overset{46}{\cancel{92}}}{1} = 46$ $\frac{2}{5} \times \frac{\overset{15}{\cancel{75}}}{1} = 30$ $\frac{2}{3} \times \frac{\overset{12}{\cancel{36}}}{1} = 24$

4.10 a. 90 pages
   b. 5 pencils
   c. 72 pieces
   d. 16 oz.
   e. 18 cookies
   f. 6 people

4.11 a. =   ≠   =
   b. ≠   =   ≠
   c. <   >   >
   d. ≥ , >   ≤ , <   ≤ , <

4.12 a. ×, ×   ÷, ÷   +, ×
      b. + or −, ×   −, ×   ×, −

4.13 a. $\overline{RS} \perp \overline{XY}$ or $\overline{XY} \perp \overline{RS}$
      b. $\overleftrightarrow{MN} \parallel \overleftrightarrow{CD}$
      c. $\Delta EFG \sim \Delta MNO$
      d. $\angle OPR \cong \angle ABC$
      e. $\overrightarrow{CF}$

4.14 a. 132   48   9   5   150
      b. $4 \times [3 + (6 \times 2)] = 4 \times (3 + 12) =$
          $4 \times 15 = 60$
          $[8 \times (2 \times 5)] - 15 = (8 \times 10) - 15 =$
          $80 - 15 = 65$
          $36 - [(4 \times 2) + 2] = 36 - (8 + 2) =$
          $36 - 10 = 26$

4.15   Suggested Answers
      a. 6 $15 - 7$ $12 \div 2$
      b. 15 $\frac{30}{3}$ $10 + 5$
      c. 4.5 or $4\frac{1}{2}$ $\frac{9 \times 0}{2}$ 2(2.25)

4.16 a. 60   60   24
          30/31   12   365(366)
          10   20   100   1,000
      b. 12   36   3   5,280
          144   9   4,840   640
      c. 16   2,000   16
          2   2   4
          12   1,728   27
          8   4

4.17 a. 2   36   2,000   10
      b. $2\frac{1}{2}$ 6   2
      c. $1\frac{1}{3}$ $\frac{3}{4}$ 36,500

4.18 a. 11 ft. 24 in. = 13 ft.
          20 lb. 21 oz. = 21 lb. 5 oz.
          6 gal. 6 qt. = 7 gal. 2 qt.
          20 yd.² 11 ft.² = 21 yd.² 2 ft.²
      b. 3 yr. 40 da.   4 mi 5,012 ft.
          4 yd.³ 19 ft.³   2 decades 7 yr.
      c. 15 bu. 6 pk = 16 bu. 2 pk.
          8 qt. 48 oz. = 9 qt. 16 oz.
          90 yd. 12 ft. = 94 yd.
          10 T. 2,500 lb. = 11 T. 500lb.
      d. 3 mi. 82 ft.

          $5\overline{)6 \text{qt. 3 oz.}} \rightarrow \begin{array}{c} 1 \text{ qt. 7 oz.} \\ 5\overline{)5 \text{ qt. 35 oz.}} \end{array}$

          $6\overline{)1 \text{ mi.}^2 \text{ 45 ac.}} \rightarrow \begin{array}{c} 114\frac{1}{6} \text{ ac.} \\ 6\overline{)685 \text{ ac.}} \end{array}$
          3 T. 159 lb.

4.19 a. 21.36   74.559   96.88
      b. 30.9   18.43   4.84   5.5
      c. 60.88   16.221   37.327   88.481   6.399
      d. 68.9   38.7   5.29   .414   2.655

4.20 a. 51   12.894   6.8302   2.744   29.36

      b. 28.2 $18\frac{3}{5} = 19$ $12.2\frac{1}{3} = 12.2$ $1.42\frac{2}{3} = 1.43$ 140
      c. 157.5   45.12   .1633   3.114   .85653
      d. .126 $.95\frac{8}{9} = .96$ 22.5   1.9 $77\frac{1}{7} = 77$
      e. .06   2.1   .6   200   7.1

Part Five

5.1   a. .5   .25   .75
      b. .2   .4   .6   .8
      c. .125   .375   .625   .875

5.2   a. $\frac{4}{5}$ .8, $\frac{3}{4}$ .75, $\frac{5}{6}$ .8$\overline{33}$, $\frac{7}{8}$ .875, $\frac{4}{5}$ .8
      b. $\frac{1}{2}$ .5, $\frac{3}{8}$ .375, $\frac{1}{4}$ .25, $\frac{7}{8}$ .875, $\frac{2}{5}$ .4
      c. $\frac{2}{5}$ .4, $\frac{2}{5}$ .4, $\frac{3}{4}$ .75, $\frac{1}{2}$ .5, $\frac{7}{10}$ .7

5.3   a. 1.25   .675   .15625   6
      b. 2.875   2.875   6.9   5.04
      c. 5.1   4.9   2.1 $.016\overline{6}$
      d. 11.6   6.85   .9375   .025

5.4   11, 14, 25   8, 9, 0   28, 21, 77   4, 8, 5
5.5   10, 5, 7, 4, subtract 4
      63, 9, 108, 5, divide by 9

5.6   Suggested Answers.
      a. $14 - 5 = 9$ $9 + 9 = 18$
          $14 - 8 = 6$ $7 + 5 = 12$
      b. $18 \div 6 = 3$ $9 \times 8 = 72$
          $55 \div 5 = 11$ $7 \times 10 = 70$

5.7   11, 22, 33, 44, 55, 66, 77, 88, 99, 110, 121, 132
      12, 24, 36, 48, 60, 72, 84, 96, 108, 120, 132, 144

5.8   a.   b.   c.   d.

          2^2, 3 3^3 3^2, 5 2^3, 7

5.9   a. 154.6   35   .036   720.04
      b. 2,056   5,290   92.18   54,600

5.10 5.300   9.480   .052   5.060   6.940
      .052   5.06   5.3   6.94   9.48

5.11 25%   60%   6%   100% 50% 67% 45%

136

5.12
$$a + 275 = 349$$
$$a + 275(-275) = 349 - 275$$
$$a = 74$$

$$x - 76 = 151$$
$$x - 76(+76) = 151 + 76$$
$$x = 227$$

$$y \times 18 = 126$$
$$y \times 18(\div 18) = 126 \div 18$$
$$y = 7$$

$$b \div 9 = 37$$
$$b \div 9(\times 9) = 37 \times 9$$
$$b = 333$$

5.13
a.   mm   cm   dm   m   km
b.   mL   cL   dL   L   kL
c.   mg   cg   dg   g   kg
d.

← smaller   larger →

5.14   multiply, divide

5.15   a. 7   b. 3
       c. 7   d. 343

5.16 $(5 \times 10^8) + (2 \times 10^7) + (6 \times 10^6) + (3 \times 10^5) +$
$(1 \times 10^4) + (2 \times 10^3) + (8 \times 10^2) + (9 \times 10^1) +$
(7×10^0)

5.17

5.18   a. 15°
       b. 15°
       c. 1,000
       d. 1,000

5.19   a. yes
       b. yes

5.20   a. 4:00 P.M. November 7
       b. 9:00 P.M. May 4
       c. 1:00 A.M. April 1

5.21   a. 3   b. 5   c. 2
       d. 4   e. 3   f. 6

5.22   1 hour, no, 7 months

5.23   a. 6:00 P.M.   b. 9:15 A.M.
       c. 6:00 P.M.   d. 9:30 A.M.
       e. 7:45 A.M.   f. 8:00 A.M.
       g. 2:00 A.M.   h. 10:45 P.M.
       i. 11:00 A.M., July 8   10:00 A.M., July 8
       j. 10:00 P.M., March 14   8:00 P.M., March 14
       k. no - It is 6:00 A.M.
           The friend might be sleeping
       l. no - It is 7:00 P.M.
           It is past business hours.
       m. j

5.24   a. 5   9
       b. 4   11
       c. 2   7
       d. 3   10
       e. 6   12
       f. 1   8

5.25   Suggested Answer.
       a.   Sixth Grade Favorite Fruits
       b.   100%
       c.   10
       d.   yes
       e.   6
       f.   teacher check

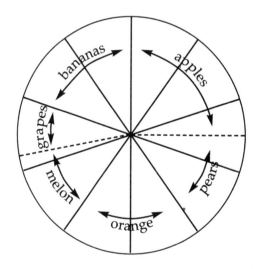

137

Part One

1.1   a.   four hundred eighty-six thousand
       b.   nine hundred forty-five
       c.   three hundred twenty-nine billion
       d.   nine hundred seventy-nine thousand
       e.   fifty-five million
       f.   six hundred twenty-seven trillion

1.2   a.   three-ninths
          seven and four-fifths
          eight percent
       b.   six cubed (to the third power)
          nine to the fifth power
       c.   seventy-two percent
          eight-hundredths
          six-tenths
       d.   five and four-hundredths
          nine and thirty-five thousandths
       e.   eight hundred forty-six thousandths
          ten to the seventh power
       f.   negative seven
          three out of nine
          eleven out of fifteen
       g.   thirty-six and five-tenths percent
          fourteen and one-half percent
       h.   thirty-four and seven-eighths percent
          thirty-three hundredths (repeating decimal)

1.3   a. $(5 \times 1{,}000{,}000) + (6 \times 100{,}000) +$
          $(8 \times 10{,}000) + (2 \times 1{,}000) + (3 \times 100) +$
          $(9 \times 10) + (7 \times 1)$
       b. $(9 \times 1{,}000{,}000{,}000) + (3 \times 100{,}000{,}000) +$
          $(8 \times 10{,}000{,}000) + (2 \times 1{,}000{,}000) +$
          $(5 \times 100{,}000) + (7 \times 10{,}000) +$
          $(6 \times 1{,}000) + (3 \times 100) + (0 \times 10)$
          $+ (4 \times 1)$

1.4   a.   4   3
          4   64
       b.   6   5
          6   7,776
       c.   7   2
          7   49
       d.   10   5
          10   100,000

1.5   a. $(8 \times 10^4) + (5 \times 10^3) + (6 \times 10^2) +$
          $(0 \times 10^1) + (4 \times 10^0)$
       b. $(2 \times 10^6) + (2 \times 10^5) + (8 \times 10^4) +$
          $(6 \times 10^3) + (3 \times 10^2) + (9 \times 10^1) +$
          (1×10^0)

       c. $(9 \times 10^{11}) + (5 \times 10^{10}) + (6 \times 10^9) +$
          $(3 \times 10^8) + (8 \times 10^7) + (4 \times 10^6) +$
          $(6 \times 10^5) + (7 \times 10^4) + (2 \times 10^3) +$
          $(5 \times 10^2) + (4 \times 10^1) + (8 \times 10^0)$

1.6   a.
```
   15    (+1)       15
   15    (+2)      × 3
 + 15    (+3)       45
  ———
   45
```

       b.
```
   28    (+1)       28
   28    (+2)      × 4
   28    (+3)      112
 + 28    (+4)
  ———
  112
```

       c.
```
   67               67
 + 67              × 2
  ———              ———
  134              134
```

       d.
```
   59    (+1)       59
   59    (+2)      × 5
   59    (+3)      295
   59    (+4)
 + 59    (+5)
  ———
  295
```

1.7   a.
```
(1)    32                          4
      − 8                        8)32
            24                    32
(2)        − 8                    ——
                 16               0
(3)             − 8
                      8
(4)                 − 8
                       0
```

       b.
```
(1)    208                          4
      − 52                       52)208
            156                    208
(2)        − 52                    ———
                 104               0
(3)             − 52
                       52
(4)                  − 52
                        0
```

       c.
```
(1)    87                          3
      − 29                       29)87
            58                    87
(2)        − 29                   ——
                 29               0
(3)             − 29
                   0
```

d.
$$84$$
(1) -14

$$\begin{array}{r} 6 \\ 14\overline{)84} \\ \underline{84} \\ 0 \end{array}$$

(2)
$$\begin{array}{r} 70 \\ -14 \end{array}$$

(3)
$$\begin{array}{r} 56 \\ -14 \end{array}$$

(4)
$$\begin{array}{r} 42 \\ -14 \end{array}$$

(5)
$$\begin{array}{r} 28 \\ -14 \end{array}$$

(6)
$$\begin{array}{r} 14 \\ -14 \\ 0 \end{array}$$

1.8 a. 60   66   96   100   84
     b. 120   90   108   77   121
     c. 108   48   132   110   99
     d. 88   33   81   144   72

1.9 a. 2   2   -5
     b. 5   -7   -8
     c. 3   2   -8
     d. -1   -4   -5

1.10 a. positive
      b. negative
      c. positive, negative

1.11 a. 0   -5   2   -4   -1
          7   -1   11   -2   16
      b. 4   -3   -1   11   subtract 7
          -1   -4   -3   4   subtract 4
      c. 13   3   -2   10
          1   -7   5   -1

1.12 a. 4, 9, 25, 36, 49, 64, 81, 100, 121, 144
      b. 12, 11, 10, 9, 8, 7, 6, 5, 3, 2

1.13 $\sqrt{49}$ $\sqrt{81}$ $\sqrt{25}$ $\sqrt{36}$ $\sqrt{121}$

1.14 a. A   315   C   544
      b. D   42   A   29
      c. D   28   C   75

1.15 a. $9(3 + 2) = 45$ $3(25 + 50) = 225$
      b. $5(12 + 8) = 100$ $7(11 + 14) = 175$
      c. $12(7 + 5) = 144$ $8(15 + 13) = 224$

1.16 a. 35   150
      b. 1,037   12
      c. 1,295   1,245   10,373   95,966   916,321
      d. $\frac{5}{8}$ $1\frac{7}{24}$ 1 $9\frac{11}{18}$ $26\frac{1}{18}$ $32\frac{3}{5}$
      e. 156.6   40.294
      f. 3   -3   -8   5

g. 44%   80%   103%   61   80
h. 6.23   62.817   82.72   10.342   28.087
i. 5 wk. 9 da. = 6 wk. 2 da.
    16 sq. yd. 14 sq. ft. = 17 sq. yd. 5 sq. ft.
    16.2 m
    7.3 mg
    33 min. 79 sec. = 34 min. 19 sec.

Part Two

2.1 a. 10
     b. A-2, C-1, E-1, H-1, I-1, M-2, T-2
     c. A-2:10, C-1:10, E-1:10, H-1:10, I-1:10,
         M-2:10, T-2:10
     d. A-20%, C-10%, E-10%, H-10%, I-10%
         M-20%, T-20%
     e. A, M, T
         C, E, H, I
     f. A, M, T, C, E, H, I

2.2 a. yes
     b. 1:9
     c. yes

2.3 Possible Answers:
     a.

     b. 40
     c. A-6, C-4, E-5, H-2, I- 5, M- 8, T-10
     d. A-6:40, C-4:40, E-5:40, H-2:40, I-5:40,
         M-8:40, T-10:40
     e. T, H
     f. T, M, A, E, I, C, H
     g. yes A, M, T were selected most often
              C, E, H, I were selected least often
     h. probably not exactly the same,
         but A, M, or T would probably be
         selected the most times

2.4 a. There are 10 colors.
         The color red is worn 3 times.
         The probability is 3:10. $\frac{3}{10} = .3 = .30 = 30\%$
     b. The are 100 pieces of candy.
         There are 18 pieces of cherry candy.
         The probability is 18:100. $\frac{18}{100} = .18 = 18\%$

2.5 Possible Answers.

a.
math	that	ache	meat	mitt
heat	tact	came	hate	itch
them	time	mite	team	etch
mate	chat	maim	emit	tame

b. A-13, C-6, E-13, H-9, I-6, M-13, T-20

c. 80

d.

	ratio	fraction	decimal	percent	norm percent
A	13:80	$\frac{13}{80}$	.162 = .16	16%	20%
C	6:80	$\frac{6}{80}\left(\frac{3}{40}\right)$	.075 = .08	8%	10%
E	13:80	$\frac{13}{80}$	.162 = .16	16%	10%
H	9:80	$\frac{9}{80}$	.112 = .11	11%	10%
I	6:80	$\frac{6}{80}\left(\frac{3}{40}\right)$	.075 = .08	8%	10%
M	13:80	$\frac{13}{80}$	.162 = .16	16%	20%
T	20:80	$\frac{20}{80}\left(\frac{1}{4}\right)$	.25	25%	20%
				100%	100%

e. yes

f. yes except E

g. There were more E's and T's in the words.

2.6 a. Norm Ratios for MATHEMATIC
A-2:10, C-1:10, E-1:10,
H-1:10, I-1:10, M-2:10,
T-2:10

b. 10

c. 7

d. see graph

2.7 a. 100

b.
lighting	10
landscaping	15
pool	25
courts	20
equipment	30

c. 10:100   15:100   25:100
20:100   30:100

d. $\frac{10}{100} = \frac{100}{1,000}$ $\frac{15}{100} = \frac{150}{1,000}$
$\frac{25}{100} = \frac{250}{1,000}$ $\frac{20}{100} = \frac{200}{1,000}$
$\frac{30}{100} = \frac{300}{1,000}$

e. pool   equipment
250 votes   300 votes

2.8 Possible answers

a. A 16%, C 8%,
E 16%, H 11%,
I 8%, M 16%,
T 25%

b. 7 letters
7 bars
0-30% by 5's

c. 7 letters
7 lines
0–30% by 5's

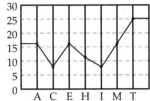

2.9 a. lighting 10:100 = 10%
landscaping 15:100 = 15%
pool 25:100 = 25%
courts 20:100 = 20%
equipment 30:100 = 30%

b. 5 choices
5 bars
⊙ = 5%
lighting
lands.
pool
courts
equip.

2.10 a. 1,267 $\frac{1}{15}$ 2.49   9%

b. 3,447   10,737   5.84   5.372   45%

c. 237,538   4.67 $\frac{2}{12} = \frac{1}{6}$ $\frac{7}{16}$ $\frac{11}{24}$ 8.61

d. 12 cu. yd. 3 cu. ft.
9 sq. ft. 53 sq. in.
23 gal. 2 qt.
7 da. 17 hr.

e. 18.4 m 4.31 L   59 mg   5 bu. 3 pk.
15 decades 6 yrs.

f. $1\frac{1}{2}$ $4\frac{3}{5}$ $1\frac{3}{6} = 1\frac{1}{2}$ $11\frac{3}{8}$ 24   3

g. 5.89   21.088   8.24   6.54 $7\frac{13}{24}$

Part Three

3.1 a. 10

b. meter - yard, liter - quart, gram - ounce

c. milli, centi, deci, deca, hecto, Kilo

d.
mm	cm	dm	m	Km
mL	cL	dL	L	KL
mg	cg	dg	g	Kg

e. divide
divide
multiply
multiply

3.2 a. 2   8   3   5   6   4   7

b. 2   8   3   5   6   4   7

3.3 a. 2   8   3   5   6   4   7

b. 2   8   3   5   6   4   7

3.4

	kilo	hecto	deca	meter	deci	centi	milli
a.				5	4	7	
b.					3	8	6
c.			8	0	5		
d.	5	4	7	6			
e.				8	3	7	

3.5　a.　M　　M　　D
　　　b.　M　　D　　D
　　　c.　M　　D　　M

3.6　a.　100　　100　　1,000
　　　b.　10　　1,000　　100
　　　c.　10　　100　　10

3.7　a.　35 mm　　370 m　　4 dm
　　　b.　.500 (.5) kL　6.3 dL　　2,340 mL
　　　c.　5,420 g　　1.342 g　　.75 dg

3.8　a.　60.96 cm　　13.71 m
　　　b.　168.945 Km　　15.24 cm
　　　c.　4.73 L　　5.4432 Kg
　　　d.　17.616 L　　510.3 g

3.9　a.　.5295 oz.　　4.728 in.
　　　b.　103.6162 lb.　　1.1296 oz.
　　　c.　7.264 qt.　　9.92 mi.
　　　d.　9.513 qt.　　15.3104 yd.

3.10　Suggested Answers:
　　　a.　2 qts = 1.892 = 2 L
　　　b.　11 in. = 27.94 = 28 cm
　　　c.　6 in. = 15.24 = 15 cm
　　　d.　84 in. = 213.36 = 213 cm or 2.13 m
　　　e.　5 lb. = 2.268 = 2 kg
　　　f.　32 oz. = 1 qt. = .946 L = .9 L
　　　g.　2 mi. = 3.218 = 3 km

3.11　4°C　　　32°C　　　46°F　　　78°F

3.12　greatest common factor
　　　Suggested Answer: simplify fractions

3.13　least common multiple
　　　Suggested Answer: common denominator

3.14　a.　1, ③, 9　　　9, 18, 27, ㊱…
　　　　　1, 2, ③, 4, 6, 12　　12, 24, ㊱, 48, …
　　　b.　1, ②, 3, 6　　　6, 12, 18, ㉔, 30, 36, …
　　　　　1, ②, 4, 8　　　8, 16, ㉔, 32, 40, …
　　　c.　1, ②, 5, 10　　　10, 20, 30, 40, 50, 60, ⑦⓪, 80, 90, …
　　　　　1, ②, 7, 14　　　14, 28, 42, 56, ⑦⓪, 84, 98, …
　　　d.　1, 2, ④, 8, 16　　　16, 32, 48, 64, ⑧⓪, 96, 112, …
　　　　　1, 2, ④, 5, 10, 20　　20, 40, 60, ⑧⓪, 100, 120, …
　　　e.　1, ③, 5, 15　　　15, 30, 45, 60, 75, ⑨⓪, 105, 120, …
　　　　　1, 2, ③, 6, 9, 18　　18, 36, 54, 72, ⑨⓪, 108, 126
　　　f.　①, 2, 4　　　4, 8, 12, 16, 24, 28, 32, ㊱, 40, …
　　　　　①, 3, 9　　　9, 18, 27, ㊱, 45, 54, …

3.15　a.　$1\frac{5}{36}$　　$\frac{19}{24}$　　$\frac{48}{70}=\frac{24}{35}$　　$\frac{29}{80}$　　$\frac{31}{90}$　　$\frac{7}{36}$
　　　b.　$\frac{4}{9}$　　$\frac{3}{20}$　　$\frac{7}{25}$　　$\frac{5}{12}$　　$4\frac{4}{5}$　　$\frac{21}{20}=1\frac{1}{20}$

3.16

30		45		28		70	
2　15	2, 3, 5	3　15	3², 5	2　14	2², 7	2　35	2, 5, 7
3　5		3　5		2　7		5　7	
5　1		5　1		7　1		7　1	

3.17　a.　2, 3, 5　　　3², 5
　　　　　3, 5
　　　　　15
　　　b.　2², 7　　　2, 5, 7
　　　　　2, 7
　　　　　14
　　　c.　2, 3, 5　　　2, 5, 7
　　　　　2, 5
　　　　　10

3.18　a.　2, 3, 5,　　　3², 5
　　　　　2, 3², 5
　　　　　90
　　　b.　2², 7　　　2, 5, 7
　　　　　2², 5, 7
　　　　　140
　　　c.　2, 3, 5　　　2, 5, 7
　　　　　2, 3, 5, 7
　　　　　210

3.19　$\frac{37}{45}$　　$\frac{59}{90}$　　$\frac{11}{24}$　　$\frac{29}{45}$　　$\frac{5}{6}$　　$\frac{10}{77}$
　　　　　　　　　　　　　　　　　　　$\frac{16}{21}$　　$\frac{3}{4}$

3.20　a.　140　　208　　729　　30
　　　b.　1,755　7,182　179,694　182,250　3,105,648
　　　c.　11.5　31.32　.090　2.888　.03618
　　　d.　6　　56　　$\frac{1}{3}$　　10　　35
　　　e.　112　231　$1\frac{3}{4}$　　54
　　　f.　22　　24　　35　　54
　　　g.　12 ft. 20 in. = 13 ft. 8 in.
　　　　　88 wk. 40 da. = 93 wk. 5 da.
　　　　　81.5 m
　　　　　65.8 cg
　　　　　19.23 kL

Part Four

4.1　a.　$\frac{7}{21}=\frac{1}{3}$　　$\frac{9}{12}=\frac{3}{4}$　　$\frac{8}{12}=\frac{2}{3}$
　　　b.　$\frac{16}{28}=\frac{4}{7}$　　$\frac{15}{30}=\frac{1}{2}$　　$\frac{4}{14}=\frac{2}{7}$
　　　c.　$\frac{50}{100}=\frac{1}{2}$
　　　d.　$\frac{24}{40}=\frac{3}{5}$

4.2 | 3 | 6 | 4 | 12

4.3 | $3\frac{1}{3}$ | $4\frac{1}{5}$ | $16\frac{2}{3}$ | $12\frac{1}{4}$ | $3\frac{3}{5}$

4.4 a. 6 apples
 b. 4 oz.
 c. 25, $\frac{1}{2}$
 d. $\frac{1}{3}$ of 26 = $8\frac{2}{3}$ There cannot be $\frac{2}{3}$ of a person.

4.5 a. $\frac{2 \times a}{3} = 16$
 b. $\frac{\frac{1}{3}(2 \times a)}{\frac{3}{1}} = 16 \times 3$
   $2 \times a = 48$
 c. $2(\div 2) \times a = 48 \div 2$
   $a = 24$
 d. 24
 e. $\frac{2}{3}$ of 24 = 16

4.6 a. 32, 32
 b. 35, 35
 c. 16, 16
 d. 21, 21
 e. 45, 45
 f. 21, 21
 g. 16, 16
 h. 14, 14

4.7 a. 28 cards
 b. 24 qt.

4.8 a. 10 | 16 | 10.5 | 30 | 16
 b. 3 | 40.5 | 2.976 | 1.75 | 12
 c. 25.76 | 20 | 5.76 | 10.8 | 1.44
 d. $\frac{2}{3} \times 21 = 14$
 e. $.5 \times 60 = 30$
 f. 6 students

4.9 a. 70, 70
 b. 31.25, 31.25
 c. 32, 32
 d. 70, 70
 e. 60, 60
 f. 144, 144

4.10

	ratio	decimal	percent
$\frac{1}{2} =$	1:2	.5	50%
$\frac{1}{4} =$	1:4	.25	25%
$\frac{3}{4} =$	3:4	.75	75%
$\frac{1}{5} =$	1:5	.2	20%
$\frac{2}{5} =$	2:5	.4	40%
$\frac{3}{5} =$	3:5	.6	60%
$\frac{4}{5} =$	4:5	.8	80%
$\frac{1}{8} =$	1:8	.125	13%
$\frac{3}{8} =$	3:8	.375	38%
$\frac{5}{8} =$	5:8	.625	63%
$\frac{7}{8} =$	7:8	.875	88%
$\frac{1}{3} =$	1:3	$.\overline{333}$	33%
$\frac{2}{3} =$	2:3	$.\overline{666}$	67%
$\frac{1}{6} =$	1:6	$.1\overline{66}$	17%
$\frac{5}{6} =$	5:6	$.8\overline{33}$	83%

4.11 a. 2:3 | $\frac{8}{12} = \frac{2}{3}$ | .666 | 67%
 b. 4:5 | $\frac{4}{5}$ | .8 | 80%
 c. 1:8 | $\frac{1}{8}$ | .125 | 13%

4.12 a. $\frac{5}{6} \times 24 = 20$ glasses
   Solving as a repeating decimal would not give an exact answer. $.833 \times 24 = 19.992$
 b. $87.5 \times 56 = 49$ Decimal solution easier with calculator
   $\frac{7}{8} \times 56 = 49$ Fraction solution easier without calculator
 c. $.25 \times a = 17$ $a = 68$ Decimal solution easier with calculator
   $\frac{1}{4} \times a = 17$ $a = 68$ Fraction solution easier without calculator

4.13 a. 36,000,000 | 584,000,000,000
 b. 46,400,000 | 3,100,000
 c. 540,000,000 | 3,680,000,000

4.14 | 17 | 66 | 240 | 93 | 75

4.15 a. 2.70 = 2.7 | 36.10 = 36.1 | .800 = .8
   7.500 = 7.5 | .3000 = .3
 b. 3.480 = 3.48 | .3200 = .32 | 41.070 = 41.07
   .470 = .47 | 6.040 = 6.04

4.16 a. 3.9 | 2.6 | .4 | 9.7 | 4.4
 b. 7.02 | 89.62 | 36.29 | .07 | 6.06

4.17 a. 9   6   3   27   2

b. $9\frac{2}{5} = 9$ $35\frac{5}{6} = 36$ $190\frac{2}{3} = 191$

   $10\frac{5}{9} = 11$ $47\frac{3}{8} = 47$

c. $2.8\frac{2}{3} = 2.9$ $.7\frac{2}{5} = .7$ $1.1\frac{6}{8} = 1.2$

   $51\frac{3}{7} = 51$ $.19\frac{1}{2} = .20$

d. 10 $\frac{1}{16}$ 12 $\frac{1}{6}$ $4\frac{1}{2}$

e. 129   125   24   35

f. 1.6   3.8   .46   .62

g.
```
      2 da. 9 hr.
   4)9 da. 12 hr.
     8     36

      1 lb. 10½ oz.
   2)3 lb.  5  oz.
     2     21

        .5 m
     7)3.5 m

        .6 kg
     6)3.6 kg
```

Part Five

5.1 a. even, even, odd

b. an even number (0, 2, 4, 6, 8)
0, 5
0
total a multiple of 3
total a multiple of 9
are divisible by 2 and 3

c. does not, does not, does not

5.2 a. E   O   E
O   E   E

b. 2, 5, 10   2   3   2, 3, 5, 6, 9, 10
3, 5   2   2, 3, 5, 6, 10   2, 3, 6, 9

c. C 16   D 36
A 30   A 48
C 15   D 75

5.3 a.
```
   36        36
   36       × 4
   36       144
 + 36
  144

   78        78
 + 78       × 2
  156       156
```

```
   27        27
   27       × 3
 + 27        81
   81
```

b. (1) 92 − 23 = 69   23)92 → 4
(2) 69 − 23 = 46   92
(3) 46 − 23 = 23   0
(4) 23 − 23 = 0

(1) 56 − 14 = 42   14)56 → 4
(2) 42 − 14 = 28   56
(3) 28 − 14 = 14   0
(4) 14 − 14 = 0

(1) 117 − 39 = 78   39)117 → 3
(2) 78 − 39 = 39   117
(3) 39 − 39 = 0   0

5.4 a. 10, 8, 14, 5 - subtract 7
b. 5, 13, 4, 6 - add 5
c. 21, 5, 12, 9 - divide by 3
d. 2, 32, 7, 72 - multiply by 8

5.5 a. 5
b. 8
c. 10
d. 1
e. 11
f. 2
g. 3
h. 7
i. 4
j. 6
k. 12
l. 9

5.6 a. 6   11, 15
    b. 4   12, 14
    c. 1   8, 9
    d. 5   10, 13
    e. 3   7
    f. 2   14, 16

5.7 each listed shape must be different
    a. 1   (2 & 3 are same)
    b. 4   (5 & 6 are same)
    c. 1 + 4   (2 & 5, 3 & 5 are same)
    d. 1 + 6   (2 & 4, 3 & 5 are same)
    e. 1 + 4 + 6   (2, 4, 5 & 5, 6, 3 are same)
    f. 1 + 4 + 2 + 5   (2, 4, 6, 3 & 3, 4, 6, 1 are same)
    g. 1 + 4 + 2 + 5 + 6   (all sections except 1 same
                                  all sections except 2 same)
    h. 1 + 2 + 3 + 4 + 5 + 6   (all sections)

5.8 a. 2:8
       1/4
    b. 25%
       75%
    c. 1:4 (1 possibility out of 4 throws)
    d. 4 cm (50% of 8 cm = 4 cm)
    e. 4:8
       $\frac{1}{2}$
       1:2 (1 possibility out of 2 throws)

5.9
    20
    24

Each corner represents one square
unit but two linear units.

5.10 a. $21.74 − ($8.32 + $5.16 + $3.29) = N
       $21.74 − $16.77 = N
       $4.97 = N (amount spent at snack bar)

    b. $D = RT$ $D = RT$
       $D = 54 \cdot 3\frac{1}{2}(3.5)$ $D = 64 \cdot 2\frac{3}{4}(2.75)$
       $D = 189$ mi. $D = 176$ mi.
       First car travelled 13 miles
       farther then the second car.

    c. 1st day - 4:5 = 80% passed
       2nd day - 9:10 = 90% passed
       3rd day - 3:4 = 75% passed
       80 + 90 + 75 = 245 ÷ 3 = 81.66 or 82
       The average was above 80%.

    d. 36 cu in.
       × 25
       900 cu. in.
       The supplier should use
       the first box (1,000 cu. in.)

    e. $A = L \times W$ $A = L \times W$
       $A = 11 \times 10$ $A = 9 \times 8$
       $A = 110$ sq. ft. $A = 72$ sq. ft.
       110 + 72 = 182 sq. ft.
       182 sq. ft. × $2.94 = $535.08

    f. $\frac{5}{8} \times 12$ oz. $= 7\frac{1}{2}$ or 7.5 oz.
       7.5 oz. × 10 boxes = 75 oz.
       There were 75 oz. of cereal all together.
       Divide 75 oz. by 12 oz.
       (amount to fill a whole box).
       $75 \div 12 = 6\frac{1}{4}$ boxes

    g. $P = s + s + s$ $P = s + s + s$
       $P = 8 + 8 + 12$ $P = 10 + 10 + 15$
       $P = 28$ cm $P = 35$ cm
       28:35 = 4:5

5.11 a. $1\frac{13}{24}$ $\frac{13}{18}$ $7\frac{1}{10}$ $14\frac{2}{9}$ $\frac{7}{15}$ $1\frac{17}{24}$

    b. 11.152   7.15   3.35   6.681
                                           12.89

    c. 96%   27%
       42 hr. 90 min. = 43 hr. 30 min.
       1 qt. 26 oz.

    d. 21   30   23   14
    e. 2   6   80   90
    f. 265,650   9.996   166
       $.15\frac{7}{24} = .15$ $.03\frac{43}{85} = .04$
    g. 30   25   15   3

Math 609 Answer key

Part One

1.1   0, 1, 2, 3, 4, 5, 6, 7, 8, 9

1.2   a. one hundred forty billion
b. two hundred forty-one trillion
c. five hundred eighty-two sextillions

1.3   a. 259,000,000,000,000
b. 371,000,000,000,000,000,000,000
c. 903,000,000,000,000,000,000,000,000

1.4   3, 11, 19, 29

1.5   2, 3, 3

2	18
2	9
3	3
3	1

1.6   2, 3   3
2   2, 3^2

1.7   a. 2, 5   2   2, 5^2 50
b. 2, 3   2 $2^2, 3^2$ 36
c. 2, 7   2   2, 7^2 98

1.8   a. two cubed, five   2   40
b. three squared, seven   3   63
c. two squared, three squared, five   2, 3   180

1.9   a. 637,294,000,000   473,092,116,000,000
b. 390,000,000,000   216,840,000,000,000

1.10   a. ten to the fifth power   10   100,000
b. ten to the eighth power   10   100,000,000

1.11   a. $637{,}294 \times 10^6$ $473{,}092{,}116 \times 10^6$
b. 39×10^{10} $21{,}684 \times 10^{10}$

1.12   a. 8, 5
b. 12, 7

1.13   a. $\frac{5}{9}$ b. $\frac{6}{7}$ c. $\frac{9}{18} = \frac{1}{2}$ d. $\frac{5}{6}$

1.14   a. $.\overline{555}$ b. $.857 \frac{1}{7}$ c. $\frac{9}{18} = \frac{1}{2} = .5$ d. $.8\overline{33}$

1.15   a. 56%   b. 86%   c. 50%   d. 83%

1.16   a. 4:9   four of nine   b. $\frac{4}{9}$ four ninths
c. $.\overline{44}$ forty-four hundredths
d. 44%   forty-four percent

1.17   a. 8:8   b. $\frac{5}{5}$
c. 1.0   d. 100%

1.18   a. 1:2 $\frac{1}{2}$ .5   50%   7:8 $\frac{7}{8}$ .875   88%
b. 3:5 $\frac{3}{5}$ .6   60%   3:4 $\frac{3}{4}$ .75   75%
c. 9:10 $\frac{9}{10}$ .9   90%   1:3 $\frac{1}{3}$ $.\overline{33}$ 33%
d. 1:8 $\frac{1}{8}$ .125   13%   3:10 $\frac{3}{10}$ .3   30%

1.19   a. 378,284,109   386,284,019   386,284,190
387,284,196   478,284,190
b. 63,145   592,145   1,463,592
14,638,592   592,145,638

1.20   a. $\frac{12}{24}$ $\frac{18}{24}$ $\frac{14}{24}$ $\frac{8}{24}$ $\frac{9}{24}$ $\frac{20}{24}$
$\frac{1}{3}$ $\frac{3}{8}$ $\frac{1}{2}$ $\frac{7}{12}$ $\frac{3}{4}$ $\frac{5}{6}$
b. 6:18   8:18   9:18   5:18   3:18   12:18
1:6   5:18   1:3   4:9   1:2   2:3

1.21   a. .300   .850   .670   .400   .395   .700
.3   .395   .4   .67   .7   .85
b. .670   .030   .508   .300   .267   .053
.03   .053   .267   .30   .508   .67

1.22   6%   7%   15%   34%   89%   91%

1.23 $1\frac{2}{3}$ 5.74   42.036 $6\frac{3}{8}$ 3.4 $29\frac{1}{4}$

1.24 $1\frac{1}{2}$ $1\frac{5}{9}$ $1\frac{2}{3}$ 3 $3\frac{4}{7}$ $15\frac{1}{2}$

1.25   145%   328%   136%   249%   151%   538%

1.26   a. 6.704   395%   12.54   4,546   46%   1.78
b. $1\frac{1}{10}$ $11\frac{11}{12}$ $6\frac{3}{8}$ $\frac{2}{5}$ $7\frac{11}{24}$ $6\frac{5}{18}$

1.27 $1\frac{5}{6}$ $6\frac{2}{7}$ $4\frac{5}{8}$ .333   11.024   5.131

Part Two

2.1   a. 7.128   13,578   38.3
b. 1.695 = 1.70   1,640,782   33.392 = 33.39
c. 12   .2142 = .21   10.842 = 10.84

2.2   a. 1.25   7.325   4.65
b. 3.625   137.25   14.985 (3.33 × 4.5)
c. .475   2.4   33.3 (6.66 ÷ .2)

2.3   a. 13 loaves
b. 16 containers
c. suggested answer
1 box cookies   2 orange juice   1 bread
d. 50% of 2.54 = 1.27
19 ÷ 1.27 = 14 boxes

2.4   Answer may vary.
a. 1,000   1,000
b. 10   100
c. 2   80
d. $\frac{1}{2}$ $\frac{1}{5}$

2.5   a.   1:2
      b.   1:6
      c.   4:10 (2:5)
      d.   3:15 (1:5)

2.6   a.   1) $\frac{1}{8}, \frac{7}{8}$ Any   2) $\frac{2}{8}, \frac{6}{8}$
           3) $\frac{3}{8}, \frac{5}{8}$ order: 4) $\frac{4}{8}, \frac{4}{8}$
      b.

      c. $\frac{4}{12}, \frac{6}{18}, \frac{8}{24}, \frac{10}{30}$

                                    10 customers
           30 doughnuts
      d. $9 \times 8 = 72$ sq. in. $\frac{1}{4}$ of 72 = 18 sq. in.
           possible answer $L = 6$ in. $w = 3$ in.

2.7   a.   2   6
      b.   3   9
      c.   5   8
      d.   1   10
      e.   4   7

2.8   a.   4   8
      b.   5   7
      c.   2   6
      d.   1   9
      e.   3   10

2.9   a.   4   6
      b.   3   5
      c.   2   7
      d.   1   8

2.10 a.   10°   acute
      b.   180°   straight
      c.   90°   right
      d.   140°   obtuse
      e.   105°   obtuse
      f.   55°   acute

2.11 oval, circle

2.12 a.   3   b.   4
      c.   1   d.   2

2.13 a.   180°   b.   360°   c.   360°

2.14 a.   3, 6
      b.   2, 5
      c.   1, 4

2.15 a.   4, 6
      b.   1, 8
      c.   2, 7
      d.   3, 5

2.16 a.   congruent   b.   concentric   c.   similar

2.17 a.   b.   c.

2.18

2.19 a.   red   b.   orange
      c.   brown   d.   yellow
      e.   blue   f.   green

2.20 sphere

2.21 a.   rectangle
      b.   square
      c.   triangle
      d.   pentagon

2.22 a.   1   b.   8   c.   3   d.   7
      e.   4   f.   2   g.   6   h.   5

2.23 a.   line RT   b.   line segment MN
      c.   ray BC   d.   angle XYZ   e.   similar
      f.   congruent   g.   triangle EFG
      h.   parallel   i.   perpendicular

2.24 a.   4, 4
      b.   ∠CDE or ∠DEF
      c. $\overline{CD}$, $\overline{FE}$
      d. $\overline{DE}$
      e.   no
      f.

2.25 a.   =   ≠   =
      b.   =   ≠   ≠
      c.   <   <   >
      d.   <   >   >

2.26 a.   16 ≤ 16, 17, 18, 19 < 20
      b.   9 ≥ 9, 8, 7, 6 > 5
      c.   12 ≤ 12, 18, 24 < 30
      d.   13 ≥ 13, 11, 7, 5 > 3

2.27 $\frac{3}{5} = \frac{18}{30}$ $\frac{2}{3} = \frac{20}{30}$ $\frac{5}{6} = \frac{25}{30}$ $\frac{7}{10} = \frac{21}{30}$ $\frac{1}{2} = \frac{15}{30}$ $\frac{7}{15} = \frac{14}{30}$

      $\frac{7}{15}$ $\frac{1}{2}$ $\frac{3}{5}$ $\frac{2}{3}$ $\frac{7}{10}$ $\frac{5}{6}$

2.28 a.   =   >   <   >
      b.   >   =   =   <

2.29 a. $\frac{3}{5}$ (>, =, $\bigcirc$<) $\frac{5}{8}$ Jose
      b. $\frac{7}{8}$ (>, =, $\bigcirc$<) $\frac{4}{5}$ too little

146

Part Three

3.1 a. $23 + 22 + 34 + 27 + x = 145$
$106 + x = 145$
$106(- 106) + x = 145 - 106$
$x = 39$ papers

b. $15 + 4 + c = 125$
$19 + c = 125$
$19(- 19) + c = 125 - 19$
$c = \$106$

c. $2 + 4 + y + y = 12$
$6 + 2y = 12$
$6(- 6) + 2y = 12 - 6$
$2y = 6$
$2(\div 2)y = 6 \div 2$
$y = 3$ miles

d. $12 \div (10 - 2) = b$
$12 \div 8 = b$
$1\frac{1}{2}$ cans $= b$

e. $5 + 8 + 7 + a = 25$
$20 + a = 25$
$20(- 20) + a = 25 - 20$
$a = 5$

3.2 a. $\frac{2}{3} = \frac{8}{q}$
$2q = 24$
$2(\div 2)q = 24 \div 2$
$q = 12$ oranges

b. $\frac{4}{6} = \frac{r}{15}$
$60 = 6r$
$60 \div 6 = 6(\div 6)r$
10 pennies $= r$

3.3 $\overline{XY}$, $\overline{YZ}$, $\overline{XZ}$

3.4 a. $\overline{MN}$, $\overline{NO}$, $\overline{MO}$
b. $\frac{AB}{MN} = \frac{2}{3}$
$\frac{8}{MN} = \frac{2}{3}$
$24 = 2$ min.
$24 \div 2 = 2(\div 2)MN$
12 in. $= \overline{MN}$

c. $\frac{BC}{NO} = \frac{2}{3}$
$\frac{11}{NO} = \frac{2}{3}$
$33 = 2\overline{NO}$
$33 \div 2 = 2(\div 2) \cdot \overline{NO}$
16.5 in. $= \overline{NO}$

d. $\frac{AC}{MO} = \frac{2}{3}$
$\frac{14}{MO} = \frac{2}{3}$
$42 = 2\overline{MO}$
$42 \div 2 = 2(\div 2) \cdot \overline{MO}$
21 in. $= \overline{MO}$

3.5

60	60	24
30/31	12	365
10	20	100
1,000	1	

3.6

12	36	3	5,280
	144		9
	4,840		640

3.7

16	2,000	16	2
2	4		12
	1,728		27

3.8 a. $V = l \cdot w \cdot h$
$V = 12 \cdot 8 \cdot 10$
$V = 960$ cu. ft.

b. $V = l \cdot w \cdot h$
$400 = 10 \cdot w \cdot 8$
$400 = 80 \cdot w$
$400 \div 80 = 80(\div 80) \cdot w$
5 yd. $= w$

c. $V = l \cdot w \cdot h$
$540 = l \cdot 15 \cdot 6$
$540 = l \cdot 90$
$540 \div 90 = l \cdot 90(\div 90)$
6 in. $= l$

d. $V = l \cdot w \cdot h$
$84 = 4 \cdot 3 \cdot h$
$84 = 12 \cdot h$
$84 \div 12 = 12(\div 12) \cdot h$
7 ft. $= h$

3.9 a. length   width   perimeter rectangle
    b. rate   time   amount
    c. side   perimeter square
    d. length   width   area rectangle
    e. side   perimeter triangle
    f. base   height   area triangle
    g. side   area square
    h. length   width
                  height   volume rect. prism
    i. pi (3.14)   diameter   circumference circle
    j. rate   time   distance
    k. side   volume of cube

3.10 a. $n = 7 \times [3 + (5 \times 2)]$
       $n = 7 \times (3 + 10)$
       $n = 7 \times 13$
       $n = 91$

       $n = [14 - (2 \times 3)] + 6$
       $n = (14 - 6) + 6$
       $n = 8 + 6$
       $n = 14$

       $n = 53 - [2 \times (7 + 4)]$
       $n = 53 - (2 \times 11)$
       $n = 53 - 22$
       $n = 31$

    b. $n = [5 + (2 \times 20)] \div 9$
       $n = (5 + 40) \div 9$
       $n = 45 \div 9$
       $n = 5$

       $n = [49 \div (3 + 4)] - 3$
       $n = (49 \div 7) - 3$
       $n = 7 - 3$
       $n = 4$

       $n = [(18 + 5) \times 2] - 12$
       $n = (23 \times 2) - 12$
       $n = 46 - 12$
       $n = 34$

3.11 a. $n = 3 + 5 \times 4 + 6$
       $n = 3 + 20 + 6$
       $n = 29$

       $n = 9 \times 7 - 8 \div 4$
       $n = 63 - 2$
       $n = 61$

       $n = 79 - 6 \times 8 - 15$
       $n = 79 - 48 - 15$
       $n = 16$

    b. $n = 14 + 3 \times 5 - 7$
       $n = 14 + 15 - 7$
       $n = 22$

$n = 48 \div 6 - 3 \times 2$
$n = 8 - 6$
$n = 2$

$n = 36 \div 2 - 13 - 5$
$n = 18 - 13 - 5$
$n = 0$

3.12 a. $A = l \cdot w$
       $A = 32 \cdot 120$
       $A = 3{,}840$ sq. ft.   4 bags

    b. $A = r \cdot t$
         $33 = r \cdot 4$
     $33 \div 4 = r \cdot 4(\div 4)$
        $8\frac{1}{4} = r$ $8\frac{1}{4}$ problems per hour

    c. $V = l \cdot w \cdot h$
      $180 = 6 \cdot 5 \cdot h$
      $180 = 30 \cdot h$
  $180 \div 30 = 30(\div 30) \cdot h$
      6 in. $= h$

    d. $P = 4s$
       $P = 4 \cdot 420$
       $P = 1{,}680$ yd.

    e. $D = r \cdot t$
       $90 = r \cdot 1.5$
   $90 \div 1.5 = r \cdot 1.5(\div 1.5)$
   60 mph $= r$

    f. $P = \pi d$
       $P = 3.14 \times 1{,}682$ ft.
       $P = 5{,}281.48$ or $5{,}280$ ft. or 1 mile

    g. $A = \frac{1}{2} bh$
       $A = \frac{1}{2} 6 \cdot 4$
       $A = \frac{24}{2}$
       $A = 12$ sq. ft.

    h. $V = l \cdot w \cdot h$
       $V = 4 \cdot 3 \cdot 2$
       $V = 24$ cu. in.   24 blocks

    i. $A = l \cdot w$
       $A = 14 \cdot 11$ (12 in. tiles = 1 sq. ft.)
       $A = 154$ sq. ft.   154 tiles

    j. $D = r \cdot t$
      $27 = r \cdot \frac{1}{2}$ hr.
    $27 \cdot 2 = r \cdot \frac{1}{2}(\frac{2}{1})$
   54 mph $= r$

3.13 a.
$$53 = [n \cdot (13 - 7)] + 5$$
$$53 = (n \cdot 6) + 5$$
$$53 - 5 = (n \cdot 6) + 5(-5)$$
$$48 = n \cdot 6$$
$$48 \div 6 = n \cdot 6(\div 6)$$
$$8 = n$$

$$33 = n \cdot [3 + (2 \times 4)]$$
$$33 = n \cdot (3 + 8)$$
$$33 = n \cdot 11$$
$$33 \div 11 = n \cdot 11(\div 11)$$
$$3 = n$$

$$5 = [(2 \times 15) + n] \div 9$$
$$5 = (30 + n) \div 9$$
$$5 \times 9 = (30 + n) \div 9 (\times 9)$$
$$45 = 30 + n$$
$$45 - 30 = 30(-30) + n$$
$$15 = n$$

b.
$$12 + [n \cdot (8 - 3)] = 32$$
$$12 + (n \cdot 5) = 32$$
$$12(-12) + (n \cdot 5) = 32 - 12$$
$$n \cdot 5 = 20$$
$$n \cdot 5(\div 5) = 20 \div 5$$
$$n = 4$$

$$22 + [n \cdot (8 \div 2)] = 46$$
$$22 + (n \cdot 4) = 46$$
$$22(-22) + (n \cdot 4) = 46 - 22$$
$$n \cdot 4 = 24$$
$$n \cdot 4(\div 4) = 24 \div 4$$
$$n = 6$$

$$[3 \cdot (4 + 8)] + n = 40$$
$$(3 \cdot 12) + n = 40$$
$$36 + n = 40$$
$$36(-36) + n = 40 - 36$$
$$n = 4$$

3.14 a. $x =$ David's cards $4x =$ Jason's cards
$$x + 4x = 55$$
$$5x = 55$$
$$5x(\div 5) = 55 \div 5$$
$$x = 11 \quad 4x = 44$$

b. $x =$ art mural $2x =$ science project
$$x + 2x = 45$$
$$3x = 45$$
$$3(\div 3)x = 45 \div 3$$
$$x = 15 \quad 2x = 30$$

c. $x =$ last year $x + 18 =$ second year
$$x + x + 18 = 110$$
$$2x + 18 = 110$$
$$2x + 18(-18) = 110 - 18$$
$$2x = 92$$
$$x = 46 \quad x + 18 = 64$$

Part Four

4.1 a. +2   -4
     b. -5   -3
     c. -1   -3
     d. +2   +6

4.2 a. 6   7   8
     b. -5   -8   -5
     c. 5   2   -6
     d. 3   -7   -4

4.3 a. ⑤   3   ②
     b. $⑤$ $⑦$ $⑫$
     c. 6   ④   2
     d. ㉔   3   ㉑
     e. -4°   -2°   -6°

4.4 a. 3, 2, -2, -5   b. 2, 7, 12, -3
     c. 0, -13, 1, -10   d. 5, 1, 9, 12

4.5 a. P   4
         P   3
         C
     b. N   2
         P   1
         B
     c. P   3
         N   4
         D
     d. N   1
         N   3
         A

149

4.6 a. -2, -1, 0, 1, 2

 -3,-2 -2,-1 -1,0 0,1 1,2

 b. 5, 4, 3, 2, 1, 0

 2,5 1,4 0,3 -1,2 -2,1 -3,0

 c. -5, -4, -3, -2, -1, 0

 0,-5 1,-4 2,-3 3,-2 4,-1 5,0

 d. 4, 3, 2, 1, 0, -1, -2

 0,4 -1,3 -2,2 -3,1

 -4,0 -5,-1 -6,-2

 e. 5, 3, 1, -1, -3, -5

 6,5 4,3 2,1 0,-1 -2,-3 -4,-5

4.7 a. I   b. P   c. I   d. I   e. P

4.8 a. Gp I - 15   18   20   ⓴   21   23   25

 Gp II - 13   14   17   ⑰   23   23   25

 Gp III - 18   19   19   ㉒   23   23   25

 Gp IV - 15   16   20   ㉑   21   23   24

 b. 20 + 17 + 22 + 21 = 80 ÷ 4 = 20

 c. Gp I - 5   Gp II - 3   Gp III - 4   Gp IV - 5

 d. Gp II

 e. 14 15 17 18 19 20 20 21 21 22 23 23 24 25 25

 10, 5

 f. The scores could be the same.

 It depends on the scores of the norm group.

4.9 a. $\frac{2}{3}$ $.\overline{66}$ 67% $\frac{3}{7}$ .428   43%

 b. $\frac{3}{5}$ .6   60% $\frac{3}{8}$ .375   38%

 c. $\frac{1}{5}$ .2   20% $\frac{7}{10}$ .7   70%

4.10 a. 1:5   20%   3:5   60%   1:5   20%

 b. 1:10   10%   3:10   30%   6:10   60%

 c. 1:7   14%   4:7   57%   2:7   29%

 d. 184

 0:5   0%   3:5   60%   2:5   40%

4.11 a. $.45 \times 40 = 18$ pages

 b. $.75 \times 16 = 12$ times

 c. $.85 \times 20 = 17$ questions

4.12 a. 100

 b. 5 + 25 + 18 + 15 = 63   63:100   63%

 5 + 8 = 13   13:100   13%

 20   20:100   20%

 4   4:100   4%

 c. earning money

 d. $\frac{20}{100} = \frac{x}{1,000}$

 $20,000 = 100x$

 200 students $= x$

4.13 25, 9, 81, 100, 16, 49, 121, 4, 36, 64, 144

4.14 4, 7, 9, 11, 2

 5, 10, 3, 12, 6, 8

4.15 16, 25

 4, 5

 4.5 - suggested answer

Part Five

5.1 a. 1.   45.   930.   4,326.

 b. 8 people

 c. 3

 d. 6,283 or 6,823

 e. 23, 29

 f. yes   yes   yes   yes   yes   yes

5.2 a. 232   5,867   8,806   4,638   2,925   51,688

 b. 216,007   4,018,702 $56\frac{4}{7}$ $302\frac{5}{8}$

 $1,699\frac{2}{5}$ $2,031\frac{3}{4}$

 c. 18   54 $64\frac{20}{84}$ $270\frac{9}{16}$

5.3 a.   56   b.   177

         56   − 59   (1)

         56   118

       + 56   − 59   (2)

         224   59

                            − 59   (3)

                              0

5.4   15, 4, 10, 9, 13, subtract 8
          18, 9, 30, 2, 42, divide by 6

5.5   a.   38.56   .405   12.907   .168   .7056
                 1.91

      b.   11.194   .33726 $1.27\frac{3}{5}$ $.012\frac{8}{29}$
                        2.2   4.43

5.6   a.   56,000   480   91,800   4

      b.   8.35   41.32   .095   .006

5.7   a.   suggested answers: $\frac{7}{7}$ $\frac{8}{7}$
                              $\frac{7}{8}$ $9\frac{7}{8}$

      b.   270   810   450   0   630   270

      c.   1, 2, 3, 6   1, 7   1, 2, 4, 8   1, 2, 4, 8, 16   1, 3, 7, 21

      d. 2^2, 3   2, 3^2 2^3, 3 3^3 2, 3, 5

5.8   6
     80-90

     "Sixth Grade
     Spelling Scores
     May and June"

5.9   a.   1 $\frac{11}{12}$ $1\frac{1}{5}$ $17\frac{1}{5}$ $15\frac{3}{5}$ $6\frac{23}{24}$

      b.   0 $2\frac{1}{3}$ $3\frac{1}{2}$ $5\frac{7}{9}$ $7\frac{11}{24}$ $3\frac{5}{6}$

5.10   a.   seven-eighths $9\frac{1}{2}$

       b.   nine-hundredths   4.5   ($4\frac{5}{10}$)

       c.   three and two-thirds $\frac{15}{16}$

       d.   eight and five hundred seven-thousandths
                  .0008

5.11   a.   1, 2, ④, 8   1, 2, 3, ④, 6, 12

       b.   1, ③, 9   1, ③, 5, 15

       c.   1, 2, 3, ⑥, 9, 18   1, 2, 3, 5, ⑥, 10, 15, 30

       d.   1, 2, ④, 8, 16   1, 2, ④, 5, 10, 20

5.12   a.   4, 8, 12, 16, ⑳   10, ⑳

       b.   6, 12, ⑱   9, ⑱

       c.   8, 16, ㉔   12, ㉔

       d.   10, 20, ㉚   ㉚

5.13   a. $\frac{1}{3}$ 2   4   34   3   35

       b. $\frac{7}{10}$ 15 $\frac{1}{16}$ 14 $\frac{5}{16}$ 4

5.14   a.   429   1,590

       b.   814   1,776

       c.   DCXLIII   MMIV

       d.   CCCXCIX   MDXII

5.15   a.   XI   V   LXX   III

       b.   XXVI   IV   XXI   VIII

5.16 $1\frac{1}{4}$ 4,505   6.8   116
       $-\frac{1}{2}$ + 2,875   9.4)63.9.2   × 75
       $\frac{3}{4}$ 7,380   8,700
                                      + 64
                                      8,764

5.17   a.   28,000   1,000,000   459,000,000

       b.   3,600   289,300   782,196,000

          6.38   28.42   94.64

       c.   76   825   40

          53   64   716

5.18   a.   3,000,000   70,000,000

       b.   2,000   20,000

       c.   4,000   6,000,000

5.19   millimeter , centimeter , decimeter , meter
      decameter , hectometer , kilometer

5.20   < , = , = , < , = , > , < , =

5.21   suggested answer

      a.   millimeter   meter   meter

      b.   millimeter   kilometer   centimeter

      c.   meter   centimeter   kilometer

5.22   a.   8 qt. 2 pt. = 9 qt.
          11 da. 27 hr. = 12 da. 3 hr.
          4 lb. 11 oz.
          3 T. 1805 lb.

      b.   24 yr. 510 da. = 25 yr. 145 da.
          27 qt. = 6 gal. 3 qt.
          42 sq. ft. = 4 sq. yd 6 sq. ft.

                 1 yd. 2 ft.
           4)6 yd. 2 ft.
            4
            2 yd. + 2 ft. = 8 ft.

5.23   a.   4 yd. 3 in.
          −   8 in.
          3 yd. 31 in.

                          8 ft.
                           0

       b. $\frac{1}{4}$ × 16 = 4 oz.

       c.   5 × 40 + 3 = nickels
               203 = nickels
         20 nickels = 1 dollar
           $10 + 3 nickels = $10.15
        20)203

       d.   4:48 P.M., P.S.T. (+ 3 hrs.) 7:48 P.M., E.S.T.

       e.   west

       f.   .09   = 9¢
         85)7.85

Part One

1.1 a. 29   20   27
    b. 32   61   91   42

1.2 a. 204   180   194
    b. 1,228   2,312   21,558

1.3 a. 36   49   46   56   17
    b. 338   934   838   128   174
    c. 1,376   7,127   3,059   2,277

1.4 a. 501   b. 38   c. 119   d. 83

1.5 a. 168   140   368   186   406   585
    b. 2,872   902   4,263   1,144   1,552
    c. 16,476   24,535   48,804   16,488

1.6 a. $4\frac{3}{4}$ $3\frac{3}{8}$ $13\frac{5}{6}$ 19 $20\frac{2}{4}(\frac{1}{2})$
    b. 118 $78\frac{3}{8}$ $162\frac{2}{6}(\frac{1}{3})$ 77
    c. 406 $1,213\frac{2}{3}$ 243 $2,038\frac{2}{4}(\frac{1}{2})$

1.7 a. 522   294
    b. $4\frac{5}{6}$ $11\frac{6}{8}(\frac{3}{4})$
    c. 2.947
    d. $71\frac{3}{5}$

1.8 a. 4.04   1.5   .84   1.11   1.53
    b. .118   .523   1.457   .499
    c. 9.48   9.77   4.335   8.804

1.9 a. .63   .62   .08   .35
    b. .37   .35   .44   .212
    c. 2.3   2.17   .76   8.54

1.10 a. 3.5   6.3   2.88   7.11
     b. .0192   2.212   43.76   .00438
     c. .4   .08 $.07\frac{2}{5}$ .309
     d. .8   3.8 $8\frac{1}{9}$ 2

1.11 a. 24   368   .119   6.17
     b. 17   125   .07   .219
     c. 448   435   1.2   .0084
     d. $6\frac{5}{8}$ 112   .06   .023

1.12 a. 24   b. 138   c. 3,789   d. 5.9
     $\times 5$ $\times 5$ $\times 3$ $\times 6$
     120   690   11,367   35.4

1.13 a. 4   12   20   32
        80   160   240   360
        400   1,200   2,000   2,800
     b. 14   28   49   63
        70   210   350   490
        2,100   2,800   4,200   5,600

1.14 a. 1,000   1,500   2,500   3,000   4,000   4,500
     b. 800   2,400   3,200   4,800   5,600   7,200

1.15 a. 27   72   18   45   0
     b. 120   60   180   270   150
     c. 1,200   1,800   2,400   3,600   4,800

1.16 a. 400   600   900   100   800   700
     b. 500   300   700   200   200   700

1.17 a. 29 R65   22R252   11 R602
     b. 27 R197   11 R38   10 R477
     c. 15 R265   57 R78   13 R112
     d. 28 R168   10 R626   21 R177
     e. 13 R159   14 R466   10 R325
     f. 11 R275   31 R33   20 R26

Part Two

2.1 a. b. c. d. e.

2.2 a.   b.

    c. (=)

2.3
a. $\frac{3}{4}$ b. $1\frac{7}{12}$ e. $2\frac{1}{6}$ d. $3\frac{1}{2}$ c. $4\frac{2}{3}$

2.4 a.
    b.
    c.
    d.

2.5 a.
    b. $\frac{1}{4}$ a. $\frac{1}{3}$

    c. $\frac{7}{12}$

    d. greater than
    e. greater than
    f. common denominator

2.6 a. 6, 12, 18, 24, 30 …   10, 20, 30, …
    b. 30

2.7 a. 4, 8, 12, 16, 20, 24, 28, 32, 36
       9, 18, 27, 36, …   12, 24, 36, …
    b. 36

2.8 a. $1\frac{1}{2}$ $1\frac{29}{40}$ $\frac{3}{4}$ $1\frac{23}{30}$ $1\frac{2}{7}$
    b. $\frac{1}{16}$ $\frac{1}{18}$ $\frac{3}{8}$ $\frac{1}{18}$ $\frac{1}{6}$

2.9 a. $7\frac{7}{8}$ $8\frac{7}{10}$ $7\frac{5}{6}$ $10\frac{5}{8}$ $11\frac{13}{18}$
    b. $5\frac{1}{6}$ $1\frac{1}{10}$ $4\frac{5}{48}$ $7\frac{9}{20}$ $12\frac{11}{24}$

2.10 a. $7\frac{19}{40}$ $11\frac{1}{12}$ $18\frac{5}{12}$ $8\frac{17}{24}$ $9\frac{1}{6}$

   b. $3\frac{9}{10}$ $3\frac{7}{9}$ $8\frac{13}{14}$ $6\frac{7}{8}$ $3\frac{5}{12}$

2.11 a. $\frac{3}{15}$ $4\frac{5}{8}$

   b. nine-tenths   three and five-sevenths

2.12 a. one and five-eighths

   b. nine and two-ninths

   c. three-tenths

   d. one and two-thirds

2.13 a. $\frac{3}{5}$ $\frac{11}{12}$ $1\frac{2}{9}$ $\frac{6}{11}$

   b. $\frac{3}{4}$ $\frac{7}{10}$ $\frac{13}{16}$ $\frac{5}{7}$

   c. $\frac{1}{4}$ $\frac{7}{16}$ $\frac{2}{15}$ $\frac{1}{6}$

   d. $\frac{1}{8}$ $\frac{2}{5}$ $\frac{1}{9}$ $\frac{11}{24}$

2.14 $\frac{3}{16}$ $\frac{4}{21}$ $\frac{20}{27}$ $\frac{5}{18}$ $\frac{12}{25}$

2.15 $1\frac{3}{8}$ 2 $4\frac{9}{10}$ 3 $2\frac{4}{7}$

2.16 a. $13\frac{1}{2}$ 65 25 54 $4\frac{8}{9}$

   b. 49 $6\frac{2}{3}$ 7 $\frac{25}{48}$ $\frac{1}{4}$

2.17 a. 2,400   6,000   1,200

   b. 300   2,100   2,400

   c. 1,200   800   700

2.18 $\frac{8}{5}$ $\frac{1}{7}$ $\frac{3}{14}$ $\frac{4}{27}$ $\frac{1}{12}$ $\frac{2}{1}$ or 2

2.19 $6 \div \boxed{\frac{3}{5}}\,\frac{5}{3}$ $\frac{14}{15} \div \boxed{10}\,\frac{1}{10}$ $5 \div \boxed{2\frac{1}{2}}\,\frac{2}{5}$

   $\frac{7}{12} \div \boxed{\frac{15}{16}}\,\frac{16}{15}$ $3\frac{7}{8} \div \boxed{9}\,\frac{1}{9}$

2.20 a. 10 2 $1\frac{1}{10}$ $\frac{8}{9}$

   b. $\frac{2}{15}$ $2\frac{1}{2}$ $6\frac{2}{3}$ $1\frac{4}{9}$

   c. $1\frac{1}{6}$ 7 4 $4\frac{2}{3}$

   d. $\frac{5}{8}$ 32 $\frac{3}{4}$ $\frac{2}{15}$

2.21 a. 8

   b. 2,100

   c. $\frac{1}{3}$

   d. 9

   e. $2\frac{1}{4}$

   f. $37\frac{1}{2}$

   g. $2\frac{1}{10}$

   h. 6

2.22 $48\frac{13}{100}$ $7\frac{16}{100}$ $3\frac{4}{100}$ $19\frac{20}{100}$ $5\frac{96}{100}$

2.23 $160.79 $6.44 $291.84 $2.63

2.24 a. $5 $7 $10 $9

   b. $200 $500 $5,400 $400

2.25 a. $.83\frac{2}{6} = \$ .83$ $3.12\frac{6}{9} = \$3.13$
   $4.56\frac{2}{4} = \$4.57$ $7.90\frac{4}{5} = \$7.91$

   b. $\frac{.66\frac{2}{3}}{3)\$200} = \$.67$ for one lb. $.67 \times 2 = \$1.34$
   for two lb.

   c. no $\frac{\$33.54\frac{2}{4}}{4)\$134.18}$

   $33.54 $33.54 $33.55 $33.55

Part Three

3.1 a. $<, <, >, <$

   b. $32, $23, $20, $16, decreased

3.2 a. 7, 5, 8

   b. 6, $\frac{2}{5}$, 9

3.3 a. 1) 8, 9, 10, 11   2) 4, 5, 6, 7
   3) 16, 20, 24, 28   3) 4, 5, 6, 7

   b. inverse operations

3.4 a. $9 < b < 14$
   $b = 10, 11, 12,$ or 13

   b. $2 < b < 6$
   $b = 3, 4,$ or 5

   c. $18 < b < 20$
   $b = 18, 19,$ or 20

   d. $95 + 82 + 91 + 88 = 356 \div 4 = 89$
   $95 + 82 + 91 + 96 = 364 \div 4 = 91$
   $89 \le b \le 91$
   $b = 89, 90,$ or 91

   e. $\$2.50 \times 4 = \$10.00$
   $\$4.25 \times 4 = \$17.00$
   $\$10.00 \le b \le \$17.00$

   f. $75 + 85 + 100 = 260$
   $90 + 100 + 120 = 310$
   $260 \le b \le 310$

3.5
42900	315,000	5,2720	6870,000
$\times$ 500	$\times$ 7,000	$\times$ 30	$\times$ 20,000
214,500	2,205,000	158,160	13,740,000

3.6 a.   4 200
   $\times$ 3,400
   16 800
   126 000
   142,800

   b.   16,000
   $\times$ 57,000
   112,000
   800,000
   912,000

   c.   8 500
   $\times$ 2,400
   34000
   170 000
   204,000

   d.   38,000
   $\times$ 63,000
   114,000
   2 280,000
   2,394,000

3.7 a. cylinder   b. sphere   c. cone

3.8 a. 6
　　b. EFGH
　　c. $A = lw$
　　　 $A = 9 \cdot 7$
　　　 $A = 63$ sq. in.
　　d. 126 sq. in.
　　e. DCGH
　　f. $A = lw$
　　　 $A = 9 \cdot 8$
　　　 $A = 72$ sq. in.
　　g. 144 sq. in.
　　h. BCGF
　　i. $A = lw$
　　　 $A = 8 \cdot 7$
　　　 $A = 56$ sq. in.
　　j. 112 sq. in.
　　k. 382 sq. in.

3.9

Area of ABCD = 12 sq. in.,
　　　EFGH = 12 sq. in. Total 24 sq. in.
Area of ABFE = 24 sq. in.,
　　　DCGH = 24 sq. in. Total 48 sq. in.
Area of ADHE = 18 sq. in.,
　　　BCGF = 18 sq. in. Total 36 sq. in.
　　　　　Total Surface Area 108 sq. in.

3.10 11 ft. 17 in. = 12 ft. 5 in.
　　　2 lb. 12 oz.
　　　15 wk. 20 da. = 17 wk. 6 da.
　　　3 gal. 2 qt.

3.11 $\dfrac{19 \text{ min.}}{5)\overline{95 \text{ min.}}}$　　$\dfrac{4\frac{2}{3} \text{ ft.}}{3)\overline{14 \text{ ft.}}}$　　$\dfrac{8 \text{ mm}}{9)\overline{72 \text{ mm}}}$

3.12 a. 3　　3:05
　　　b. 5　　6
　　　c. 4　　SW
　　　d. 6　　$2\frac{1}{2}$ in.
　　　e. 2　　70°
　　　f. 1　　50 mph

3.13

3.14

3.15 a. millimeters, centimeters, decimeter
　　　b. 2.5 (2.54)
　　　c. inch

3.16 7.62　　2.758　　58.42　　6.304

3.17

3.18 a. -11, -10, -5, -3, -2, 0, 1, 6, 7, 9, 15
　　　b. -856, -601, -315, 276, 453, 500, 1,904

3.19 date line on vertical number line

-3500		
	3200 B.C. Hieroglyphic Writing	6
	2700 B.C. First Pyramids	4
-3000		
-2500		
-2000		
	1800 B.C. Abraham in Canaan	1
-1500	1500 B.C. First American Civilization	5
	1250 B.C. Moses at Mt. Sanai	9
-1000	1000 B.C. King David	8
-500	520 B.C. Age of Confucius	2
	400 B.C. Start of Great Wall of China	10
	340 B.C. Alexander the Great	3
0	55 B.C. Julius Caesar	7
	100 A.D. Acts of the Apostles	11
500	400 A.D. Barbaric Invasions	13
	611 A.D. Muhammad	20
1000	1000 A.D. Crusades	15
	1350 A.D. Bubonic Plague	14
1500	1492 A.D. Columbus	16
	1500 A.D. Michelangelo	19
	1776 A.D. American Revolution	12
	1927 A.D. Lindbergh's Flight	18
2000	1961 A.D. First Man in Space	17

154

3.20 a. 8, 15   45, 9
     b. 14, 6   6, 2
     c. 78, 8, 5

3.21 a. D, 72   b. C, 437   c. A, 27

3.22 a. $3(4 + 2) = 18$ $(9 \times 4) + (9 \times 3) = 63$
     b. $4(9 + 6) = 60$ $(7 \times 2) + (7 \times 8) = 70$

3.23   0, 2, 4, 6, 8 or even number
     0, 5
     0
     add up to a multiple of 3
     add up to a multiple of 9
     divisible by both 2 and 3

3.24

	2	5	10	3	9	6
522	✓			✓	✓	✓
690	✓	✓	✓	✓		✓
984	✓			✓		✓
1,425		✓		✓		

Part Four

4.1

		fraction	decimal	percent
1:2 =		$\frac{1}{2}$	.5	50%
1:4 =		$\frac{1}{4}$	.25	25%
3:4 =		$\frac{3}{4}$	.75	75%
1:5 =		$\frac{1}{5}$	.2	20%
2:5 =		$\frac{2}{5}$	.4	40%
3:5 =		$\frac{3}{5}$	.6	60%
4:5 =		$\frac{4}{5}$	.8	80%
1:8 =		$\frac{1}{8}$	.125	$12\frac{1}{2}\%$, 13%
3:8 =		$\frac{3}{8}$	.375	$37\frac{1}{2}\%$, 38%
5:8 =		$\frac{5}{8}$	.625	$62\frac{1}{2}\%$, 63%
7:8 =		$\frac{7}{8}$	.875	$87\frac{1}{2}\%$, 88%
1:3 =		$\frac{1}{3}$	$.\overline{333}$	33%
2:3 =		$\frac{2}{3}$	$.\overline{666}$	67%
1:6 =		$\frac{1}{6}$	$.1\overline{66}$	17%
5:6 =		$\frac{5}{6}$	$.8\overline{33}$	83%

4.2   a. 30:50 $\frac{3}{5}$ .6   60%
     b. 4:16 $\frac{1}{4}$ .25   25%
     c. 60:180 $\frac{1}{3}$ $.\overline{33}$ 33%
     d. 21:28 $\frac{3}{4}$ .75   75%

4.3   a. 18:22 $\frac{18}{22}$

$$\begin{array}{r} 81\frac{18}{22} = 82\% \\ 22\overline{)18.00} \\ \underline{17\ 60} \\ 40 \\ \underline{22} \\ 18 \end{array}$$

     b. 32:45 $\frac{32}{45}$

$$\begin{array}{r} .71\frac{5}{45} = 71\% \\ 45\overline{)32.00} \\ \underline{31\ 50} \\ 50 \\ \underline{45} \\ 5 \end{array}$$

     c. 67:75 $\frac{67}{75}$

$$\begin{array}{r} 89\frac{25}{75} = 89\% \\ 75\overline{)67.00} \\ \underline{60\ 00} \\ 7\ 00 \\ \underline{6\ 75} \\ 25 \end{array}$$

     d. 12:13 $\frac{12}{13}$

$$\begin{array}{r} 92\frac{4}{13}\ 92\% \\ 13\overline{)12.00} \\ \underline{11\ 70} \\ 30 \\ \underline{26} \\ 4 \end{array}$$

4.4   a. line
     b. Oct. 1
       Oct. 22
       Oct. 15
       Oct. 8
       Oct. 29
     c. Brown Family Grocery Bills

4.5   a. bar
     b. 6, 7, 5
     c. 3, 1
     d. Jeff's Baskets Per Game

4.6   a. circle
     b. see graph

     c. Restaurant Sales
       for One Week

4.7   a.   picture graph or pictograph
     b.   June
         July
         May
         March
         April
     c.   Houses Sold in Five Months

4.8 a. 56 R252   53 R365   96 R504
    b. 188 R173   239 R3   81 R436
    c. 46 R586   121 R499 56 R212
    d. 102 R813   73 R36   63 R78

4.9 a. B, O   O B
    b. BOA, BAO, OBA, OAB, ABO, AOB
    c. TMD, TDM, MTD, MDT, DMT, DTM

4.10 a. mode   24 boxes
     b. mean   74°F
     c. median   60, 72, 75, ⑦⑥ 83, 89, 94 Betsy

4.11 a. 3:5   60%
     b. 2:3   67%

4.12 a.
$$45 + x = 102$$
$$45(-45) + x = 102 - 45$$
$$x = 57$$

$$x - 88 = 185$$
$$x - 88(+88) = 185 + 88$$
$$x = 273$$

$$y \div 4 = 28$$
$$y \div 4(\times 4) = 28 \times 4$$
$$y = 112$$

b.
$$36 \cdot c = 216$$
$$36(\div 36) \cdot c = 216 \div 36$$
$$c = 6$$

$$4a = 92$$
$$4(\div 4) \cdot a = 92 \div 4$$
$$a = 23$$

$$81 = s^2$$
$$9 = s$$

c.
$$x + x + x + 14 = 20$$
$$3x + 14 = 20$$
$$3x + 14(-14) = 20 - 14$$
$$3x = 6$$
$$3(\div 3) \cdot x = 6 \div 3$$
$$x = 2$$

$$(2 \cdot y) + (2 \cdot 3) = 14$$
$$2 \cdot y + 6 = 14$$
$$2 \cdot y + 6(-6) = 14 - 6$$
$$2y = 8$$
$$2(\div 2) \cdot y = 8 \div 2$$
$$y = 4$$

$$x = \tfrac{1}{2}(7 \times 8)$$
$$x = \tfrac{1}{2} \times 56$$
$$x = \tfrac{1}{2} \times \tfrac{56}{1}$$
$$x = 28$$

4.13 a.
$$\tfrac{1}{3} = \tfrac{x}{45}$$
$$3x = 45$$
$$3(\div 3) \cdot x = 45 \div 3$$
$$x = 15$$

$$\tfrac{12}{18} = \tfrac{2}{a}$$
$$12a = 36$$
$$12(\div 12) \cdot a = 36 \div 12$$
$$a = 3$$

$$\tfrac{b}{20} = \tfrac{4}{5}$$
$$5b = 80$$
$$5(\div 5) \cdot b = 80 \div 5$$
$$b = 16$$

b.
$$\tfrac{2}{y} = \tfrac{3}{6}$$
$$12 = 3y$$
$$12 \div 3 = 3(\div 3) \cdot y$$
$$4 = y$$

$$\tfrac{2}{6} = \tfrac{3}{c}$$
$$2c = 18$$
$$2(\div 2) \cdot c = 18 \div 2$$
$$c = 9$$

$$\tfrac{3}{5} = \tfrac{x}{15}$$
$$45 = 5x$$
$$45 \div 5 = 5(\div 5) \cdot x$$
$$9 = x$$

c.
$$\tfrac{z}{8} = \tfrac{9}{12}$$
$$12z = 72$$
$$12(\div 12) \cdot z = 72 \div 12$$
$$z = 6$$

$$\tfrac{5}{10} = \tfrac{4}{c}$$
$$5c = 40$$
$$5(\div 5) \cdot c = 40 \div 5$$
$$c = 8$$

$$\tfrac{9}{x} = \tfrac{3}{8}$$
$$72 = 3x$$
$$72 \div 3 = 3(\div 3) \cdot x$$
$$24 = x$$

4.14 a.

$$\frac{2}{5} = \frac{4}{w} \quad \text{(width)}$$
$$2w = 20$$
$$2(\div 2) \cdot w = 20 \div 2$$
$$w = 10 \text{ in.}$$

$$\frac{2}{5} = \frac{6}{l} \quad \text{(length)}$$
$$2l = 30$$
$$2(\div 2) \cdot l = 30 \div 2$$
$$l = 15 \text{ in.}$$

 b. $128 \div 8 = x$ (number of pieces)
$$16 = x$$

4.15 a. $5 \times 8 = 4 \times 10$ $\qquad \frac{15}{3} = 20 \div 4$
 b. $6^2 = 4 \times 9$ $\qquad 9 + (-6) = \frac{12}{4}$
 c. $9 + 8 = 8 + 9$ $\qquad 4(2 \times 8) = (4 \times 2) \times 8$

4.16 a.

$$A = l \cdot w$$
$$108 = 12 \cdot w$$
$$108 \div 12 = 12(\div 12) \cdot w$$
$$9 \text{ cm} = w$$

 b.

$$P = 4s$$
$$28 = 4s$$
$$28 \div 4 = 4(\div 4) \cdot s$$
$$7 \text{ yd.} = s$$

 c.

$$D = r \cdot t$$
$$310 = 62 \cdot t$$
$$310 \div 62 = 62(\div 62) \cdot t$$
$$5 \text{ hr.} = t$$

 d. $C = \boldsymbol{\pi} d$
$$C = 3.14 \cdot 7$$
$$C = 21.98 \text{ mm}$$

 e.

$$P = 2l \cdot 2w$$
$$22 = (2 \cdot l) + (2 \cdot 4)$$
$$22 = 2 \cdot l + 8$$
$$22 - 8 = 2 \cdot l + 8(-8)$$
$$14 = 2l$$
$$14 \div 2 = 2(\div 2) \cdot l$$
$$7 \text{ ft.} = l$$

 f. $A = \frac{1}{2} bh$
$$A = \frac{1}{2} (6 \times 4)$$
$$A = \frac{1}{2} \cdot 24$$
$$A = 12 \text{ sq. yd.}$$

4.17 a.

$$\frac{5}{12} = \frac{x}{60} \quad \text{(number of push-ups)}$$
$$300 = 12x$$
$$300 \div 12 = 12(\div 12) \cdot x$$
$$25 \text{ push-ups} = x$$

 b.

$$\frac{8}{10} = \frac{x}{120} \quad \text{(number of cookies)}$$
$$960 = 10x$$
$$960 \div 10 = 10(\div 10) \cdot x$$
$$96 \text{ cookies} = x$$

Part Five

5.1 a. 56
 b. 81
 c. 280
 d. 4,800

5.2 a. 70 $\qquad$ .9 $\qquad$ 5,000
 b. .06 $\qquad$ 30,000 $\qquad$ 400,000,000

5.3 a. $39 + 63 = 102$
 b. $\frac{5}{8} - \frac{1}{2} = \frac{1}{8}$
 c. $.6 \times .05 = .03$
 d. $18 \div 9 = 2$
 e. $8 \le 8, 9, 10, 11 < 12$
 f. $25 \ge 25, 20, 15, 10 > 5$

5.4 a. 10 $\qquad$ 1,000,000
 b. 67 $\qquad$ 76
 c. 2, 4, 10, 20
 d. 1, 3, 5, 15
 e. 2
 f. odd
 g. $5\frac{1}{2}$ hr.
 h. 6 mo.

5.5 possible answers

 a. *or*

 obtuse acute $\qquad$ right right

 b.

 c.

 d.

 rectangle (or square)

e.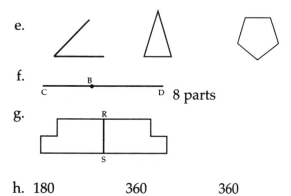

f.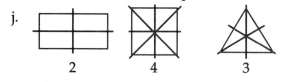

B
C ———————— D 8 parts

g.
R
S

h. 180   360   360

i. The area of one face is A = s², A = 49 sq. in.
A square has 6 faces. 6 × 49 = 294 sq. in.
Total surface area 294 sq. in.

j.

2   4   3

5.6 a. 80 days = y

b.   8 = 25% of y
          $8 = \frac{1}{4} \cdot y$
          $8 \times 4 = (4 \cdot \frac{1}{4}) \cdot y$
          32 cats = y

c.   6 = .4 of y
          $6 = \frac{2}{5}$ of y
          $6 \times 5 = (5 \cdot \frac{2}{5}) \cdot y$
          30 = 2y
          15 in. = y

d. $10 = \frac{2}{3}$ of y
          $10 = \frac{2}{3} \cdot y$
          $10 \cdot 3 = (3 \cdot \frac{2}{3}) \cdot y$
          30 = 2 · y
          15 cats = y

e. $12 = \frac{3}{4}$ of y
          $12 = \frac{3}{4} \cdot y$
          $12 \cdot 4 = (4 \cdot \frac{3}{4}) \cdot y$
          48 = 3y
          16 hot dogs = y

f. $4 = \frac{1}{3}$ of y
          $4 = \frac{1}{3} \cdot y$
          $4 \times 3 = (3 \cdot \frac{1}{3}) \cdot y$
          12 books = y

5.7 a. 2 in.
     b. 4 cm
     c. 40 mm

5.8 a. 439 $1\frac{3}{5}$ 41%
     b. $24.25   18.49   3 gal. 1 qt.
     c. 10,681 $1\frac{1}{3}$ 25%
     d. $23.35   9.64   9 cm 1 mm

5.9 a. 2,778 $8\frac{13}{24}$ 69%
     b. $14.76   10.819   4 yd. 23 in.
     c. 3,971 $5\frac{1}{2}$ 24%
     d. $44.58   3.788   7 g 5 dg

5.10 a. 80   .9   6   250%   30,000   450
         800   9   60   2500%   300,000   4500
         8,000 90 600 25,000% 3,000,000 45,000

     b. .8   .009 $\frac{3}{50}$ 2.5%   300   4.5
         .08   .0009 $\frac{3}{500}$ .25%   30   .45
         .008 .00009 $\frac{3}{5,000}$ .025%   3   .045

5.11 a. 15,322   8   45%
     b. $1.74   17.014   24 qt. (6 gal.)
     c. 449,595   3   84%
     d. $61.03   1.6682   120 cm (1 m 2 dm)

5.12 a. $\frac{3}{4} \times \overset{25}{\underset{1}{100}} = 75¢$

     b. 9 × 10 = 90 quarters
         4 qtr. = 1 dollar $22.50
         Betsy has $22.50.   4)90

     c. $3.20 = .50 + .30 + .50 + x
                 $3.20 = 1.30 + x
         $3.20 − 1.30 = 1.30(− 1.30) + x
                 $1.90 = x (amount Jason has)

     d. $100 − (40 − 3 − .05) =
         $100 − $36.95 = $63.05

     e. 10% of $123,000 = x
         .10 × 123,000 = x
                 12,300 = x (commission paid)

     f.   .8
         3.5.)$2.8.0   .8 = .80 or 80¢ per pound
                 2 8 0

     g.   3.333 = $3.33
         6)$20.000

     h. x = $2.75 + (5 × $1.25)
        x = $2.75 + 6.25
        x = $9.00 charge for 6 hours

i. $\frac{1}{4}$ of \$6.24 $= x$

$\overset{1}{\underset{1}{\frac{1}{4}}} \times \overset{1.56}{\cancel{6.24}} = x$

     \$1.56 $= x$ charge for sub

j. $\overset{.02}{48)\overline{.96}}$ $= .02$ or 2¢ per ounce

k.   2 people

l. $\overset{.57}{6)\overline{\$13.42}}$ \$ .57 = 1 pencil $\times$ 9 = \$5.13

5.13 a.   381 $12\frac{1}{2}$ 14%
      b.   \$1.83   69   4 in.
      c.   85 $\frac{3}{4}$ 12%
      d.   \$1.32   .14   3 cups or $1\frac{1}{2}$ pts.

Self Test 1

1.01 0 1 2 3 4 5 6 7 8 9

1.02 units   thousands   millions

1.03 8,952,138 millions
      386   units
      54,392   thousands

1.04 a. nine hundred thirty-five thousand
          eight hundred forty-seven
      b. three hundred forty-seven million
          nine hundred sixty-five thousand

1.05 221,735,946

1.06 a. nineteenth   forty-seventh
      b. three hundred fifty-eighth

1.07 a. 2,776   256,348
      b. 995   59,279

1.08 a. 1, 3, 9, - C   1, 13 - P
      b. 1, 2, 3, 6, 9, 18 - C   1, 3, 7, 21 - C

1.09 a. addend   b. minuend
          addend   subtrahend
          sum   difference

1.010 a. multiplicand   b.   quotient
          multiplier   divisor dividend
          product

1.011 a. tens $\underline{19}$ ones $\underline{11}$ 234 10,943 1,529
      b. 846   1,206   244   2,306
      c. 3,430   21,238   471,588
      d. 120 R3   96   107 R2

Self Test 2

2.01 a. =   =   ≠
      b. >   <   >

2.02 a. + , −   × , ×   + , ×
      b. × , ×   − , ÷   × , ×

2.03 a. 4, 7, 11 - 7, 4, 11
          11, 4, 7 - 11, 7, 4
      b. 7, 9, 63 - 9, 7, 63
          63, 7, 9 - 63, 9, 7

2.04 a. 5,634   b. 8,458
      c. 17,664   d. 147

2.05 fraction bar   numerator
                      denominator

2.06 c   b   a

2.07 seven-ninths   three and two-fifths

2.08 $\frac{6}{7}$ $5\frac{3}{8}$

2.09 6   4   2

2.010 10   6   15

2.011 $2\frac{1}{4}$ 1 $8\frac{1}{2}$

2.012 $\frac{1}{2}$ $\frac{2}{3}$ $\frac{3}{4}$

2.013 $\frac{1}{2}$ 1 $1\frac{3}{7}$ $\frac{1}{4}$ $\frac{1}{5}$ $\frac{1}{4}$

2.014 28, 35   9,999   9,998

2.015 <

2.016 248,967 248,976 284,679 284,769 429,786

Self Test 3

3.01 $\frac{405}{1,000}$ $\frac{9}{10}$ $\frac{72}{100}$ $\frac{8}{100}$

3.02 a. six-tenths   thirty-five hundredths
      b. two hundred forty-nine thousandths

3.03 .6   .022   .03   .168

3.04 $8\frac{5}{10}$ $5\frac{2}{1,000}$ $14\frac{36}{100}$ $2\frac{13}{1,000}$

3.05 a. three and seven-tenths
          nine and twenty-six hundreths
      b. four and twelve thousandths

3.06 8.0   46.00   57.000

3.07 a. $\frac{7}{100}$ $\frac{80}{100}$ $\frac{390}{1,000}$ $\frac{40}{1,000}$
      b. $6\frac{1}{100}$ $9\frac{72}{1,000}$ $17\frac{280}{1,000}$ $24\frac{30}{1,000}$

3.08 a. .80   .30   .70   .10
      b. .600   .710   .020   .900

3.09 a. 8.070 .500 .900 .070 .234 .030
      b. .030 .07 .234 .50 .9 8.07

3.010 a. 41.742   b. 18.758

3.011 seven hundred thirty-nine billion

3.012 ten thousandths   hundred thousandths

3.013 1,602   33.112   9.06   2.451
      1,602   33.112   22.64   5.300

3.014 31   15

3.015 a. Four times two is not equal to fifty-six
          divided by eight.
      b. $7 - 2 > 4 + 0$

3.016 a.

$$N + 79 = 132$$
$$N + 79(-79) = 132 - 79$$
$$N = 53$$
$$53 + 79 = 132$$

b.

$$N - 63 = 151$$
$$N - 63(+63) = 151 + 63$$
$$N = 214$$
$$214 - 63 = 151$$

Self Test 4

4.01   20,223   609,245   1,949,472

4.02   a.   40, 80, 120, 160, 200, 240, 280, 320, 360
        b.   70, 140, 210, 280, 350, 420, 490, 560, 630

4.03   Zero (0)

4.04   21 R15   11 R52   22 R14

4.05   48   86
     336   7)336   1,806   21)1,806

4.06   54 R3   54   40 R13   40
                 ×6   24)973   ×24
                 324   960
                 + 3   + 13
                 327   973

4.07   a.   6,400   883,000   35,200
        b.   81,000   316,000   470,000

4.08   a.   695   200   b.   2,143   7,000
               + 500   − 5,000
               700   2,000

4.09   a.   2,368   40   b.   52   50
               × 60   8)400
               2,400

4.010   a.   130 students
        b.   4,000 cars
        c.   120 push-ups
        d.   20 boxes

Self Test 5

5.01   a.   567,112,816   567,212,416
                     576,112,416   576,131,426
        b.   hundred millions
        c.   place holder

5.02   a.   seventh
        b.   1, 2, 4, 5, 10, 20
        c.   8, 16, 24, 32, 40, 48, 56, 64, 72

5.03   8   12   5   7
        1   13   4   20

5.04   a.   2,841   4,162   b.   47
                       + 2,841   2,491   53)2,491
                       7,003

5.05 $35 + 25 < 40 + 25$

5.06 $96 \times 8 =$ $96 \cdot 8 =$ $96(8) =$

5.07   c   a   c   a   b   b

5.08   6   16   3   6

5.09 $\frac{2}{5}$ mile

5.010   a.   .563   .040   .670   .800   .048
        b.   .04   .048   .563   .67   .8

5.011   a. $\frac{1}{6}$ $\frac{1}{2}$ $1\frac{1}{3}$ $1\frac{2}{3}$
        b.   .03   .06   .08   .10

5.012   a. $59,000 < 62,000$ $61,000 < 62,000$
        b. $43,000 < 62,000$ $70,000 > 62,000$

5.013 $N = 4 + (2 \times 4) + (4 - 2)$
        $N = 4 + 8 + 2$
        $N = 14$ birds

Self Test 1

1.01 18.   4.   1,392.   608.

1.02 a. ten   b. ten   c. tenths'

1.03 five hundred sixty billion, three hundred twenty-four million, one hundred ninety-eight thousand, seven

1.04 $\frac{8}{100}$ $\frac{276}{1,000}$ $\frac{4,205}{10,000}$ $\frac{73,184}{100,000}$

1.05 a. .90   .20   .70
      b. .600   .090   .530
      c. .0300   .5270   .4010

1.06 $\cancel{00}$,290,463 $\cancel{0}$,350   807,321

1.07 .8$\cancel{0}$ .056   .07$\cancel{0}$

1.08 600   900   371,000

1.09 a. 21, 24, 27, 30, 33, 36, 39, 42
      b. 12, 24, 36, 48, 60 ,72, 84, 96

1.010
$$\begin{array}{cccc} 15 & 1 & 5 & 3 \\ \underline{\times 1} & \underline{\times 15} & \underline{\times 3} & \underline{\times 5} \end{array}$$
1, 3, 5, 15

1.011 a. 1, 2, 3, 6 - C   1, 3, 9 - C
       b. 1, 13 - P   1, 3, 7, 21 - C

1.012 a.
```
   ┌────┐
   │ 15 │
 ┌─┬────┤
 │3│ 5  │
 ├─┼────┤
 │5│ 1  │    3, 5
 └─┴────┘
```
       b.
```
   ┌────┐
   │ 28 │
 ┌─┬────┤
 │2│ 14 │
 ├─┼────┤
 │2│ 7  │
 ├─┼────┤
 │7│ 1  │    2, 2, 7
 └─┴────┘
```
       c.
```
   ┌────┐
   │ 84 │
 ┌─┬────┤
 │2│ 42 │
 ├─┼────┤
 │2│ 21 │
 ├─┼────┤
 │3│ 7  │
 ├─┼────┤
 │7│ 1  │    2, 2, 3, 7
 └─┴────┘
```
       d.
```
   ┌─────┐
   │ 150 │
 ┌─┬─────┤
 │2│ 75  │
 ├─┼─────┤
 │3│ 25  │
 ├─┼─────┤
 │5│ 5   │
 ├─┼─────┤
 │5│ 1   │    2, 3, 5, 5
 └─┴─────┘
```

Self Test 2

2.01 $\frac{2}{3}$ $1\frac{1}{9}$ $\frac{2}{3}$ $2\frac{1}{2}$

2.02 10   4   9   20

2.03 3, 6, 9, 12, 15
      4, 8, 12, 16, 20
      12
      12

2.04 a. $1\frac{5}{24}$ $\frac{19}{20}$ $1\frac{3}{14}$ $1\frac{1}{6}$
      b. $\frac{9}{16}$ $\frac{1}{2}$ $\frac{13}{20}$ $\frac{1}{24}$

2.05 19 R28   56   25 R3   14 R32

2.06 a. 3   4 3^4 81
      b. 7   3 7^3 343
      c. 3, 7   2, 2 $3^2 \times 7^2$ 441
      d. 2, 5   3, 2 $2^3 \times 5^2$ 200

2.07 a. five cubed $5 \times 5 \times 5$ 125
      b. nine squared 9×9 81
      c. six cubed $6 \times 6 \times 6$ 216
      d. two to the fifth power
          $2 \times 2 \times 2 \times 2 \times 2$ 32

2.08 ten

2.09 a. ten cubed $10 \times 10 \times 10$ 1,000
      b. ten to the fifth power
          $10 \times 10 \times 10 \times 10 \times 10$ 100,000

2.010 10^4

Self Test 3

3.01 a. 90   62   45   55
      E, E, E   O, O, E   E, O, O   O, E, 0
      b. even   even   odd
          even   even   odd

3.02 a. 890   5,640   37,180
      b. 2,400   38,000   926,300
      c. 7,000   29,000   483,000

3.03 C - 1, 2, 3, 6   P - 1, 11
      C - 1, 2, 7, 14   P - 1, 19

3.04 a.
```
   ┌─────┐
   │ 225 │
 ┌─┬─────┤
 │3│ 75  │
 ├─┼─────┤
 │3│ 25  │
 ├─┼─────┤
 │5│ 5   │
 ├─┼─────┤
 │5│ 1   │   3² × 5²
 └─┴─────┘
```
$3^2 \times 5^2$
      b.
```
   ┌─────┐
   │ 196 │
 ┌─┬─────┤
 │2│ 98  │
 ├─┼─────┤
 │2│ 49  │
 ├─┼─────┤
 │7│ 7   │
 ├─┼─────┤
 │7│ 1   │   2² × 7²
 └─┴─────┘
```
$2^2 \times 7^2$

3.05 $\frac{1}{8}$ $\frac{2}{8}$ $\frac{3}{8}$ $\frac{4}{8}$ $\frac{5}{8}$ $\frac{6}{8}$ $\frac{7}{8}$ $\frac{8}{8}$

3.06 $\frac{7}{12}$ $\frac{2}{3}$ $\frac{3}{4}$ $\frac{5}{6}$

3.07 a. = $1 \times 15 = 15$ $5 \times 3 = 15$
          = $2 \times 24 = 48$ $8 \times 6 = 48$
      b. ≠ $1 \times 24 = 24$ $6 \times 8 = 48$
          ≠ $4 \times 20 = 80$ $5 \times 10 = 50$

3.08 a. $10\frac{3}{4}$ $14\frac{4}{9}$ $14\frac{1}{2}$ $17\frac{2}{5}$
      b. $9\frac{1}{6}$ $13\frac{1}{2}$ $11\frac{1}{2}$ $6\frac{1}{24}$

3.09 a. 6,000,000 + 9,000,000   15
      b. 429,000,000 + 211,000,000   640
      c. 6,000,000 − 2,000,000   4
      d. 70,000,000 − 31,000,000   39

Self Test 4

4.01 a. 33.875   14.245
    b. 7.877   21.26

4.02 a. 8.4 (M) 16 (E) 5.4 (L) 12 (E) 9.6 (L) 20.8 (M)
    b. 23.4 (M)   8 (E)

4.03 2.268   45.58   .01885   .00344

4.04 a. Twenty-seven plus thirty-eight is not equal to fifty-seven.
    b. Forty-three is less than fifty-two
    c. Nine divided by three is greater than nine times zero.

4.05 a. $21 > 19$
    b. $14 - 8 = 6$
    c. $7 \times 5 \neq 4 \times 9$

4.06 $\neq$ N   = Y

4.07 2   7
     12   9

4.08 a.
$$351 + N = 624$$
$$351(-351) + N = 624 - 351$$
$$N = 273$$
$$351 + 273 = 624$$

    b.
$$593 = 327 + N$$
$$593 - 327 = 327(-327) + N$$
$$266 = N$$
$$593 = 327 + 266$$

    c.
$$N - 247 = 194$$
$$N - 247(+247)\ 194 + 247$$
$$N = 441$$
$$441 - 247 = 194$$

    d.
$$480 = N - 158$$
$$480 + 158 = N - 158(+158)$$
$$638 = N$$
$$480 = 638 - 158$$

4.09 a. $7\frac{3}{4}$ $13\frac{7}{8}$ $7\frac{1}{2}$ $13\frac{7}{9}$
    b. $14\frac{3}{7}$ $20\frac{2}{5}$ $5\frac{3}{8}$ $8\frac{7}{12}$
    c. $6\frac{2}{3}$ $4\frac{3}{5}$ $1\frac{1}{2}$ $7\frac{8}{9}$

4.010 41   119 R2   155 R1   94 R2

5.02 a. $\frac{5}{8} = \frac{25}{40}$ $\frac{7}{10} = \frac{38}{40}$ Ruth swam the furthest.

    b.
$$2\frac{1}{3} = \frac{4}{12}$$
$$+ 1\frac{1}{4} = \frac{3}{12}$$
$$3\frac{7}{12}$$

$$5$$
$$- 3\frac{7}{12}$$
$$1\frac{5}{12}$$

5.03 365   3   2
     16   5,280   60
     9   30 - 31   4

5.04 a. 4, 9
    b. fluid units

5.05 a. B.C.
    b. A.M.   P.M.
    c. Gregorian

5.06 1 decade

5.07 a. 604
    b. 9,863
    c. 40, 48, 56, 64, 72
    d. 13, 17, 19, 23
    e. 3.376
    f. $2\frac{7}{8}$
        suggested answers g. and h.
    g. 24,670   02,467
    h. 3.029   3.290
    i. 3
    j. $(18 \div 3) + (2 \times 5) =$
          6   +   10   = 16
    k.
$$N + 49 = 123$$
$$N + 49(-49) = 123 - 49$$
$$N = 74$$

5.08 a. $\frac{1}{2} = \frac{9}{18}$ $\frac{2}{3} = \frac{12}{18}$ $\frac{5}{6} = \frac{15}{18}$ $\frac{7}{9} = \frac{14}{18}$ $\frac{11}{18}$
    b. $\frac{1}{2}$ $\frac{11}{18}$ $\frac{2}{3}$ $\frac{7}{9}$ $\frac{5}{6}$

5.09 $\frac{5}{8}$ $12\frac{3}{5}$ $16\frac{1}{10}$ $2\frac{1}{2}$ $4\frac{1}{2}$ $8\frac{3}{8}$

5.010 O   O   E   E

5.011 $(2 \times 15) + (2 \times 21) - 5 =$
        30   +   42 $- 5 = 67$ points

Self Test 5

5.01 a. seven tenths - .7 - $\frac{7}{10}$ - .70
    b. seven hundredths - .07 - $\frac{7}{100}$ - .070
    c. seven thousandths - .007 - $\frac{7}{1,000}$ - .0070
    d. one-fourth - $\frac{1}{4}$ - $\frac{3}{12}$ - $\frac{5}{20}$
    e. two-fifths - $\frac{2}{5}$ - $\frac{8}{20}$ - $\frac{12}{30}$
    f. three-eighths - $\frac{3}{8}$ - $\frac{6}{16}$ - $\frac{15}{40}$

Self Test 1

1.01 a. 144   123   92   20 R7
      b. 268   75 R3   32   93 R3

1.02 a. 320   4,270   18,290
      b. 1,000   8,700   32,600
      c. 6,000   26,000   527,000

1.03 120   240   30   180

1.04 90   70   60   50

1.05 a. $\frac{7}{12}$ $\frac{11}{24}$ $\frac{9}{16}$ $\frac{1}{2}$
      b. $\frac{9}{2} = 4\frac{1}{2}$ 12 $\frac{5}{2} = 2\frac{1}{2}$ $\frac{18}{5} = 3\frac{3}{5}$
      c. $\frac{11}{20}$ $\frac{2}{5}$ $\frac{13}{16}$ $\frac{5}{18}$

1.06 21 pennies   12 cupcakes
      10 glasses   9 bags

1.07 15   25

1.08 $56 \div 7 = 8$ $75 = 150 \div 2$

1.09 a. subtract $18 + N = 53$
                            $18 + N (- 18) = 53 - 18$
                            $N = 35$
          divide $N \times 6 = 114$
                            $N \times 6 (\div 6) = 114 \div 6$
                            $N = 19$
      b. multiply $43 = N \div 5$
                            $43 \times 5 = N \div 5 (\times 5)$
                            $215 = N$
          add $N - 394 = 218$
                            $N - 394 (+ 394) = 218 + 394$
                            $N = 612$

1.010 1,480,282   78,367   73,600   1,228,003

1.011 143   52   305   48

1.012 ten billions   hundred millions
       ten thousands   one millions

Self Test 2

2.01 $\frac{35}{4}$ $\frac{23}{3}$ $\frac{85}{8}$ $\frac{11}{5}$

2.02 a. $7\frac{1}{2}$ $10\frac{1}{2}$ $\frac{1}{2}$
      b. $\frac{3}{4}$ $4\frac{3}{10}$ 40
      c. $\frac{10}{27}$ $1\frac{1}{9}$ 24

2.03 a. 35   7   8   16
      b. 9   15   8   24

2.04 a. $7 \times 8 \neq 6 \times 9$
      b. $18 - 9 > 16 \div 2$

2.05 even   odd   even

2.06 four-ninths   seven and two-thirds

2.07 $<$ $=$ $<$ $>$

2.08 $\frac{7}{9} = \frac{14}{18}$ $\frac{2}{3} = \frac{12}{18}$ $\frac{5}{6} = \frac{15}{18}$ $\frac{1}{2} = \frac{9}{18}$ $\frac{1}{2}$ $\frac{2}{3}$ $\frac{7}{9}$ $\frac{5}{6}$

2.09 a. $(24 + 36) + 3 = 60 + 3 = 63$
      b. $(15 + 25) + 8 = 40 + 8 = 48$
      c. $(38 + 2) + (13 + 27 = 40 + 40 = 80$
      d. $(35 + 55) + (8 + 22) = 90 + 30 = 120$

2.010 .310   .034   .215   .600   .157
       .034   .157   .215   .31   .6

2.011 a. .7   .1   .5   .7
       b. .11   .36   .67   .10

2.012 Name: <u>Cars on Freight Train</u>

2.013 2,385   19,832   111,034
       .1944   .003807   3.402

Self Test 3

3.01 a. $44\frac{4}{8} = 45$ $49\frac{2}{5} = 49$ $135\frac{5}{6} = 136$
      b. $.52\frac{1}{9} = .52$ $.7\frac{4}{7} = .8$ $.71\frac{1}{4} = .71$

3.02 .125(.13)   .666(.67)   .5   .6

3.03 a. 29,000,000   29
      b. 730,000,000,000   730

3.04 119
      941

3.05 $2,115 < 2,252 < 2,521$

3.06 14   14, 15, 16, 17   18
      25   25, 24, 23, 22   21

3.07 a.

          $2^2 \times 3$ 2×3^2

      b. $2^2, 3$ $2, 3^2$
          2^2 3^2
          —— $2^2, 3^2, 36$

3.08 $\frac{29}{36}$ $1\frac{1}{24}$ $\frac{17}{18}$ $\frac{1}{40}$ $\frac{17}{30}$ $\frac{13}{20}$

3.09 a. Five plus seven is not equal to three times six.

b. Fifteen divided by three is less than two times four.

3.010 a. $7 + 8 = 5 \times 3$

b. $4 \times 9 > 40 - 8$

3.011 116,211

$$\begin{array}{r} 64,000 \\ +52,000 \\ \hline 116,000 \end{array}$$

477,375

$$\begin{array}{r} 764,000 \\ -286,000 \\ \hline 478,000 \end{array}$$

Self Test 4

4.01 a. 49,000   6,800

b. 349,100   .45

c. .089   .0763

d. 9.38   .08502

4.02 a. 7

b. 11

c. 13

d. 1

e. 12

f. 10

g. 14

h. 4

i. 6

j. 9

k. 3

l. 2

m. 5

n. 8

4.03 a. 6   e. 4

b. 3   f. 2

c. 1   g. 5

d. 7

4.04 a. $\overline{EF} \perp \overline{RS}$

b. $\angle XYZ \cong \angle LMN$

4.05 a.

40	
2	20
2	10
2	5
5	1

$40 = 2^3 \times 5$

b.

56	
2	28
2	14
2	7
7	1

$56 = 2^3 \times 7$

c. 2^3

4.06 a. 369,000,000   369 millions

b. 526,000,000,000   526 billions

4.07 a. 800,000,000 8×10^8

b. 60,000,000,000 6×10^{10}

4.08 a. five times ten to the sixth power

b. seventy-six times ten to the third power (ten cubed)

4.09 a. $\frac{1}{6}$ $\frac{1}{3}$ $\frac{1}{2}$

b. 6   12   18

4.010 a. $\frac{11}{15}$ $9\frac{1}{8}$ $15\frac{3}{4}$ $9\frac{23}{24}$ $16\frac{3}{18} = 16\frac{1}{6}$

b. $6\frac{2}{3}$ $3\frac{4}{7}$ $3\frac{3}{5}$ $8\frac{7}{18}$ $5\frac{11}{20}$

Self Test 5

5.01 a. 1,058

b. .561

5.02 a. 10,699 $\frac{5}{6}$ 30.53 $4\frac{4}{15}$

b. 7,542 $\frac{1}{6}$ 58.46 $8\frac{9}{15} = 8\frac{3}{5}$

5.03 ordinal

5.04 $\frac{2}{3}$ $\frac{3}{8}$ 9   49

5.05 10,000   100,000   10,000,000

5.06 three and nine tenths

two and six ten thousandths

5.07 d   g   e

5.08 .3000   .5480   .0470

5.09 28.854   4.778

5.010 $(2 \times 18) + (2 \times 12) + 15 = N$

$36 \quad + \quad 24 \quad + 15 = N$

$75 \text{ boxes} = N$

5.011 $<$ $>$ $<$ $=$

5.012 a.

$\frac{1}{3} \times 4.80 = \$1.60$ model car

$\frac{1}{4} \times 4.80 = \$1.20$ glue

$\frac{1}{8} \times 4.80 = \$\ .60$ paint

$\$3.40$

$\$4.80 - \$3.40 = \$1.40$ hot dog & soda

b. 8 gallons = 32 qts.   32 qts. $\div$ 2 = 16

multiply by 16

c. $\frac{6}{20}$ $(>, =, \boxed{<})$ $\frac{8}{25}$ second day

5.013 a. $\frac{8}{12}$

b. $2^5 = 32$

c. $97 > 96 > 95$

d.

Self Test 1

1.01 $\frac{3}{12} = \frac{1}{4}$

1.02 a. $\frac{1}{3}$ 14 $\frac{1}{3}$ $3\frac{1}{3}$

     b. 6 $5\frac{1}{2}$ 9 $\frac{3}{8}$

1.03 $\frac{5}{2}$ $\frac{9}{4}$ $\frac{1}{8}$ $\frac{1}{27}$

1.04 a. 12 $\frac{1}{15}$ 16 $\frac{1}{14}$

     b. $\frac{2}{5}$ $\frac{16}{21}$ $1\frac{3}{4}$ $\frac{27}{32}$

1.05 a. $12 \div \frac{1}{4} = \frac{12}{1} \times \frac{4}{1} = 48$ people

     b. $\frac{5}{8} \div 10 = \frac{5}{8} \times \frac{1}{10} = \frac{1}{16}$ of a box

1.06 a. a center point

     b. degrees

     c. vertex

     d. protractor

1.07 a. S   b. E   c. I

1.08   Line AB is parallel to line MR.

1.09 a. $\angle$ angle – Distance between two rays with a common end points

     b. $\cong$ congruent – identical in form and size

     c. $\leftrightarrow$ line – a series of dots that has no beginning or end

     d. $\parallel$ parallel – lines the same distance apart along their entire length

     e. $\perp$ perpendicular – lines that form square corners where they meet

     f. $\rightarrow$ ray – a line with one end point

     g. — line segment – a part of a line that begins and ends with end points

1.010 a. 60°   acute

      b. 110°   obtuse

      c. 165°   obtuse

      d. 30°   acute

Self Test 2

2.01   9 $2\frac{1}{4}$ $\frac{5}{6}$ $\frac{6}{7}$

2.02

2.03 a. 12 in.   b.   14 in.
      6 sq. in.   6 sq. in.

2.04 a. P = 2L + 2W   A = L W
     b. P = 4S   A = S²

2.05 a. 26 in.   40 sq. in.
     b. 38 yd.   78 sq. yd.

2.06 a.   A = L W
          $42 = 7 \cdot N$
      $42 \div 7 = (7 \div 7) \cdot N$
       6 in. = N (width)

     b.   A = L W
          $135 = N \cdot 9$
      $135 \div 9 = N \cdot (9 \div 9)$
      15 yd. = N (length)

2.07 a.   P = 2L + 2W
        $32 = (2 \cdot 11) + (2 \cdot N)$
        $32 = 22 + (2 \cdot N)$
    $32 - 22 = (22 - 22) + (2 \cdot N)$
        $10 = 2 \cdot N$
     $10 \div 2 = (2 \div 2) \cdot N$
       5 mi. = N (width)

     b.   P = 2L + 2W
        $56 = (2 \cdot N) + (2 \cdot 13)$
        $56 = (2 \cdot N) + 26$
    $56 - 26 = (2 \cdot N) + (26 - 26)$
        $30 = 2 \cdot N$
     $30 \div 2 = (2 \div 2) \cdot N$
      15 in. = N (length)

2.08 a. P = 4S   A = S²
      $P = 4 \cdot 9$ A = 9²
      P = 36 ft.   A = 81 sq. ft.

     b. P = 4S   A = S²
      $P = 4 \cdot 13$ A = 13²
      P = 52 in.   A = 169 sq. in.

2.09 a. five and three-hundredths
      three hundred fifty-six thousandths

     b. $\frac{7}{1,000}$ $6\frac{345}{1,000}$

2.010   2.456   .02232   .23042

2.011 $.51\frac{5}{8} = .52$ $15.6\frac{2}{6} = 15.6$ $.016\frac{2}{24} = .016$

2.012   .375   .8 $.\overline{33}$ .5

2.013   5.375   12.8 $9.\overline{33}$ 7.5

2.014 $4 \div 3$ $3\overline{)4}$ $1\frac{1}{3}$ $1.\overline{33}$ 1.33…

2.015 a.   70.32   630   958
      b.   .843   8.931   .0071

Self Test 3

3.01 a. 20.9 12 3,240 $2.1\frac{5}{9} = 2.2$
     b. .2 $2.5\frac{19}{29} = 2.6$ .02 30

3.02 a. 3 b. 1 c. 4 d. 2

3.03 $439{,}268{,}735 < 493{,}628{,}735 < 934{,}628{,}735 < 943{,}268{,}375$

3.04 a. $(7 \times 5) - (9 \times 3) = 35 - 27 = 8$
     b. $(8 \times 0) + (6 + 4) = 0 + 10 = 10$

3.05 a. 360° b. 360°
     c. 180° d. 180°

3.06 a. 6 b. 4 c. 1 d. 3 e. 2 f. 5

3.07 a. base = 6 in.   height 3 in.
     b. $P = S + S + S$ $A = \frac{1}{2} B \times H$
     c. $P = 4 + 5 + 6$ $A = \frac{1}{2} B \times H$
        $P = 15$ in. $A = \frac{1}{2} (6 \times 3)$
          $A = \frac{1}{2} \times 18$
          $A = 9$ sq. in.

3.08 $\frac{8}{9} = \frac{16}{18}$ $\frac{2}{3} = \frac{12}{18}$ $\frac{13}{18} = \frac{13}{18}$ $\frac{1}{2} = \frac{9}{18}$ $\frac{5}{6} = \frac{15}{18}$
      $\frac{1}{2}$ $\frac{2}{3}$ $\frac{13}{18}$ $\frac{5}{6}$ $\frac{8}{9}$

3.09 .043 = .043, .5 = .500, .3 = .300, .38 = .380, .43 = .430
      .043, .3, .38, .43, .5

3.010 $42 \geq 42$ 35 $28 > 21$

3.011 $\frac{4}{10} = \frac{6}{15}$ $\frac{5}{9} < \frac{7}{12}$ $\frac{4}{5} < \frac{7}{8}$
       $60 = 60$ $60 < 63$ $32 < 35$

3.012
18	
2	9
3	3
3	1
$2, 3^2$

27	
3	9
3	3
3	1
3^3

3.013 $2, 3^2$ 3^3
       3^2
       9

3.014 $1\frac{5}{24}$ $1\frac{5}{12}$ $4\frac{7}{36}$ $\frac{1}{6}$ $\frac{3}{16}$ $3\frac{1}{2}$

Self Test 4

4.01 11 yr. 4 mo. 8 yd. 3 in. 37 lb. 13 oz. 28 pt.

4.02 7 da. 18 hr. 4 lb. 9 oz. 1 ft. $3\frac{4}{5}$ in. 2 yr. $5\frac{2}{3}$ mo.

4.03 a. 1 qt. 20 oz. b. 13 yd. 4 in.
      c. yes: He will use 4 lb. 15 oz. d. 15 hr.

4.04 $D = R \times T$ $A = R \times T$

4.05 a. $D = R \times T$ b. $A = R \times T$
        $D = 48 \times 5$ $A = 8.35 \times 5$
        $D = 240$ mi. $A = \$41.75$
     c. $D = R \times T$
          $177 = N \times 3$
          $177 \div 3 = N \times (3 \div 3)$
          59 mph = N (rate)
     d. $A = R \times T$
          $150 = N \times 30$
          $150 \div 30 = N \times (30 \div 30)$
          5 epm = N (rate)

4.06 5 ten millions
      6 hundred billions

4.07 5×10^6 4×10^{11}

4.08 a. 1,179 $300 + 500 + 400 = 1{,}200$
     b. 34,538 $70{,}000 - 40{,}000 = 30{,}000$
     c. 228,656 $7{,}000 \times 30 = 210{,}000$
     d. 1901 $6{,}000 \div 3 = 2{,}000$

4.09 $7 + [9 - 3 \times 2] = 7 + (9 - 6) = 7 + 3 = 10$
      $[(4 + 8) \times 3] \div 9 = (12 \times 3) \div 9 = 36 \div 9 = 4$

4.010 $49 \div 7 + 6 \times 3 = 7 + 18 = 25$
       $26 - 2 \times 8 + 13 = 26 - 16 + 13 = 23$

4.011 9   8   10

4.012 =   >   =

4.013 $\frac{2}{8} = \frac{N}{12}$
       $24 = N \cdot 8$
       $24 \div 8 = N \cdot (8 \div 8)$
       $3 = N$
       $\frac{2}{8} = \frac{1}{4}$ $\frac{3}{12} = \frac{1}{4}$

       $\frac{2}{4} = \frac{N}{10}$
       $20 = N \cdot 4$
       $20 \div 4 = N \cdot (4 \div 4)$
       $5 = N$
       $\frac{2}{4} = \frac{1}{2}$ $\frac{5}{10} = \frac{1}{2}$

       $\frac{9}{12} = \frac{N}{16}$
       $144 = N \cdot 12$
       $144 \div 12 = N \cdot (12 \div 12)$
       $12 = N$
       $\frac{9}{12} = \frac{3}{4}$ $\frac{12}{16} = \frac{3}{4}$

4.014
$$\frac{2}{5} = \frac{12}{N}$$
$$2 \cdot N = 60$$
$$(2 \div 2) \cdot N = 60 \div 2$$
$$N = 30 \text{ black pencils}$$
$$\frac{3}{4} = \frac{9}{N}$$
$$3 \cdot N = 36$$
$$(3 \div 3) \cdot N = 36 \div 3$$
$$N = 12 \text{ subtraction problems}$$

Self Test 5

5.01 $\underline{8}$ 2^3 $3\overline{)24}$ $\frac{16}{2}$

    $\underline{20}$ 20.00 $5(2^2)$ $\frac{40}{2}$

5.02   a. $\frac{3}{8} \times 24 = 9$

    b. $.41 + .05 = .46$

    c. $\overleftrightarrow{AB} \perp \overleftrightarrow{CD}$

    d. $\triangle RST \cong \triangle XYZ$

    e. $A = \frac{1}{2}BH$

    f. $8 \le 8, 10, 12, 14 < 16$

5.03 $1\frac{2}{5}$ $1\frac{2}{5} \div \frac{1}{4} = \frac{7}{5} \times \frac{4}{1} = \frac{28}{5} = 5\frac{3}{5}$

5.04   20 $\overset{5}{\cancel{20}} \times \frac{5}{\underset{2}{\cancel{8}}} = \frac{25}{2} = 12\frac{1}{2}$

5.05   a.   3 cookies   3 cookies

    b.   27 pennies   27 pennies

5.06 $\frac{4}{6} = \frac{N}{18}$

        $6 \cdot N = 72$

    $(6 \div 6)N = 72 \div 6$

        $N = 12$

    $\frac{4}{6} = \frac{2}{3}$ $\frac{12}{18} = \frac{2}{3}$

        $\frac{3}{N} = \frac{4}{12}$

        $36 = 4 \cdot N$

    $36 \div 4 = (4 \div 4) \cdot N$

        $9 = N$

    $\frac{3}{9} = \frac{1}{3}$ $\frac{4}{12} = \frac{1}{3}$

        $\frac{N}{9} = \frac{6}{27}$
        $54 = N \cdot 27$
    $54 \div 27 = N \cdot (27 \div 27)$
        $2 = N$
    $\frac{2}{9} = \frac{2}{9}$ $\frac{6}{27} = \frac{2}{9}$
        $\frac{8}{10} = \frac{12}{N}$
    $8 \cdot N = 120$
    $(8 \div 8) \cdot N = 120 \div 8$
        $N = 15$
    $\frac{8}{10} = \frac{4}{5}$ $\frac{12}{15} = \frac{4}{5}$

5.07
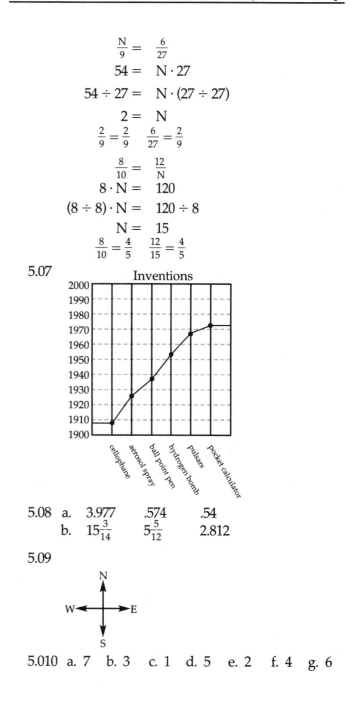

5.08   a.   3.977   .574   .54
    b. $15\frac{3}{14}$ $5\frac{5}{12}$ 2.812

5.09

5.010   a. 7   b. 3   c. 1   d. 5   e. 2   f. 4   g. 6

Self Test 1

1.01 a. 431,000,000,000,000,000,000,000
      b. 692,000,000,000,000,000,000

1.02 a. 744×10^9 b. 424×10^{12}

1.03 a. 632 quintillion
      b. 296 sextillion

1.04   426 thousand (3 zeros) $\times$ 1 billion (9 zeros) =
        426 trillion (12 zeros)

1.05 a. .5   .25   .75
      b. .2   .4   .6   .8
      c. .125   .375   .625   .875
      d. $.\overline{33}$ $.\overline{66}$ $.1\overline{66}$ $.8\overline{33}$

1.06 a. $3\frac{1}{4}$ $7.\overline{33}$ $8\frac{3}{4}$
      b. 9.4 $6\frac{1}{2}$ 11.625

1.07   (.825)

1.08 $\frac{6}{N} = \frac{2}{3}$
           $18 = 2 \cdot N$
      $18 \div 2 = (2 \div 2) \cdot N$
           $9 = N$
      _____
           $\frac{5}{N} = \frac{10}{12}$
           $60 = 10 \cdot N$
      $60 \div 10 = (10 \div 10) \cdot N$
           $6 = N$
      _____
           $\frac{3}{N} = \frac{4}{5}$
           $15 = 4 \cdot N$
      $15 \div 4 = (4 \div 4) \cdot N$
      $3\frac{3}{4} \, (3.75) = N$
      _____
           $\frac{8}{N} = \frac{2}{3}$
           $24 = 2 \cdot N$
      $24 \div 2 = (2 \div 2) \cdot N$
           $12 = N$

1.09 a. similar   b. vertex   c. vertices

1.010 a. $\frac{EF}{JK} = \frac{2}{3}$
              $\frac{2}{JK} = \frac{2}{3}$
              $6 = 2 \cdot JK$
         $6 \div 2 = (2 \div 2) \cdot JK$
              $3 = \overline{JK}$

b. $\frac{FG}{KL} = \frac{2}{3}$
        $\frac{4}{KL} = \frac{2}{3}$
        $12 = 2 \cdot KL$
   $12 \div 2 = (2 \div 2) \cdot KL$
        $6 = \overline{KL}$

c. $\frac{EG}{JL} = \frac{2}{3}$
        $\frac{5}{JL} = \frac{2}{3}$
        $15 = 2 \cdot JL$
   $15 \div 2 = (2 \div 2) \cdot JL$
   $7\frac{1}{2} \, (7.5) = \overline{JL}$

1.011 a. $\frac{AB}{RS} = \frac{6}{9} = \frac{2}{3}$ 2:3

b. $\frac{BC}{ST} = \frac{2}{3}$
        $\frac{9}{ST} = \frac{2}{3}$
        $27 = 2 \cdot ST$
   $13\frac{1}{2} \, (13.5) = \overline{ST}$

c. $\frac{AC}{RT} = \frac{2}{3}$
        $\frac{7}{RT} = \frac{2}{3}$
        $21 = 2 \cdot RT$
   $21 \div 2 = (2 \div 2) \cdot RT$
   $10\frac{1}{2} \, (10.5) = \overline{RT}$

Self Test 2

2.01 a. base 10
          10
      b. meter, liter, gram
      c. milli, kilo
      d. yard, quart, ounce
      e. 100
          1,000

2.02 0

2.03 a. 3
      b. 4
      c. 1
      d. 2

2.04

square

2.05 a. $\overline{OF} \parallel \overline{MN}$
      b. $\triangle ABC \sim \triangle XYZ$

2.06 P = Sum of sides
P = 5 + 7 + 3 + 4 + 2 + 3
P = 24 ft.

A = LW   A = LW
A = 5 · 3   A = 4 · 3
A = 15 sq. ft.   A = 12 sq. ft.
A = 15 sq. ft. + 12 sq. ft.
A = 27 sq. ft.

2.07 <   <

2.08 13 thousand 13×10^3
22 thousand   22 thousand
19 million   19 million
21 million $(7 \times 3) \times 10^6$

2.09 $30 \leq 30,\ 32,\ 34 < 36$

2.010 $2[(5 \times 35) + 43 + 48] =$
$2(175 + 43 + 48) =$
$2 \times 266 =$
532 papers

2.011 MCCCXLV

2.012 1,509

2.013 a. $45\frac{1}{8} = 45$ $76\frac{4}{5} = 77$ $318\frac{2}{3} = 319$

b. $14\frac{7}{27} = 14$ $69\frac{1}{83} = 69$

Self Test 3

3.01 a. 5   b. 1   c. 2   d. 3   e. 4
circle   circle   square   rectangle   triangle

3.02
a. square pyramid
b. triangular pyramid
c. triangular prism
d. rectangular prism

3.03

3.04 $V = L \times W \times H$

3.05 $V = L \cdot W \cdot H$
$V = 6 \times 3 \times 4$
$V = 72$ cu. ft.

3.06 $V = S^3$

3.07 $V = S^3$
$V = 5^3$
$V = 125$ cu. in.

3.08 $\frac{2}{5}$ $\frac{2}{3}$ $\frac{3}{5}$ $4\frac{1}{4}$ $4\frac{2}{3}$

3.09 a.

	60
2	30
2	15
3	5
5	1

	84
2	42
2	21
3	7
7	1

$2^2, 3, 5$ $2^2, 3, 7$

b. $2^2 \times 3 = 12$
c. $\frac{60}{84} = \frac{5}{7}$

3.010 a. $1\frac{1}{10}$ $9\frac{5}{24}$ b. 8.658
18.53
c. $\frac{1}{3}$ $2\frac{11}{12}$ d. .356   15.444
e. 6   18
f. $\frac{1}{6}$ $1\frac{3}{5}$ g. $.36\frac{4}{8} = .37$ $.41\frac{2}{9} = .41$

3.011 a. 7
b. 1
c. 11
d. 12
e. 9
f. 2
g. 5
h. 6
i. 10
j. 3
k. 4
l. 8

3.012 $C = \pi d$

3.013 $C = \pi d$
$C = 3.14 \cdot 6$
$C = 18.84$ meters

Self Test 4

4.01 a. mode   b. mean   c. median

4.02 a. 16   b. 18   c. 18

4.03   a.   9   Crew A   5, 6, 6, 7, 8   Crew B   14, 17
      b.   7   Crew A   5, 6, 6   Crew B   7, 8, 14, 17
      c.   median

4.04   a.   1,239   907   303,408 $16.\overline{33}$
      b.   16.62   5.23   26.256   .485
      c. $3.2 + 4.625 = 7.825$ $7.75 - 2.6 = 5.15$
      d. $6.25 \times 8.5 = 53.125$ $(2 \times 14) \div 9 = 3.\overline{11}$

4.05   a. $.25 \times 56 = 14$ b. $.6 + .5 = 1.1$

4.06   a. $\frac{8}{24} = \frac{1}{3} = \frac{4}{12}$ $\frac{4}{24} = \frac{1}{6} = \frac{2}{12}$
          $\frac{6}{24} = \frac{1}{4} = \frac{3}{12}$ $\frac{2}{24} = \frac{1}{12}$ $\frac{4}{24} = \frac{1}{6} = \frac{2}{12}$
      b.   12   e.   Sarah's Day
      c.   & d.

sleeping	4
eating	2
school	3
chores & homework	1
recreation	2

4.07   a. $8 \times [(6 - 3) + (12 - 5)] = 8 \times (3 + 7) =$
            $8 \times 10 = 80$
         $[(9 + 5) - (3 + 4)] \div 7 = (14 - 7)] \div 7 =$
            $7 \div 7 = 1$
      b. $4 \times 8 - 7 \times 4 + 6 \div 2 = 32 - 28 + 3 = 7$
         $35 - 2 \times 5 + 9 \div 3 + 12 =$
            $35 - 10 + 3 + 12 = 40$

Self Test 5

5.01   a.   11
      b.   7,9   plus 2, minus 1
      c.   6.301
      d. $1\frac{1}{2}$ or 1.5
      e.   69
      f.   eight and six-hundredths   12.004

5.02   a.   .800   2.300   .060   .560   2.180
      b.   .06   .56   .8   2.18   2.3

5.03   a.   9.82 $\begin{array}{r} 9.82 \\ -\ 6.28 \\ \hline 3.54 \end{array}$

      b. $8\frac{1}{3} \times \frac{3}{5} = \frac{\overset{5}{\cancel{25}}}{\cancel{3}} \times \frac{\overset{1}{\cancel{3}}}{\cancel{5}} = 5$

         $5 \div \frac{3}{5} = \frac{5}{1} \times \frac{5}{3} = \frac{25}{3} = 8\frac{1}{3}$

5.04   a. $2,900 - 2,600 = 300$ mi.
      b. $2,900 \div 10 = 290$ miles/days

5.05   a. $13 \le 13$, 17, $19 < 23$
      b. $15 \ge 15$, 14, $12 > 10$
      c.   9   1, 3, 9
          12   1, 2, 3, 4, 6, 12
      d.

	28	
2	14	
2	7	
7	1	2^2, 7

      e. $\frac{1}{4} \times 36 = 9$ inches
      f. $\frac{1}{8} + \frac{1}{8} + \frac{1}{2} = \frac{3}{4}$ gal
         1 gal. = 4 qt.
         $\frac{3}{4}$ of 4 qt. = 3 qt.
      g. $\frac{7}{7}$, $\frac{8}{14}$, $\frac{1}{4}$

5.06   a.   perpendicular
      b. $V = L \times W \times H$
         $V = 8 \times 5 \times 3$
         $V = 120$ cu. ft.
      c. $4{:}8 = \frac{4}{8} = \frac{1}{2}$ $5 \div 10 = \frac{5}{10} = \frac{1}{2}$ similar
      d. $C = \pi d$
         $C = 3.14 \times 6$
         $C = 18.84$ in.
      e.   4, 5, none

5.07   a. $D = R \times T$ b. $A = R \times T$
            $720 = R \times 12$ $A = 2 \times 30$
       $720 \div 12 = R \times 12 (\div 12)$ $A = 60$ pages
       60 mph = R

5.08   a.   3 da.   5 hr.
           6 da.   18 hr.
        + 9 da.   15 hr.
         18 da.   38 hr.   = 19 da. 14 hr.
      b. $36 \times 4 = 144$ in.
             18 lengths
           $8\overline{)144}$

5.09   2,709

5.010 a.   to measure the large distances in space
       b.   light travelling six trillion miles in
            one year
       c.   suggested answer - distance to a star

5.011 a.   580   25 $1,600
       b.   7.08   .05 $3.40

Self Test 1

1.01 a. 4.6   2.0   .3   29.5
     b. 6.10   .29   41.04   6.29

1.02   6   18   242   14

1.03 a. 3.2   2.6   1.0
     b. .46   63.22   7.62

1.04 $64\frac{3}{6} = 65$ $104\frac{1}{9} = 104$ $126\frac{4}{5} = 127$

1.05 $14\frac{2}{28} = 14$ $46\frac{53}{63} = 47$

$$\begin{array}{r} 14 \\ \times\ 28 \\ \hline 392 \\ +\ \ 2 \\ \hline 394 \end{array} \qquad \begin{array}{r} 46 \\ \times\ 63 \\ \hline 138 \\ +\ 2760 \\ \hline 2{,}898 \\ +\ \ 53 \\ \hline 2{,}951 \end{array}$$

1.06 a. eight and three thousandths
     b. 7.034

1.07   ones   thousandths   tenths

1.08   100   1,000   10

1.09   6.906   10.31   1.89   18.66

1.010   102,312   .5622   4.0768

1.011 $.20\frac{5}{9} = .21$ $22.4\frac{2}{3} = 22.5$ $7.1\frac{33}{54} = 7.2$

1.012 a. 0, 2, 4, 6, 8
      b. 0, 5
      c. 0
      d. add up to a multiple of 3
      e. add up to a multiple of 9
      f. divisible by both 2 and 3

1.013

	2	5	10	3	9	6
459				✓	✓	
450	✓	✓	✓	✓	✓	✓
455		✓				
288	✓			✓	✓	✓
430	✓	✓	✓			
93				✓		

Self Test 2

2.01   30, 60, 105, 135

2.02   1, 3, 5, 15

2.03

		12	
	2	6	
	2	3	
	3	1	

$2^2, 3$

	15	
3	5	
5	1	

$3, 5$

		18	
	2	9	
	3	3	
	3	1	

$2, 3^2$

		24
2	12	
2	6	
2	3	
3	1	

$2^3, 3$

2.04 a. $2^2, 3$ 3, 5
          $2^2, 3, 5$
          60

     b. $2^2, 3$ 3, 5
          3
          3

2.05

	PF	PF		LCM		GCF
18/24	$2, 3^2$	$2^3, 3$	$(2^3 \cdot 3^2)$	72	(2, 3)	6

2.06 $1\frac{1}{45}$ $\frac{19}{36}$ $\frac{17}{36}$ $\frac{13}{40}$

2.07 $\frac{1}{3}$ 39   6 $1\frac{1}{7}$

2.08   .5   .4   .75   .875 $.\overline{66}$

2.09   6.6   9.25 $11.1\overline{66}$ 8.5

2.010 $\frac{7}{8}$ $\frac{1}{5}$ $\frac{1}{3}$ $\frac{3}{4}$

2.011   .875   .35   5.25   .4

2.012   6.240   .040   .600   3.800

2.013   2,730   4,500   9,000   8,020

2.014   .37   .4   .469   2.047   2.46

2.015 $\frac{1}{2} = \frac{12}{24}$ $\frac{5}{6} = \frac{20}{24}$ $\frac{5}{8} = \frac{15}{24}$ $\frac{1}{3} = \frac{8}{24}$ $\frac{3}{4} = \frac{18}{24}$

$\frac{1}{3}, \frac{1}{2}, \frac{5}{8}, \frac{3}{4}, \frac{5}{6}$

2.016   .500   .600   .625 $.\overline{333}$ .750
        $.\overline{333}$ .500   .600   .625   .750

Self Test 3

3.01 $\frac{8}{100}$ .08   8% $\frac{26}{100}$ .26   26%

3.02   36%   92%   74%

3.03   9:100 $\frac{9}{100}$ .09   38:100 $\frac{38}{100}$ .38

3.04 $.472 = .47 = 47\%$
       $.5 = .50 = 50\%$
       $.067 = .07 = 7\%$

3.05 a. .5, 50%   .25, 25%   .75, 75%
     b. .20, 20%   .40, 40%   .60, 60%   .80, 80%
     c. .125, .13, 13%   .375, .38, 38%
        .625, .63, 63%   875, .88, 88%
     d. $.\overline{33}$, .33, 33% $.\overline{66}$, .67, 67%
        $.1\overline{66}$, .17, 17% $.8\overline{33}$, .83, 83%

3.06 $.444 = .\overline{44} = 44\%$ $.714 = .71 = 71\%$
       $.10 = 10\%$

3.07 .083 = .08 = 8%   .777 = .78 = 78%
.272 = .27 = 27%

3.08 a. variable   b. inverse operations

3.09 a.
$$x \div 7 = 23$$
$$x \div 7(\cdot\ 7) = 23 \cdot 7$$
$$x = 161$$

b.
$$\frac{2}{12} = \frac{n}{18}$$
$$36 = 12 \cdot n$$
$$36 \div 12 = 12 \cdot n(\div\ 12)$$
$$3 = n$$

3.010 a. 2   b. 5

c. 6   d. 3

e. 1   f. 4

3.011 7, 18, 1, 21 - add 6
32, 9, 40, 1 - divide by 8

3.012 $a = 9$ $b = 3$

3.013 a. perimeter - length - width -
perimeter of rectangle
b. area - side - area of square
c. area - base - height - area of triangle
d. circumference - pi (3.14) - diameter
circumference of circle
e. volume - length - width - height
volume of rectangular prism
f. distance - rate - time - distance

3.014 a.
$$D = rt$$
$$310 = r \cdot 5$$
$$310 \div 5 = r \cdot 5(\div\ 5)$$
$$62 \text{ mph} = r$$

b.
$$P = 2l + 2w$$
$$80 = (2 \cdot 22) + (2 \cdot w)$$
$$80 = 44 + (2 \cdot w)$$
$$80 - 44 = 44 + (2 \cdot w) - 44$$
$$36 = 2 \cdot w$$
$$18 \text{ in.} = w$$

Self Test 4

4.01 a, a

4.02

```
        N
        ↑
W ←———+———→ E
        ↓
        S
```

4.03
$$\frac{.75}{1} = \frac{15}{x}$$
$$.75 \cdot x = 1.5$$
$$.75 \cdot x(\div\ .75) = 1.5 \div .75$$
$$x = 2 \text{ mi.}$$

4.04 a. 45°   b. 95°   c. 165°

4.05 $\frac{15}{16}$ in., $1\frac{3}{16}$ in.

4.06 $\frac{7}{8}$ in., .875 in. $1\frac{1}{4}$ in., 1.25 in.

4.07 144   9   4,840
640   1,728   27

4.08 2   81
3,200   5
2   9,680

4.09 a. 8
b. 7
c. 6
d. 2
e. 4
f. 1
g. 5
h. 3

4.010 $C = \pi d$ $C = 2\pi r$
$A = \pi r^2$

4.011 a. $C = \pi d$
$C = 3.14 \cdot 6$
$C = 18.84$ in.

radius = 3 in.
$A = \pi r^2$
$A = 3.14 \cdot 3^2$
$A = 3.14 \cdot 9$
$A = 28.26$ sq. in.

b. diameter = 10 in.
$C = \pi d$
$C = 3.14 \cdot 10$ $C = \pi r$
$C = 31.4$ in.   or $C = 2 \cdot 3.14 \cdot 5$
$C = 31.4$ in.
$A = \pi r^2$
$A = 3.14 \cdot 5^2$
$A = 3.14 \cdot 25$
$A = 78.5$ sq. in.

4.012 divide   divide   multiply

4.013 100   1,000   10

4.014 70   .038   490   .604

4.015 80   5,000   .7   90

4.016 a. 10 $\frac{1}{10}$ .1   1

      b. $\frac{7}{10}$ .7   7

4.017   7 L 6 dL   2m 25 cm   7g 8mg
                  or
           2m 2dm 5 cm

Self Test 5

5.01   a. 8, 12, 6   3, 7
          Suggested answers b, c, d, h
      b. 3, 6, 9, 15 - multiples of 3
      c. ninth
      d. $\frac{3}{9}$ 3:12
      e. $6 \le 6, 7, 8, 9 < 12$
      f. VI   XV
      g. $3^2, 2^3$
      h. 9, 8, 12, 6, 15

5.02 $.10
       $.15
       $.50
       $.25

5.03   a. A.M., P.M.
      b. 1 to 24
      c. 8:40 A.M.   9:02 P.M.   1:30 P.M.   3:00 A.M.
      d. 20.24   3.00   12.23   11.37
      e. minute
         minutes
         minutes
      f. fifty-eight degrees, seven minutes
         ninety-four degrees, forty-one minutes

5.04   a. $5:8 = \frac{5}{8} = .625 = 63\%$
      b. $6:20 = \frac{6}{20} = \frac{3}{10} = .30 = 30\%$
      c. $8:32 = \frac{8}{32} = \frac{1}{4} = .25 = 25\%$

5.05   a. $20 - [5.26 + (2 \times 5.26)] = n$
        $20 - (5.26 + 10.52) = n$
        $20 - 15.78 = n$
        $\$4.22 = n$
      b. $135 - [(\frac{1}{5} \times 135) + (\frac{1}{3} \times 135)] = n$
        $135 - (27 + 45) = n$
        $135 - 72 = n$
        63 pages $= n$

5.06   a. a = Bette   a + 8 = Teri
          a + a + 8 = 60
            2a + 8 = 60
       2a + 8(− 8) = 60 − 8
              2a = 52
                a = 26 min.
          a + 8 = 34 min.

      b. a = Caleb   2a = Michael
          a + 2a = 48
             3a = 48
             a = 16 min.
          2a = 32 min.

5.07   a. 1,001 $8\frac{1}{12}$ 20.06   15.66
      b. 2,128 $2\frac{7}{20}$ $7\frac{1}{7}$ $2\frac{5}{6}$ 4.75
      c. 1.841   10   3   4.09
          $\frac{1}{18}$ $1\frac{3}{4}$

Math 607 Self Test Key

Self Test 1

1.01 a. millions   5,000,000
     b. trillions   9,000,000,000,000

1.02 a. two hundred eighty-five billion
     b. nine hundred fifty-six million

1.03 a. $(3 \times 1,000,000) + (2 \times 100,000) + (3 \times 10,000)$
        $+ (5 \times 1,000) + (6 \times 100) + (9 \times 10) + (8 \times 1)$
     b. $(3 \times 10^6) + (2 \times 10^5) + (3 \times 10^4) + (5 \times 10^3)$
        $+ (6 \times 10^2) + (9 \times 10^1) + (8 \times 10^0)$

1.04   110
     $- 22 = 88$ (-1)   5
       $- 22 = 66$ (-2) $22\overline{)110}$
         $- 22 = 44$ (-3)
           $- 22 = 22$ (-4)
             $22 = 0$ (-5) 5 children

1.05 14, 9, 18 - subtract 6
      32, 72, 16 - divide by 8

1.06 0, 1, 2, 3, 4
      (2,0) (3,1) (4,2) (5,3) (6,4)

1.07 a. 11, 22, 33, 44, 55, 66, 77, 88, 99, 110, 121, 132
     b. 12, 24, 36, 48, 60, 72, 84, 96, 108, 120, 132, 144

1.08 three squared
      3 is the square root of 9
      9 is the square of 3

1.09 9, 16, 25, 36, 49, 64, 81, 100, 121, 144

1.010 12, 11, 10, 9, 8, 7, 6, 5, 4, 3

1.011 $A = s^2$
       8 ft.

1.012 a. C   13   b. D   55
       c. C   12   d. A   42

1.013 a. $7(3 + 5) = 56$ b. $4(9 + 7) = 64$

1.014 20, 40, 60, 80, 100, 120, 140, 160, 180

1.015 $52\frac{5}{7} = 53$ $1{,}356\frac{2}{4} = 1{,}357$
       $21\frac{5}{28} = 21$ $89\frac{36}{41} = 90$

Self Test 2

2.01 a. whole number
     b. $+ , -$
     c. neither

2.02 a. +2   -4
     b. -1   5

2.03 a. 5   1   +5
     b. -3   -3   -1

2.04 a. x   y
     b. point of origin

2.05 a. P, N
     b. P, N

2.06 a. P   4
        N   3
       B
     b. N   1
       P   5
       C

2.07 a. (15)   8   (7 ft.)
     b. (13)   19   -6°F

2.08 a. $(2 \times 5) \times (7 \times 8) = 10 \times 56 = 560$
     b. $(13 + 37) + (24 + 16) = 50 + 40 = 90$

2.09 a. 28,755   b. 411,372   c. 235,083

2.010 8   100   eight-hundredths
       4   9   four-ninths or four out of nine

2.011

1:2	.5	50%	3:4	.75	75%
1:5	.2	20%	4:5	.8	80%
3:8	.375	38%	7:8	.875	88%
2:3	.$\overline{66}$	67%	1:6	.1$\overline{66}$	17%

2.012 a. 25%
     b. $\frac{1}{5}$
     c. 6:10 or 3:5
     d. .375

2.013 a. $18\% + 36\% = 54\%$
     b. $10\% \times 6 = 60\%$
     c. $(82\% + 93\% + 86\%) \div 3 = 87\%$

Self Test 3

3.01 $\frac{2}{5} = \frac{x}{25}$ (red)
                     (black)
           $50 = 5x$
       $50 \div 5 = 5x(\div 5)$
           $10 = x$ red pencils

3.02   a.   6

b. $3:6 = \frac{3}{6} = \frac{1}{2}$; $2:6 = \frac{2}{6} = \frac{1}{3}$; $1:6 = \frac{1}{6}$

c. $\frac{1}{2} = \frac{x}{36}$ (chocolate) (total)

$36 = 2x$

$36 \div 2 = 2x(\div 2)$

$18 = x$ (chocolate)

d. $\frac{1}{3} = \frac{x}{36}$ (sugar) (total)

$36 = 3x$

$36 \div 3 = 3x(\div 3)$

$12 = x$ (sugar)

e. $\frac{1}{6} = \frac{x}{36}$ (ginger) (total)

$36 = 6x$

$36 \div 6 = 6x(\div 6)$

$6 = x$ (ginger)

f. $18 + 12 + 6 = 36$ or 3 doz.   yes

3.03   a. $\frac{4}{5} = \frac{5}{x}$ (RS) (MN)

$25 = 4x$

$25 \div 4 = 4x(\div 4)$

$6\frac{1}{4}(6.25)$ in. $= x$ (MN)

b. $\frac{4}{5} = \frac{8}{x}$ (SD) (NO)

$40 = 4x$

$40 \div 4 = 4x(\div 4)$

10 in. $= x$ (NO)

c. $\frac{4}{5} = \frac{6}{x}$ (RD) (MO)

$4x = 30$

$4x(\div 4) = 30 \div 4$

$x = 7\frac{1}{2}$ (7.5) in.

3.04   a.   tr

b.   re

c.   ro

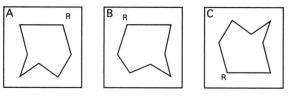

3.05

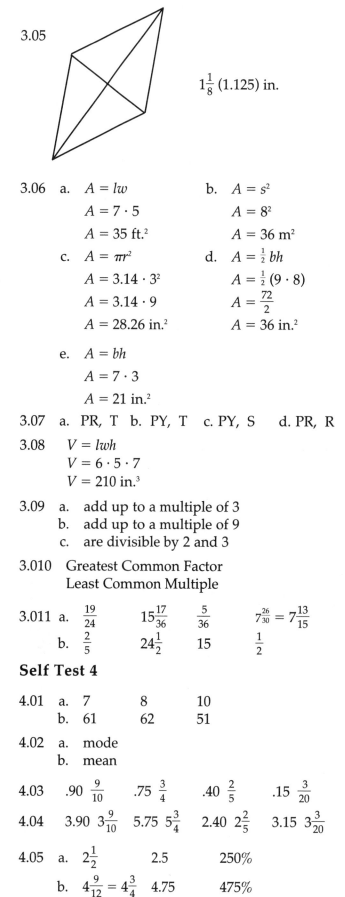

$1\frac{1}{8}$ (1.125) in.

3.06   a. $A = lw$ b. $A = s^2$

$A = 7 \cdot 5$ $A = 8^2$

$A = 35$ ft.^{2} $A = 36$ m^2

c. $A = \pi r^2$ d. $A = \frac{1}{2} bh$

$A = 3.14 \cdot 3^2$ $A = \frac{1}{2}(9 \cdot 8)$

$A = 3.14 \cdot 9$ $A = \frac{72}{2}$

$A = 28.26$ in.^{2} $A = 36$ in.^{2}

e. $A = bh$

$A = 7 \cdot 3$

$A = 21$ in.^{2}

3.07   a. PR, T   b. PY, T   c. PY, S   d. PR, R

3.08 $V = lwh$

$V = 6 \cdot 5 \cdot 7$

$V = 210$ in.^{3}

3.09   a.   add up to a multiple of 3

b.   add up to a multiple of 9

c.   are divisible by 2 and 3

3.010   Greatest Common Factor

Least Common Multiple

3.011   a. $\frac{19}{24}$ $15\frac{17}{36}$ $\frac{5}{36}$ $7\frac{26}{30} = 7\frac{13}{15}$

b. $\frac{2}{5}$ $24\frac{1}{2}$ 15 $\frac{1}{2}$

Self Test 4

4.01   a.   7   8   10

b.   61   62   51

4.02   a.   mode

b.   mean

4.03   .90 $\frac{9}{10}$ .75 $\frac{3}{4}$ .40 $\frac{2}{5}$ .15 $\frac{3}{20}$

4.04   3.90 $3\frac{9}{10}$ 5.75 $5\frac{3}{4}$ 2.40 $2\frac{2}{5}$ 3.15 $3\frac{3}{20}$

4.05   a. $2\frac{1}{2}$ 2.5   250%

b. $4\frac{9}{12} = 4\frac{3}{4}$ 4.75   475%

4.06   a. $.\overline{333}$ $.\overline{666}$ $.1\overline{66}$ $.8\overline{33}$

        b.   .125   .375   .625   .875

4.07   a.   33%   67%   17%   83%

        b.   12.5% $12\frac{1}{2}\%$ 37.5% $37\frac{1}{2}\%$

             62.5% $62\frac{1}{2}\%$ 87.5% $87\frac{1}{2}\%$

4.08   a.   5.4   15.96   52

        b. $\frac{2}{\cancel{3}} \times \frac{\overset{3}{\cancel{9}}}{1} = 6$ $\frac{1}{\cancel{4}} \times \frac{\overset{6}{\cancel{24}}}{1} = 6$ $\frac{1}{\cancel{8}} \times \frac{\overset{4}{\cancel{32}}}{1} = 4$

4.09   a.   27 subscriptions

        b.   15 cars

4.010   =   =   >   ≤ , <

4.011   × , ×   − , +

4.012 $\overrightarrow{MN} \parallel \overleftrightarrow{XY}$

4.013 $6 \times [8 + (3 \times 4)]$ 4   430

          $6 \times (8 + 12)$

            6×20

             120

4.014   4 4×0 Suggested: $8 \div 2$

4.015   16   144   640   10

4.016   5 ft. 13 in. = 6 ft. 1 in.

         3 wk 5 da.

         12 qt. 3 pt. = 13 qt. 1 pt.

         1 gal. $\frac{2}{5}$ qt.

4.017   34.778   24.85   .584   70

Self Test 5

5.01 $\frac{1}{2}$ .5 $\frac{5}{6}$ .8$\overline{33}$ $\frac{2}{5}$ .4 $\frac{5}{8}$ .625

5.02   1.275   .875   .175   1.6

5.03   15   11   20   24, 56, 32

5.04   Suggested Answers:

        $11 - 3 = 8$ $5 + 9 = 14$ $30 \div 6 = 5$ $3 \times 9 = 27$

5.05

                2, 2, 3, 3 or 2^2, 3^2

5.06 $x - 239 = 168$

     $x - 239(+ 239) = 168 + 239$

                $x = 407$

5.07   a.   154.6   35   b.   3.6   72,004

5.08   4.600   4.680   .067   .060   4.060

        .06   .067   4.06   4.6   4.68

5.09   75%   54%   100%   40%

5.010   mm   cg   dm   L   kg

5.011   multiply divide

5.012   5   4

        5   625

5.013   a.   24

        b.   15°

        c.   longitude

        d.   meridian

        e.   Prime Meridian

        f.   International Date Line

        g.   6

        h.   Possible Answers:

             Eastern, Central, Mountain, Pacific,

                   Alaskan, Hawaiian

        i.   eastern

        j.   no

5.014   a.   4, 6

        b.   1, 8

        c.   3, 5

        d.   2, 7

5.015   Suggested Answers:

        a.   Sixth Grade Favorite Vegetables

        b.   10

        c.   Teacher check

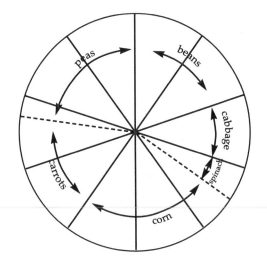

Self Test 1

1.01 a. three hundred eighty-seven million
b. five hundred eighty-six billion
c. six hundred one trillion

1.02 a. seven and four-fifths
five cubed (or to the third power)
b. sixteen and four-tenths percent
ten to the fifth power
c. eight-hundredths
negative nine
six out of eight

1.03 $(2 \times 1,000,000) + (1 \times 100,000) + (6 \times 10,000)$
$+ (8 \times 1,000) + (3 \times 100) + (9 \times 10) + (2 \times 1)$

1.04 a. 3   5   b. 10   4
3   243   10   10,000

1.05 $(5 \times 10^{10}) + (6 \times 10^9) + (3 \times 10^8) + (9 \times 10^7) +$
$(2 \times 10^6) + (1 \times 10^5) + (8 \times 10^4) + (0 \times 10^3) +$
$(9 \times 10^2) + (7 \times 10^1) + (4 \times 10^0)$

1.06 a.
```
   56        56     b.   98       98
   56      × 4          98      × 3
   56       224        + 98      294
 + 56                   294
  224
```

1.07 a.
```
   104                        4
(1)− 26                 26)104
     78                    104
(2) − 26                     0
      52
(3) − 26
      26
(4) − 26
       0
```
b.
```
   105                        3
(1)− 35                 35)105
     70                    105
(2) − 35                     0
      35
(3) − 35
       0
```

1.08 a. whole number
b. +
c. −
d. positive
e. neither

1.09 108   99   144   120   121   132

1.010 4   -2   -6

1.011 negative

1.012 3   -7   -2   2   9   -7

1.013 25   144   49

1.014 9   64

1.015 a. A 14   C 56
b. D 44   C 44

1.016 $9(3 + 2) = 45$

1.017 a. 29   14
b. 70% $1\frac{4}{15}$ $17\frac{7}{24}$ 9.708   3.53
2
c. 872,184
25 da. 30 hr. = 26 da. 6 hr.
25 gal. 5 qt. = 26 gal 1 qt.
6.2 L

Self Test 2

2.01 a. 9
b. 8
c. 7
d. 1
e. 3
f. 5
g. 4
h. 2
i. 6

2.02 a. 10
b. C - 2, E - 3, M - 1, O - 1, P - 1, N - 1, T - 1
c. C - 2:10, E - 3:10, M - 1:10, O - 1:10,
P - 1:10, N - 1:10, T - 1:10
d. E   M, O, P, N, T
e. E, C, M, O, P, N, T
f. yes, 1:9, yes
g. no

2.03 a. C - 20%, E - 30%, M - 10%, O - 10%,
P - 10%, N - 10%, T - 10%
b. 7
c. 0 - 30% by 5's

179

2.04 a. quartz - 4:20 = 2:10
turquoise - 2:20 = 1:10
mica - 8:20 = 4:10
silica - 6:20 = 3:10
b. 1:10

2.05 a. 10
b. 4 kinds of rocks
4 colors
c. & d. see graph

2.06 a. 10
b. variety - 1:10, magic - 3:10, puppet - 1:10,
catch/throw - 2:10, stories - 3:10

c. variety - $\frac{1}{10} = \frac{10}{100}$ 10 votes
magic - $\frac{3}{10} = \frac{30}{100}$ 30 votes
puppet - $\frac{1}{10} = \frac{10}{100}$ 10 votes
catch/throw - $\frac{2}{10} = \frac{20}{100}$ 20 votes
stories - $\frac{3}{10} = \frac{30}{100}$ 30 votes

2.07 a. 3,844   77   1.44
b. $8\frac{11}{20}$ $5\frac{1}{8}$ 27%   4.74
c. 4.2 dg   4 ft. 8 in.   3 wk. 5 da.

Self Test 3

3.01 a. 10
b. meter - yard, liter - quart, gram - ounce
c. any three
milli, centi, deci, deca, hecto, kilo

3.02 a. 4   3   5   7   8   2   6
b. 4   3   5   7   8   2   6

3.03

	kilo	hecto	deca	meter	deci	centi	milli
a.			3	5	2		
b.	4	6	7				
c.					9	7	8

3.04 a. D   D   M
b. 100   1,000   1,000
c. 3,400 mg   5,200 m   3 dL
.2 kL   2,400 mg   7,400 mm

3.05 a. 40.64 cm   8.226 m
b. 20.917 km   22.86 cm

3.06 11.627 qt.   8.668 in.
299.8256 lb.   .4942 oz.

3.07 –5°C   74°F

3.08 a. 1, 2,④ 8   8, 16,㉔ 32, 40, …
1, 2, 3,④ 6, 12   12,㉔ 36, 48, …
b. 1, 2,③ 6   6, 12, 18, 24,㉚ 36, 42 …
1,③ 5, 15   15,㉚ 45, 60, …

3.09

	8		
2	4		2^3
2	2		
2	1		

	20		
2	10		$2^2, 5$
2	5		
5	1		

3.010 2^3 $2^2, 5$
2^2
4

3.011 2^3 $2^2, 5$
$2^3, 5$
40

3.012 $\frac{43}{40} = 1\frac{3}{40}$ $\frac{7}{18}$ $\frac{5}{16}$ $\frac{5}{4} = 1\frac{1}{4}$

3.013 a. .30   165,594
36 yd. 8 ft. = 38 yd. 2 ft.
130.32
b. 45   48   121   15

Self Test 4

4.01 a. $\frac{6}{24} = \frac{1}{4}$ $\frac{8}{20} = \frac{2}{5}$ $\frac{9}{21} = \frac{3}{7}$
b. $\frac{18}{54} = \frac{1}{3}$

4.02 a. 6   12 $13\frac{3}{4}$ or 13.75
b. $\frac{1}{4} \times 9 = \frac{9}{4} = 2\frac{1}{4}$ 2 whole bars $\frac{1}{4}$ bar

4.03 a. 12, 12
b. 25, 25
c. 21, 21
d. 32, 32

4.04 a. 10   32.8   7.2
b. $\frac{2}{3} \times 21 = 14$ people
c. .25 × 80 = 20 planes
d. .76 × 50 = 38 students

4.05 40, 40
50, 50
36, 36

4.06 3:4   .75   75%
2:5   .4 or .40   40%
1:8   .125 $12\frac{1}{2}\%$ or 13%
5:6   .833   83%

4.07 4:16 or 1:4 $\frac{1}{4}$ .25   25%

4.08 37.5% = $\frac{3}{8}$ $\frac{3}{8} \times 48 = 18$ blue shirts

4.09   a.   683,000,000

        b.   240,000000

4.010   59   7   421

4.011   a. $3.50 = 3.5$ $9.70 = 9.7$ $.700 = .7$

        b. $7.070 = 7.07$ $.4300 = .43$ $58.210 = 58.21$

4.012   5.5   .7   .13

4.013   a.   7   16 $9\frac{4}{9}$ 6   3

        b. $13\frac{13}{48} = 13$ $.11\frac{8}{27} = .11$

        c. $\frac{1}{24}$ 4

        d.   1 wk. $1\frac{3}{8}$ da.   .8 mg

            8)9 wk. 4 da.   4)3.2 mg

              8 wk. 11 da.

Self Test 5

5.01   a.   even

        b.   an even number (0, 2, 4, 6, 8)

        c.   add up to a multiple of 3

        d.   does not

5.02   a.   E, O

        b.   2, 3, 6, 9   2, 3, 5, 6, 9, 10

        c.   C   D   A

5.03   a.   37   37

             37           $\times\, 4$

             37   148

          $+\, 37$

            148

        b.   87   3

          $-\, 29$ 29)87

               58   87

            $-\, 29$ 0

                 29

              $-\, 29$

                 0

5.04   a.   7, 8, 10 - subtract 4

        b.   48, 9, 40 - divide by 8

5.05   a.   1, 6

        b.   4, 8

        c.   3, 5

        d.   2, 7

        e.   9

5.06   a. $75\% = .75 = \frac{3}{4} = 3{:}4$

        b. $\frac{3}{4}$ of 20 cm = 15 cm

        c.   3:4 (3 possibilities out of 4 throw)

5.07   a. $\frac{1}{3}$ of 42 = 14

           $\frac{2}{7}$ of 42 = 12

           14 + 12 = 26   42 − 26 = 16

           16 pieces are cherry

        b.   ($50.00 − $42.59) ÷ 3 = N

           7.41 ÷ 3 = N

           $2.47 = N (amount each boy received)

        c. $A = lw$ $A = lw$

           $A = 10 \cdot 4$ $A = 8 \cdot 6$

           $A = 40$ sq. in. $A = 48$ sq. in.

                 40:48 = 5:6

5.08   a.   9.382 $\frac{1}{15}$ 14%   3.85 $16\frac{1}{18}$

        b.   64   45   15 $1\frac{1}{5}$

        c.   2   11   14,335   59 $7\frac{43}{65}$ or 8

Self Test 1

1.01 a. one (1)
    b. zero (0)   one (1)

1.02 two hundred eighty-seven trillion

1.03 2^2, 5

	20
2	10
2	5
5	1

1.04 2, 9   3 2^3, 9   72

1.05 two squared, seven 2   28

1.06 478,000,000,000
     659,500,000,000

1.07 ten to the fourth power   10   10,000

1.08 478×10^9

1.09 a. 7:7   b. $\frac{9}{9}$
    c. 1.0   d. 100%

1.010 a. 3:4 $\frac{3}{4}$ .75%

     b. 3:5 $\frac{3}{5}$ .6

1.011 a. 247,194,638   257,491,368

       257,491,638   275,491,638

     b. $\frac{14}{20}$ $\frac{15}{20}$ $\frac{8}{20}$ $\frac{10}{20}$
       $\frac{2}{5}$ $\frac{1}{2}$ $\frac{7}{10}$ $\frac{3}{4}$

     c. 8:12   10:12   3:12   7:12
       1:4   7:12   2:3   5:6

     d. .370   .125   .400   .510
       .125   .37   .4   .51

     e. 8%   16%   42%   47%

1.012 a. ④$\frac{1}{2}$ ⑯$\frac{2}{3}$ ㉗$\frac{5}{8}$
     b. ③72   ㉙.04   ⑦0.290
     c. ②$\frac{3}{5}$ ①$\frac{3}{5}$ ②$\frac{1}{3}$
     d. ①50%   ②12%   ③25%

1.013 a. $4\frac{5}{6}$ b. $4\frac{13}{24}$ c. .33 d. 6.754

Self Test 2

2.01 a. 90.2   518   1.350 = 1.35
     b. 11.225   48.75   2.4

2.02 a. 100   10
     b. .4   200

2.03 a. 1:5
     b. 2:12 (1:6)

2.04 a. reflection
     b. $\frac{2}{8}$ $\frac{3}{12}$ $\frac{4}{16}$ $\frac{5}{20}$

     20 cones

     5 chocolate

2.05 A line has no beginning and no end.

2.06 a. 180°   straight
     b. 40°   acute
     c. 110°   obtuse
     d. 90°   right

2.07 a. 9
     b. 7
     c. 3
     d. 8
     e. 6
     f. 5
     g. 1
     h. 2
     i. 4

2.08 sphere

2.09 a. 3
     b. 5
     c. 2
     d. 6
     e. 1
     f. 4

2.010 a. ray CD   b. angle XYZ
      c. line segment MN
      d. similar   e. parallel   f. perpendicular

2.011 a. ≠   =   <
      b. >   <   <

2.012 $16 \leq 16$, 17, 18, $19 < 20$

Self Test 3

3.01 a. $y - 12 + 3 + 4 = 123$
            $y - 5 = 123$
       $y - 5(+5) = 123 + 5$
               $y = 128$ members

     b. $5 \times 12 = 18 + 2(18) + 2 + x$
            $60 = 18 + 36 + 2 + x$
              $60 = 56 + x$
        $60 - 56 = 56(-56) + x$
       4 cookies $= x$

3.02 b = black pencils
$$\frac{2}{5} = \frac{6}{b}$$
$$2b = 30$$
$$2(\div 2)b = 30 \div 2$$
$$b = 15 \text{ black pencils}$$

3.03 $\overline{MN} = 8$ in.

3.04
$$\frac{\frac{3}{4}}{\frac{3}{4}} = \frac{YZ}{FG}$$
$$\frac{\frac{3}{4}}{\frac{3}{4}} = \frac{6}{FG}$$
$$3 \, FG = 24$$
$$\overline{FG} = 8 \text{ in.}$$

3.05
24	365	10
36	5,280	9
16	16	2
2,000	27	

3.06   a. $n = [(24 \div 3) + 7] \times 2$
$n = (8 + 7) \times 2$
$n = 15 \times 2$
$n = 30$

b. $n = 6 + [3 \times (14 - 5)]$
$n = 6 + (3 \times 9)$
$n = 6 + 27$
$n = 33$

c. $8 + [n - (15 \div 3)] = 9$
$8 + (n - 5) = 9$
$8(-8) + (n - 5) = 9 - 8$
$n - 5 = 1$
$n - 5(+5) = 1 + 5$
$n = 6$

d. $n = 13 + 4 \times 3 - 16$
$n = 13 + 12 - 16$
$n = 9$

3.07   a. $P = 2l + 2w$
$P = (2 \cdot 12) + (2 \cdot 5)$
$P = 24 + 10$
$P = 34$ ft.

b. $D = rt$
$186 = r \times 6$
$186 \div 6 = r \times 6(\div 6)$
$31 \text{ mph} = r$

c. $A = s^2$
$A = 9^2$
$A = 81$ sq. in.

d. $C = \pi d$
$C = 3.14 \times 8$ in.
$C = 25.12$ in. (25 in.)

e. $A = lw$
$112 = l \times 8$
$112 \div 8 = l \times 8(\div 8)$
14 yd. $= l$

3.08 x = first night $3x$ = second night
$x + 3x = 72$
$4x = 72$
$4(\div 4) x = 72 \div 4$
$x = 18$ students
$3x = 54$ students

Self Test 4

4.01   positive and negative whole numbers

4.02   neither

4.03   a.   positive
b.   negative
c.   positive or negative
d.   positive

4.04   a.   1, 4, 8
b.   1, -14, -7

4.05   a.   ⟨$16⟩ $4 $2   ⟨$10⟩
b.   ②   7   5

4.06   a.   2, -6, -1, -3   b.   2, 6, 0, 10

4.07
-4, -2, 0, 2, 4, 6
(-6, -4); (-4, -2);
(-2, 0); (0, 2)
(2, 4); (4, 6)

4.08   norm

4.09   random sample (survey)

4.010 a. $\frac{1}{2}$ .5   50% $\frac{1}{5}$ .2   20%
b. $\frac{1}{8}$ .125   13% $\frac{1}{3}$ $.\overline{33}$ 33%

4.011   1:5 = 20% , 1:5 = 20%, 3:5 = 60%

4.012 a.   80 × 35 = 28 cookies
b.   90 × 40 = 36 books

4.013 a.   10
b.   35 , 37 , 38 , 39 , ⟨43 , 43⟩ 45 , 45 , 46 , 48
c.   6   6:10 = 60%

4.014   perfect square

4.015   25, 81, 100, 49, 121, 36

4.016   12, 4, 9, 6, 11, 8

Self Test 5

5.01   3,122   31,354   193,732   229

5.02

69	152	
69	− 38	(1)
+ 69	114	
207	− 38	(2)
	76	
	− 38	(3)
	38	
	− 38	(4)
	0	

5.03   32, 9, 12, 4 - divide by 4

5.04   74,000
        .09
        .0846
        .0382

5.05   9.542   1.82   .028 $.090\frac{1}{3}$

5.06   1, 2, 3, ④, 6, 12   1, 2, ④, 5, 20

5.07   9, 18, 27, 36, ㊺   15, 30, ㊺

5.08 $9\frac{3}{8}$ $4\frac{1}{2}$ 70   12

5.09   a. 79   1,424
        b. DXLVII   MCCCXXIX

5.010   7 lb. 17 oz. = 8 lb. 1 oz.
        3 yr. 7 mo.
        72 yd. 40 in. = 73 yd. 4 in.

5.011   a. <   =
        b. =   <

5.012   6
        80-90

"Sixth Grade
 Spelling Scores
 January and February

5.013   a. fourteenth
        b. 2,000 cars
        c.   89
            32)2,848

Self Test 1

1.01   a.   29   27
      b.   53   87
      c.   244   219
      d.   931   20,530
      e.   63   27
      f.   638   758
      g.   455   3,407
      h.   276   4,130
      i.   3,087   18,156
      j. $7\frac{1}{4}$ $53\frac{2}{5}$
      k.   213   655

1.02   a.   864
      b.   17
      c.   235
      d. $14\frac{1}{4}$

1.03   a.   1.24   .776
      b.   1.273   12.12
      c.   4.9   .54
      d.   .35   .308
      e.   3.6   2.17
      f.   .0080   1.224
      g.   .6   .201
      h. $.5\frac{5}{6}$ $8\frac{2}{7}$

1.04   a.   65   21
      b.   10.4   2

1.05   a.   32   b.   8.4
          $\times 6$ $\times 5$
         192   42.0

1.06   a.   12   30   36   48
      b.   60   240   420   540
      c.   1,200   2,400   3,000   4,800

1.07   a.   24   72   16
      b.   140   0   350
      c.   1,000   1,500   2,500

1.08   200   600   300   900   700

1.09   a.   35 R184   23 R88
      b.   11 R378   13 R215

Self Test 2

2.01

2.02   a.
      b.

2.03 $\frac{12}{12} = 1$ $\frac{6}{8} = \frac{3}{4}$ $\frac{12}{16} = \frac{3}{4}$ $\frac{12}{10} = 1\frac{2}{10} = 1\frac{1}{5}$

2.04   a.   4, 8, 12, 16, 20, 24, 28, 32, 36, …
           6, 12, 18, 24, 30, 36, …   18, 36, …
      b.   36

2.05 $1\frac{3}{10}$ $\frac{1}{12}$ $9\frac{17}{30}$ $5\frac{5}{24}$ $11\frac{3}{10}$ $4\frac{1}{2}$

2.06   a.   eight-ninths
      b.   thirteen and one-fourth
      c.   eleven-fortieths
      d.   two and five-eighths

2.07   a. $\frac{2}{5}$ 1 $\frac{4}{5}$
      b. $\frac{3}{4}$ $\frac{7}{8}$ $\frac{5}{6}$

2.08   3 $7\frac{1}{2}$ $\frac{3}{8}$ 18

2.09 $3\frac{1}{2} \div$ ⑨ $\frac{1}{9}$ $7 \div$ ⑤⁄₈ $\frac{8}{5}$ $6 \div$ ⑤⅓ $\frac{3}{16}$

2.010   20 $\frac{2}{5}$ $8\frac{3}{4}$ $\frac{2}{7}$

2.011 $37\frac{49}{100}$ $8\frac{7}{100}$ $41\frac{70}{100}$

2.012   \$12.09   \$12.67   \$1,566.72   \$2.14

2.013   a.   \$.19   \$.25   \$.58
       b.   \$4   \$16   \$7
       c.   \$300   \$300   \$9,100

2.014   a. $.33\frac{3}{9} = \$.33$ $.56\frac{1}{5} = \$.56$ $2.39\frac{2}{3} = \$2.40$

       b. $.39\frac{2}{4}$ \$.40 for one lb.
          $4\overline{)\$1.58}$ or \$1.58 ÷ 4 = \$.79

Self Test 3

3.01   < , > , <

3.02   6, 24, 4

3.03   a.   10, 11, 12   7, 8, 9
      b.   inverse operations

3.04 $2 < b < 6$
      b = 3, 4, or 5

3.05   a.   637   b.   94   c.   7 2
        $\times$ 400 $\times$ 3,000 $\times$ 2,600
      254,800   282,000   43 2
                                        144 0
                                    187,200

3.06

Area of ABCD = 20 sq. in.,
      EFGH = 20 sq. in. Total 40 sq. in.
Area of ABFE = 35 sq. in.,
      DCGH = 35 sq. in. Total 70 sq. in.
Area of ADHE = 28 sq. in.,
      BCGF = 28 sq. in. Total 56 sq. in.
              Total Surface Area 166 sq. in.

3.07   5 yd. 3 ft. = 6 yd.
       1 wk. 4 da.
       12 pt. 3 cup = 13 pt. 1 cup

$$\begin{array}{r} 9 \text{ oz.} \\ 4\overline{)36 \text{ oz.}} \end{array}$$

3.08
a.	4	7:15
b.	2	4
c.	5	NE
d.	1	4 in.
e.	6	30°
f.	3	60 mph

3.09
a. inch
b. 15   8

3.010

3.011 -1814, -1013, -512, 0, 630, 1951

3.012 C, 9   D, 77   A, 21

3.013

	2	5	10	3	9	6
135				✓	✓	
540	✓	✓	✓	✓	✓	✓

Self Test 4

4.01
a.	4:16	$\frac{1}{4}$	.25	25%
b.	35:40	$\frac{7}{8}$	.875	88%

4.02
a. 12:15 $\frac{12}{15} = \frac{4}{5}$ .8   .80%
b. 18:21 $\frac{18}{21} = \frac{6}{7}$ .85 $\frac{5}{7}$ = 86%
                             $7\overline{)6.00}$

4.03
a. line
b. April 16
    April 2
    April 30
    April 9
    April 23
c. Library Books Loaned Per Week

4.04 76 R358   57 R922   187 R120

4.05 HCS HSC CHS CSH SHC SCH

4.06 median   55 56 (59) 60 62   Trevor

4.07 5:8 = .625 $62\frac{1}{2}$% (63%)

4.08 $(6 \cdot 3) + (6 \cdot 5) = 6(3 + 5)$ $\frac{18}{2} = 9$

4.09
a.
$$93 + x = 122$$
$$93(-93) + x = 122 - 93$$
$$x = 29$$

$$(2 \cdot a) + (2 \cdot 7) = 32$$
$$2a + 14 = 32$$
$$2a + 14(-14) = 32 - 14$$
$$2a = 18$$
$$2(\div 2) \cdot a = 18 \div 2$$
$$a = 9$$

$$7b = 56$$
$$7(\div 7) \cdot b = 56 \div 7$$
$$b = 8$$

b.
$$\frac{5}{x} = \frac{4}{8}$$
$$40 = 4x$$
$$40 \div 4 = 4(\div 4) \cdot x$$
$$10 = x$$

$$\frac{2}{6} = \frac{x}{9}$$
$$18 = 6x$$
$$18 \div 6 = 6(\div 6) \cdot x$$
$$3 = x$$

$$\frac{r}{16} = \frac{10}{20}$$
$$160 = 20r$$
$$160 \div 20 = 20(\div 20) \cdot r$$
$$8 = r$$

c.
$$A = l \cdot w$$
$$18 = 6 \cdot w$$
$$18 \div 6 = 6(\div 6) \cdot w$$
$$3 \text{ in.} = w$$

d.
$$D = r \cdot t$$
$$135 = 45 \cdot t$$
$$135 \div 45 = 45(\div 45) \cdot t$$
$$3 \text{ hr.} = t$$

e.
$$P = s + s + s$$
$$22 = 7 + 9 + s$$
$$22 = 16 + s$$
$$22 - 16 = 16(-16) + s$$
$$6 \text{ cm} = s$$

f.
$$\frac{2}{3} = \frac{x}{9} \text{ (number of lawns)}$$
$$18 = 3x$$
$$18 \div 3 = 3(\div 3) \cdot x$$
$$6 \text{ lawns} = x$$

Self Test 5

5.01 a. 210

b. 6,400

5.02 300   .07   50,000,000

5.03 a. $.7 - .5 = .2$

b. $\frac{2}{3} \times \frac{9}{14} = \frac{3}{7}$

c. $4 \leq 4, 5, 6, 7 < 8$

5.04 a. 10,000

b. 2, 6, 18

c. $5\frac{1}{2}$ hr.

d. 3 months

5.05 a.

b.

c.

d. 180°   360°   360°

5.06
$$6 = 75\% \text{ of } x$$
$$6 = \frac{3}{4} \cdot x$$
$$6 \times 4 = (4 \cdot \frac{3}{4}) \cdot x$$
$$24 = 3x$$
$$24 \div 3 = 3(\div 3) \cdot x$$
$$8 \text{ students} = x$$

5.07 a. 4 cm

b. 40 mm

5.08 700   60   25   3,000%   4,000,000   8,200
.7   .06 $\frac{1}{40}$ or .025   3%   4,000   8.2

5.09 a. $\frac{1}{4} \times 1.\overset{.25}{00} = \$.25$

b. $\$100 - (\$30 - \$7 - \$.06) =$
$\$100 - \$22.94 = \$77.06$

c. $\frac{.4}{4.5.\overline{)\$1.8.0}} = 40¢$
$\underline{1\,8\,0}$

d. $7\overline{)\$10.00} \quad 1.42\frac{6}{7} = \$1.43$

e. 3 people

5.010 a. $1\frac{7}{8}$ 7 da. 9 hr.   104%

b. $.23 $10.63   2 ft.

LIFEPAC TEST 601

1. a. 0, 1, 2, 3, 4, 5, 6, 7, 8, 9
   b. as a place holder

2. a. five hundred eighty-six thousand
   b. twenty-three billion

3. a. 56, 92 b. 29, 71
   c. 3, 61 d. 7th, 21st
   e. 2, 17 f. 9, 15

4. a. $=$ $\neq$
   b. $<$ $>$

5. $-$, $\times$ $\div$, $\times$

6. $6 \times 7 = 42$ - $7 \times 6 = 42$
   $42 \div 6 = 7$ - $42 \div 7 = 6$

7. a. 269
   b. 46
   c. 2,408
   d. 5

8. a. 1,506
```
(a) 1,506
     − 765
      741
     − 432
      309
     − 309
        0
```
   b. 4,409
```
(b) 5,438
   + 4,409
     9,847
```
   c. 1,767
```
(c)    57
    31)1,767

       31
    57)1,767
```
   d. 81 R7
```
(d)    81
      × 9
      729
      + 7
      736
```

9. 599,808   750,26012 R10 42 R10

10. 1, 2,④ 8   and   1, 2, 3,④ 6, 12

11. 24   48   16   48

12. c   b   a

13. a. seven and five-eighths $\frac{15}{16}$
    b. one-third $4\frac{1}{2}$

14. 8 5   4

15. a. $\frac{8}{8} = 1$ $1\frac{8}{15}$ $\frac{16}{10} = 1\frac{6}{10} = 1\frac{3}{5}$ $\frac{7}{9}$ $\frac{16}{24} = \frac{2}{3}$
    b. $\frac{6}{12} = \frac{1}{2}$ $\frac{8}{14} = \frac{4}{7}$ $\frac{2}{8} = \frac{1}{4}$ $\frac{4}{16} = \frac{1}{4}$ $\frac{4}{6} = \frac{2}{3}$

16. a. five hundredths
    six and three-tenths
    b. seven thousandths
    four hundred seven thousandths

17. .700 .532 .040 .731 .720
    .04 .532 .7 .72 .731

18. a. 3.527 51.47 6.182
    b. 5.34 2.37 4.406

19. a. $10,000 - 8,000 = 2,000$ sq. mi.
    b. $40 \times 20 = 800$ cookies
    c. $40 + 60 + 20 + 30 + 40 = 190$
       $190 \div 5 = 38$ plants

20. a. $8 \times 5 = 40$ $64 \div 8 = 8$
    b. $14 + 6 + 0 = 20$ $36 - 13 - 9 = 14$

21. a. $N + 57 = 93$
       $N + 57(-57) = 93 - 57$
                $N = 36$
           $36 + 57 = 93$
    b. $N - 69 = 87$
       $N - 69(+69) = 87 + 69$
                $N = 156$
           $156 - 69 = 87$

22. 33, 36, ...
    plus 6, plus 3

LIFEPAC TEST 602

1. three hundred fifteen billion, seven hundred twenty-seven million, six hundred thirty thousand, four

2. $\neq$ $>$ $=$ $<$

3. 8,602   9,342   139,650   130 R4   134 R2

4. 28,000,000,000; 46,000,000,000; 31,000,000,000
   28, 46, 31, 105

5. 286.   3,794.   8.   629,307.

6. E   E   O   E   E   O

7. $\frac{2}{3}$ 1 $1\frac{2}{3}$

8. $\frac{7}{7}$

9. a. $\frac{1}{4}$ b. $\frac{1}{4}$

10. a. $7\frac{1}{2}$ $8\frac{1}{3}$ $5\frac{5}{8}$ $\frac{23}{36}$ $1\frac{7}{40}$

   b. $7\frac{5}{8}$ $13\frac{3}{10}$ $8\frac{1}{3}$ $5\frac{5}{7}$ $8\frac{7}{9}$ $1\frac{1}{2}$

11. a. $\frac{7}{18},\frac{9}{18},\frac{12}{18},\frac{10}{18}$

   b. $\frac{7}{18},\frac{1}{2},\frac{5}{9},\frac{2}{3}$

12. a. three tenths - .3 - $\frac{3}{10}$ - .30

   b. three hundredths - .03 - $\frac{3}{100}$ - .030

   c. three thousandths - .003 - $\frac{3}{1,000}$ - .0030

13. a. 5.473   12.367   .045
    b. .068   .0504   25.848

14. a. 1, 2, 3, 6, 9, 18
    b. Suggested answers - 7, 14, 21, 28, 35, 42

15. $21 - 8 = 13$ $3 + 7 = 10$ $8 - 6 = 2$ $9 \times 0 = 0$

16. Eight plus three is greater than twelve minus two.
    $2 \times 5 \neq 12 \div 1$

17. $N + 49(- 49) = 67 - 49$
    $N = 18$
    $18 + 49 = 67$

    $314(- 148) = N + 148(- 148)$
    $166 = N$
    $314 = 166 + 148$

    $N - 36(+ 36) = 61 + 36$
    $N = 97$
    $97 - 36 = 61$

$275 + 180 = N - 180(+ 180)$
$455 = N$
$275 = 455 - 180$

18. a. 16   9   12
    b. 12   10   4
    c. 36   8   7
    d. 88 minutes

19. 2, 3   3, 2 $2^3, 3^2$ $(8 \times 9)\,72$

20. a. two to the fourth power   2   16
    b. ten cubed   10   1,000

21. $2^2 \times 3^2 \times 5$

	180
2	90
2	45
3	15
3	5
5	1

LIFEPAC 603

1. .2   .3   .6   .8   .9

2. .320, .207, .500, .020, .460 .02, .207, .32, .46, .5

3. eight and five hundredths

4. a. 3.722   b. 4.769   c. .00144

5. a. 5 b. 3   c. 5
   d. 125   e. five cubed or
   five to the third power

6.

	12
2	6
2	3
3	1

2^2, 3

	18
2	9
3	3
3	1

2, 3^2

7. 2^2, 3   2, 3^2
   2^2, 3^2
   2^2, 3^2, 36

8. Circled: $5 \cdot 9 = 45$ $2^3 = 8$

9. $12 + 9 = N$ $21 = N$
   $35 - 16 = N$ $19 = N$
   $11 + 32 = N$ $43 = N$
   $8 + 2 = N$ $10 = N$

10. $N \times 6 (\div 6) = 108 \div 6$
       $N = 18$
       $18 \times 6 = 108$

       $N \div 9 (\times 9) = 13 \times 9$
       $N = 117$
       $117 \div 9 = 13$

11. $=$ $6 \times 12 = 72$ $9 \times 8 = 72$
       $<$ $7 \times 5 = 35$ $4 \times 9 = 36$

12. $.42\frac{6}{7} = .43$ .625

13. three and four-fifths

14. $\frac{15}{20}, \frac{10}{20}, \frac{18}{20}, \frac{16}{20}$ $\frac{1}{2}, \frac{3}{4}, \frac{4}{5}, \frac{9}{10}$

15. a. $\frac{3}{18} = \frac{1}{6}$ $\frac{6}{18} = \frac{1}{3}$ $\frac{9}{18} = \frac{1}{2}$

    b. $\frac{1}{6} = \frac{④}{24}$ $\frac{1}{3} = \frac{⑧}{24}$ $\frac{1}{2} = \frac{⑫}{24}$

16. $15\frac{3}{40}$ $7\frac{2}{5}$ 21   42 $\frac{5}{24}$
    3   7   45

17. a. 5
    b. 10
    c. 8
    d. 2
    e. 3
    f. 7
    g. 9
    h. 1
    i. 4
    j. 6

18. Name: <u>Drinks Sold at Game</u>

19. a. $(37 + 13) + 5 = 50 + 5 = 55$
    b. $6 + (18 + 32) = 6 + 50 = 56$

20. 3 yd.   84 da.   20 qt.
    4 decades   2 lb.

21. 15

22. 3,700   50.8   .16   .00406

23. $29\frac{5}{8} = 30$ $188\frac{2}{5} = 188$ $24\frac{15}{23} = 25$ $14\frac{10}{42} = 14$

24. a.   9, 10, 11
    b.   16, 14, 12

25. 400,000,000,000
    four hundred billions
    4×10^{11}

26. 6,788   4,000   5,121   8,000
           + 3,000   − 3,000
             7,000   5,000

LIFEPAC 604

1. 4.719   4.71   1.476   .47112

2. 642   800   9.43   .005

3. $6.1\frac{2}{6} = 6.1$ $2.15\frac{3}{4} = 2.16$ $31.4\frac{1}{3} = 31.4$ $3.65\frac{1}{2} = 3.66$

4. .413   .300   .430   .320
    .3   .32   .413   .43

5. a. $1\frac{5}{24}$ $10\frac{19}{20}$ $5\frac{1}{24}$ $1\frac{5}{6}$
    b. $\frac{4}{15}$ 20   3 $2\frac{1}{4}$

6. $\frac{10}{12}$ $\frac{8}{12}$ $\frac{6}{12}$ $\frac{9}{12}$
    $\frac{1}{2}$ $\frac{2}{3}$ $\frac{3}{4}$ $\frac{5}{6}$

7. a. .625   b. $.\overline{33}$

8. a. >   =
    b. N = 6   N = 25

9. 64   32   25   81

10.

	18
2	9
3	3
3	1

2, 3²

	27
3	9
3	3
3	1

3³

11. 2, 3²   3³
    3²
    9

12. a. S   b. E   c. I

13. a. 140°   obtuse
    b. 25°   acute
    c. 90°   right

14. 12 (linear) in.   5 sq. in.

15. a. 8
    b. 3
    c. 1
    d. 5
    e. 7
    f. 4
    g. 2
    h. 6

16. a. $A = \frac{1}{2}BH$ A = 18 sq. in.
    b. $D = R \times T$ D = 312 mi.
    c. $A = LW$ W = 5 yd.

17. $[(8 \times 5) \div 10] + 15 = (40 \div 10) + 15 =$
    $4 + 15 = 19$
    $6 \times [5 + (2 + 2)] = 6 \times (5 + 4) = 6 \times 9 = 54$
    $4 \times 3 + 12 \div 6 = 12 + 2 = 14$
    $35 - 6 \times 5 + 9 = 35 - 30 + 9 = 5 + 9 = 14$

18. a. $\frac{2}{5} = \frac{N}{15}$ (pennies) (dimes)
    $30 = N \times 5$
    $30 \div 5 = N \times (5 \div 5)$
    $6 = N$
    b. $\frac{2}{5} = \frac{12}{N}$ (pennies) (dimes)
    $2 \times N = 60$
    $(2 \div 2) \times N = 60 \div 2$
    $N = 30$

19. 12 ≤ 12, 14, 16 < 18

20. 8 lb. 20 oz. = 9 lb. 4 oz.

21. 4 wk. 5 da.

22. $\begin{array}{r} 4 \text{ pt } 1\frac{1}{2} \text{ cup} \\ 2\overline{)9 \text{ pt. } 1 \text{ cup}} \\ 8 \text{ pt. } 3 \text{ cup} \end{array}$

23. actual - 1,470   estimated - 1,500

LIFEPAC 605

1. a. 832,000,000,000,000
    b. 431,000,000,000,000,000

2. a. 369×10^9
    b. 575 trillions

3. light-year

4. a. 91
    $$\begin{array}{r} 91 \\ -15 \\ \hline 76 \\ -27 \\ \hline 49 \\ -49 \\ \hline 0 \end{array}$$

    b. 644
    $$\begin{array}{r} 179 \\ +644 \\ \hline 823 \end{array}$$

    c. 1,431
    $$27\overline{)1{,}431} \quad 53$$

    d. 49
    $$\begin{array}{r} 49 \\ \times 8 \\ \hline 392 \end{array}$$

5. a. 510   224,202   2.71
    b. .5
        $6.5 + 5.875 = 12.375$
        $3.2 \times 4.25 = 13.6$

6. a. 4
    b. 1
    c. 5
    d. 3
    e. 2

7. a. 74   b. 1,709   c. XXXVII   d. DCXCIII

8. a. .5   .25   .75 $.\overline{4}$ $.\overline{8}$
    b. .125   .375   .625 $.\overline{33}$ $.\overline{166}$

9. a. 7
    b. 8
    c. 4
    d. 1
    e. 3
    f. 2
    g. 6
    h. 5

10. $C = \pi d$
    $C = 3.14 \times 8$
    $C = 25.12$ in.

11. 26 in. $A = L \times W$ $A = L \times W$
    39 sq. in. $A = 6 \times 4$ $A = 5 \times 3$
                  $A = 24$ sq. in. $A = 15$ sq. in.
                  $24 + 15 = 39$ sq. in.

12. a. T, Py   b. R, Pr   c. T, Pr   d. S, Py

13. $V = L \times W \times H$
    $V = 5 \times 4 \times 7$
    $V = 140$ cu. in.

14. $V = S^3$
    $V = 3^3$
    $V = 27$ cu. ft.

15. a.   b.   c.
    triangle   square   triangle

16. a. 3
    b. 1
    c. 2

17. a. 11   b. 8   c. 11

18. a. base 10
        10
    b. meter, liter, gram
    c. milli   kilo
    d. yard   quart   ounce
    e. 100; 1,000

19. a. $\frac{4}{24} = \frac{1}{6} = \frac{2}{12}$ $\frac{2}{24} = \frac{1}{12}$ $\frac{8}{24} = \frac{1}{3} = \frac{4}{12}$
        $\frac{6}{24} = \frac{1}{4} = \frac{3}{12}$ $\frac{4}{24} = \frac{1}{6} = \frac{2}{12}$
    b. 12
    c. 1935 – 2
        1936 – 1
        1937 – 4
        1938 – 3
        1939 – 2

Math 606 Test Key

LIFEPAC 606

1. a. 1,859   3,404   56,551
    $87\frac{4}{5} = 88$ $13\frac{60}{63} = 14$
  b. 13.422   4.73   .562
    $.012\frac{1}{7} = .012$ .03
  c. $16\frac{5}{12}$ $3\frac{7}{12}$ 12 $4\frac{4}{5}$ 2

2. a. even number or 0, 2, 4, 6, 8   0, 5   0
  b. add up to a multiple of 3
    add up to a multiple of 9
    divisible by both 2 and 3

3.
PF	PF	LCM		PF	PF	GCF
②³	2², ③	24		2³	②² 3	4
3, ⑤	② 3²	90		③ 5	2, 3²	3

4. variable

5. a. $x - 47 = 95$
    $x - 47(+47) = 95 + 47$
    $x = 142$
  b. $y \cdot 9 = 135$
    $y \cdot 9(\div 9) = 135 \div 9$
    $y = 15$
  c. $\frac{n}{15} = \frac{2}{10}$
    $n \cdot 10 = 30$
    $n \cdot 10(\div 10) = 30 \div 10$
    $n = 3$
  d. $\frac{4}{12} = \frac{2}{c}$
    $4 \cdot c = 24$
    $4(\div 4) \cdot c = 24 \div 4$
    $c = 6$

6. 12, 2, 10, 8   28, 2, 49, 5

7. $\frac{9}{16}$ $1\frac{3}{16}$

8. $\frac{7}{8}$, .875

9. 144   9   640   27

10. $\frac{.5 \text{ in}}{1 \text{ mi.}} = \frac{2 \text{ in.}}{x \text{ mi.}}$
    $.5 \cdot x = 2$
    $.5(\div .5) \cdot x = 2 \div .5$
    $x = 4$ 4 miles

11. 65°   150°

12. D   M   D

13. yard, quart, ounce

14. 100   10   1,000

15. 30   12,000   5.1

16. a. 7   b. 4   c. 2
    d. 6   e. 8   f. 5
    g. 1   h. 3

17. a. $D = rt$
        $160 = r \cdot 5$
        $160 \div 5 = r \cdot 5(\div 5)$
    $32 \text{ i(items)ph} = r$
  b. $P = 2l + 2w$
        $32 = 2 \cdot 9 + 2 \cdot a$
        $32 = 18 + 2 \cdot a$
    $32 - 18 = 18(-18) + 2a$
        $14 = 2 \cdot a$
        $14 \div 2 = 2(\div 2) \cdot a$
        $7 \text{ in.} = a$

18. b

19. 5"   10"

20. $C = \pi d$ $A = \pi r^2$
    $C = 3.14 \cdot 10$ $A = 3.14 \cdot 5^2$
    $C = 31.4 \text{ in.}$ $A = 3.14 \cdot 25$
            $A = 78.5 \text{ sq. in.}$

21. a. 34%   b. 6%   c. 58%   d. 5%

22. a. 8:100 $\frac{8}{100}$ .08   b. 26:100 $\frac{26}{100}$ .26

23. a. .40 40%   b. .25 25%   c. .875 88%

24. a. 7:25 A.M.   b. 3:03 P.M.

25. a. 20.06   b. 4.15

26. a. x = Seth's candy $x + 5$ = Jenny's candy
        $x + x + 5 = 23$
        $2x + 5 = 23$
        $2x + 5(-5) = 23 - 5$
        $2x = 18$
        $2x(\div 2) = 18 \div 2$
        $x = 9$ pieces
        $x + 5 = 14$ pieces $9 + 14 = 23$
    Jenny, 14 pieces   Seth, 9 pieces
  b. x = 1st yr. $x + 4$ = 2nd yr.
        $x + x + 4 = 18$
        $2x + 4 = 18$
        $2x + 4(-4) = 18 - 4$
        $2x = 14$
        $x = 7$ days
        $x + 4 = 11$ days $7 + 11 = 18$
    1st yr., 7 days   2nd yr., 11 days

LIFEPAC 607

1. a. $(8 \times 1{,}000{,}000{,}000) + (6 \times 100{,}000{,}000) +$
    $(0 \times 10{,}000{,}000) + (3 \times 1{,}000{,}000) + (2 \times 100{,}000)$
    $+ (5 \times 10{,}000) + (1 \times 1{,}000) + (4 \times 100) +$
    $(6 \times 10) + (9 \times 1)$

    b. $(8 \times 10^9) + (6 \times 10^8) + (0 \times 10^7) + (3 \times 10^6) +$
    $(2 \times 10^5) + (5 \times 10^4) + (1 \times 10^3) + (4 \times 10^2) +$
    $(6 \times 10^1) + (9 \times 10^0)$

2. a. A 36   b.   C   16
    c. D 25   d.   A   13

3. $7(6 + 8) = 98$

4. a.
    ```
      15      15
      15     × 4
      15      60
    + 15
      60
    ```

    b. 39
      $- 13 = 26$ (1) $13\overline{)39}$ 3
      $- 13 = 13$ (2)
         $- 13 \;\; = 0$ (3)

5. a. $\frac{1}{4}$ .25   25%
    b. $\frac{7}{10}$ .7   70%

6. 75%   17%   96%   8%
    ```
        25
      × .16
       150
        25
      4.00 or 4
    ```

7. $\frac{375}{100}$ or $3\frac{3}{4}$

8. $\frac{2}{5} = \frac{x}{25}$ (bats) / (members)
    $50 = 5x$
    $50 \div 5 = 5x\ (\div 5)$
    $10 = x$

9. a. 2 10
    b. 4 8
    c. 5 6
    d. 1 9
    e. 3 7

10. a. $l \times w$ 28 m²
    b. s^2 81 ft.²
    c. πr^2 $(3.14 \times 25) = 78.5$ in.²
    d. $\frac{1}{2} bh$ $(8 \times 6) \div 2 = 24$ cm²
    e. bh 6 yd.²

11. a. 16   b. -14   c. 6
    d. 3   e. -2   f. -10

12. 3, 4, 5, 6, 7, 8
    (0,3) (1,4) (2,5) (3,6) (4,7) (5,8)

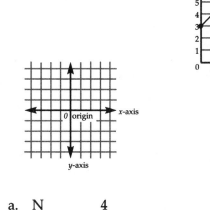

13.

14. a. N   4
        P   3
        A
    b. P   3
        N   2
        C

15. a. John had $5.00 when he went to the store. He spent $1.85. How much money does John have now?
    answer: $3.15

    b. The temperature was 12°F. During the night it fell 17 degrees. What was the temperature the next morning?
    answer: -5°F

16. a. 25   64
    b. 7   4

17. a. 24
    b. International Date Line
    c. 6
    d. no
    e. 3:00 A.M.
    f. 2:00 A.M.

18. 6 in.

19. a. $2\frac{5}{12}$ b. $12\frac{1}{4}$ c. 4.27
    d. .75   e. 11 ft. 16 in. = 12 ft. 4 in.

LIFEPAC 608

1. a. three-ninths
   b. seven-hundredths
   c. negative nine
   d. eighteen and one-half percent

2. a.
$$\begin{array}{r} 46 \\ 46 \\ 46 \\ +\ 46 \\ \hline 184 \end{array} \qquad \begin{array}{r} 46 \\ \times\ 4 \\ \hline 184 \end{array}$$

   b.
$$\begin{array}{r} 78 \\ (1)\ -\ 26 \\ \hline 52 \\ (2)\ -\ 26 \\ \hline 26 \\ (3)\ -\ 26 \\ \hline 0 \end{array} \qquad \begin{array}{r} 3 \\ 26\overline{)78} \\ \underline{78} \\ 0 \end{array}$$

3. 4, 13, 2   subtract 7

4. a. 6   b. 9

5. a. 4   b. 1
   c. 6   d. 5
   e. 2   f. 8
   g. 9   h. 7
   i. 3

6. a. p 6:20 = 3:10 n 4:20 = 2:10 d 6:20 = 3:10
   q 2:20 = 1:10 hd 2:20 = 1:10

   b. 3:10

   c. pennies, dimes, nickels, quarters, half-dollars

   d. yes
   5:19 or 1:3.8
   probably not

7. a. 10
   b. 5
   c. see graph
   d. see graph

8. a. 1:10   3:10   2:10   1:10   3:10
   b. 10   30   20   10   30

9. a. ten
   b. meter, liter, gram

10. 3 grams   5 decigrams   7 centigrams
    4 kilograms 6 hectograms   7 decagrams

11. a. D   M   D
    b. 1,000 10   1,000

12. 22.86   10.968
    4.34   16.912

13. a. 4:20 $\frac{4}{20}$ $\frac{1}{5}$
    b. $\frac{5}{8} \times 32 = 20$ dogs
    c. $\frac{3}{4} \times 9 = 6\frac{3}{4} = 6$ whole cans plus $\frac{3}{4}$ of a can

14. a.
$$\frac{2}{3} \times a = 18$$
$$\frac{2 \times a}{3} = 18$$
$$3 \times \frac{(2 \times a)}{3} = 18 \times 3$$
$$2 \times a = 54$$
$$2(\div 2) \times a = 54 \div 2$$
$$a = 27$$
$$\tfrac{2}{3} \text{ of } 27 = 18$$

   b.
$$\frac{3}{5} \times a = 9$$
$$\frac{3 \times a}{5} = 9$$
$$5 \times \frac{(3 \times a)}{5} = 9 \times 5$$
$$3 \times a = 45$$
$$3(\div 3) \times a = 45 \div 3$$
$$a = 15$$
$$\tfrac{3}{5} \text{ of } 15 = 9$$

   c.
$$8 = \frac{1}{4} \times a$$
$$8 = \frac{1 \times a}{4}$$
$$8 \times 4 = \frac{(1 \times a)}{4} \times 4$$
$$32 = 1 \times a$$
$$32 \div 1 = 1(\div 1) \times a$$
$$32 = a$$
$$8 = \tfrac{1}{4} \text{ of } 32$$

   d.
$$6 = \frac{3}{8} \times a$$
$$6 = \frac{3 \times a}{8}$$
$$6 \times 8 = \frac{(3 \times a)}{8} \times 8$$
$$48 = 3a$$
$$16 = a$$
$$6 = \tfrac{3}{8} \text{ of } 16$$

15. 16, 12, 1.8

16. 3:4 .75   75%   2:5 .4   40%
    5:6 .833 83%   7:8 .875   88% or $87\frac{1}{2}$%

17. a. 673,000,000,000,000
    b. 24,172,110,000,000
    c. 47.24
    d. 65.16

LIFEPAC 609

1. a. one
   b. zero, one

2. $2, 3^2$

	18
2	9
3	3
3	1

3. 2, 3, 5   2, 2 $2^2, 3^2, 5$ 180

4. a. 468,239,000,000
   b. 380,000,000,000

5. a. .4   40%   b. 1:4 $\frac{1}{4}$

6. a. ③.059   b. ④.21%

7. $\frac{1}{4}$ $\frac{2}{5}$ $\frac{1}{2}$ $\frac{3}{5}$ $\frac{7}{10}$ $\frac{3}{4}$

8. a. 41.835   b. 81

9. 4:10 = 2:5

10. 12
    5

11. a. 5
    b. 6
    c. 2
    d. 1
    e. 4
    f. 3

12. a. 2   b. 3   c. 1

13. a. ray RF
    b. congruent
    c. perpendicular

14. >   =   <

15. $22 + 9 + 37 + 8 + x = 110$
    $76 + x = 110$
    $76(-76) + x = 110 - 76$
    $x = 34$ mystery books

16. $\frac{RS}{XY} = \frac{2}{3}$
    $\frac{8}{XY} = \frac{2}{3}$
    $24 = 2 \cdot XY$
    $24 \div 2 = 2(\div 2) \cdot XY$
    $12 = XY$ $\overline{XY} = 12$ in.

17. 365   10   5,280
    16   9   2

18. a. $D = r \cdot t$
    $232 = r \cdot 4$
    $232 \div 4 = r \cdot 4(\div 4)$
    58 mph $= r$

    b. $P = 2 \cdot l + 2 \cdot w$
    $P = (2 \cdot 9) + (2 \cdot 5)$
    $P = 18 + 10$
    $P = 28$ ft.

    c. $C = \pi d$
    $C = 3.14 \cdot 7$
    $C = 21.98$ in.

    d. $A = s^2$
    64 sq. in. $= s^2$
    8 in. $= s$

19. $x = $ cups $3x = $ glasses

    $x + 3x = 16$
    $4x = 16$
    $4(\div 4) \cdot x = 16 \div 4$
    $x = 4$
    $3x = 12$

20. -3, -1, 1, 3, 5
    -5,-3   -3,-1   -1,1   1,3   3,5

21. 183
    20%   40%   40%

22. a. 16   36   81
    b. 5   8   12

23. 27   45

24. a. <   b. >
    c. =   d. =

25. a. 6.389   31,569   .038   .49
    b. 2 yr. 7 mo. $2\frac{7}{8}$ .9 $\frac{1}{4}$

LIFEPAC 610

1. a. $\frac{19}{20}$ $1\frac{4}{5}$ $2\frac{1}{2}$ 4.74

   b. 185%   8 gal. 1 qt.   3 lb. 11 oz.   3 in.

2. a.
$$\begin{array}{r} 2\,8 \\ \times\ \ 700 \\ \hline 19{,}600 \end{array}$$
   b.
$$\begin{array}{r} 87 \\ \times\ 5{,}000 \\ \hline 435{,}000 \end{array}$$
   c.
$$\begin{array}{r} 63 \\ \times\ 46{,}000 \\ \hline 378\ \ \ \ \\ 2\ 520\ \ \ \\ \hline 2{,}898{,}000 \end{array}$$

3.   900   8,000   600

4. a. $1.66\frac{2}{3} = \$1.67$ $.86\frac{4}{6} = \$.87$

   b. $\$1.19 = \$1$ $\$13.98 = \$14$

5. a.
$$\begin{array}{r} 40 \\ \times\ .15 \\ \hline 200 \\ 400 \\ \hline 6.00 \end{array}$$
    6 days

   b.
$$x = \text{inches}$$
$$6 = \frac{2}{3} \cdot x$$
$$3 \cdot 6 = (\cancel{3} \cdot \frac{2}{\cancel{3}}) \cdot x$$
$$18 = 2 \cdot x$$
$$18 \div 2 = 2(\div 2) \cdot x$$
$$9 = x$$

   c.
$$x = \text{bananas}$$
$$9 = \frac{3}{4} \cdot x$$
$$4 \cdot 9 = (\cancel{4} \cdot \frac{3}{\cancel{4}}) \cdot x$$
$$36 = 3 \cdot x$$
$$36 \div 3 = 3(\div 3) \cdot x$$
$$12 = x$$

6. a. 45   b. 15 R768

7. a. 22   58   59

   b. 130   778   116

   c. 2,080   13   63

   d. 2.883   7.53   1.4

   e. .9 $1\frac{1}{6}$ $\frac{5}{8}$

8. a. 6:9 $\frac{6}{9} = \frac{2}{3}$ $.\overline{666}$ 67%

   b. 12:20 $\frac{12}{20} = \frac{3}{5}$ .6   60%

9. a. GYP   GPY   YGP   YPG   PGY   PYG

   b. mode   28

   c. 3:9   33%

10.

	2	5	10	3	9	6
375		✓		✓		
540	✓	✓	✓	✓	✓	✓

11.
$$A = l \cdot w$$
$$A = 5 \cdot 3$$
$$A = 15\ (\times 2) = 30 \text{ sq. in.}$$
$$A = 7 \cdot 3$$
$$A = 21\ (\times 2) = 42 \text{ sq. in}$$
$$A = 7 \cdot 5$$
$$A = 35\ (\times 2) = 70 \text{ sq. in} \quad \text{Total} = 142 \text{ sq. in.}$$

12.

13. a.   b.   c.

14. a.
$$x + x + x + 7 = 49$$
$$3x + 7 = 49$$
$$3x + 7(-7) = 49 - 7$$
$$3x = 42$$
$$3(\div 3) \cdot x = 42 \div 3$$
$$x = 14$$

   b.
$$\frac{12}{18} = \frac{2}{3}$$
$$36 = 12 \cdot x$$
$$36 \div 12 = 12(\div 12) \cdot x$$
$$3 = x$$

15. a.
$$P = 2l + 2w$$
$$28 = (2 \cdot 8) + (2 \cdot w)$$
$$28 = 16 + 2w$$
$$28 - 16 = 16(-16) + 2w$$
$$12 = 2w$$
$$12 \div 2 = 2(\div 2) \cdot w$$
$$6 \text{ in.} = w$$

   b.
$$A = s^2$$
$$64 = s^2$$
$$8 \text{ ft.} = s$$

   c.
$$x = \text{books}$$
$$\frac{3}{8} = \frac{x}{40}$$
$$120 = 8 \cdot x$$
$$120 \div 8 = 8(\div 8) \cdot x$$
$$15 = x$$

16. $\$10 < b < \$16$

   $b = \$11, \$12, \$13, \$14 \text{ or } \$15$

17. -8, -6, -3, 0, +2, +7

18. a. bar

   b. Oct. 1, Sept. 17, Oct. 8, Sept. 24, Oct. 15

   c. Concession Stand Sales

1. a. 0, 1, 2, 3, 4, 5, 6, 7, 8, 9
   b. as a place holder

2. a. 3,<u>542</u>,816,059 - five hundred forty-two million
   b. <u>86</u>,795,283,015 - eighty-six billion

3. a. 4, 32   b. 3, 25
   c. 21, 46   d. 8th, 69th
   e. 5, 11   f. 4, 21

4. a. $=$ $\neq$
   b. $<$ $>$

5. $\div$, $\times$ $+$, $\times$

6. $5 + 8 = 13$ - $8 + 5 = 13$
   $13 - 5 = 8$ - $13 - 8 = 5$

7. a. 186
   b. 27
   c. 1,820
   d. 23

8. a. 1,180   (a) 1,180
                      $-\ 287$
                      893
                      $-\ 364$
                      529
                      $-\ 529$
                      0

   b. 5,056   (b) 2,975
                      $+\ 5,056$
                      8,031

   c. 2,457   (c)   63
                 39⟌2,457

                          39
                 63⟌2,457

   d. 126 R1   (d)   126
                        $\times\ 5$
                        630
                        $+\ 1$
                        631

9. 217,755   191,226   21 R8   18 R46

10. 1, 2, ⑤ 10 and   1, 3 ⑤ 15

11. 36   12   60   24

12. a   c   b

13. a. eight and two thirds $\frac{13}{15}$
    b. three-fifths $6\frac{1}{4}$

14. 6   5   20

15. a. $\frac{8}{10} = \frac{4}{5}$ $\frac{15}{15} = 1$ $\frac{9}{12} = \frac{3}{4}$ $\frac{20}{16} = 1\frac{4}{16} = 1\frac{1}{4}$ $\frac{6}{9} = \frac{2}{3}$

    b. $\frac{4}{20} = \frac{1}{5}$ 0 $\frac{6}{8} = \frac{3}{4}$ $\frac{9}{15} = \frac{3}{5}$ $\frac{5}{10} = \frac{1}{2}$

16. a. eight and three tenths
       sixty-five thousandths
    b. thirteen hundredths
       two hundred four thousandths

17. .240   .300   .379   .186   .400
    .186   .24   .3   .379   .4

18. a. 5.384   1.591   83.22
    b. 3.16   6.727   2.486

19. a. $600 \div 3 = 200$
    b. $300 \times 40 = 12,000$ pennies
    c. $\$23,000 - \$2,000 = \$21,000$

20. a. $6 + 8 + 9 = 23$ $4 + 6 = 10$
    b. $0 + 8 + 8 = 16$ $18 \div 6 = 3$

21. a. $N + 36 = 81$
             $N + 36(- 36) = 81 - 36$
                        $N = 45$
               $45 + 36 = 81$
    b. $N - 27 = 68$
             $N - 27(+ 27) = 68 + 27$
                        $N = 95$
             $95 - 27 = 68$

22. 30, 60, ...
    times 2, plus 2

1. forty-seven billion, three hundred six million, two hundred ten thousand, four hundred thirty-five

2. $>$ $=$ $\neq$ $<$

3. 6,365   23,722   187,407   209 R1   157 R22

4. 33,000,000,000; 22,000,000,000; 10,000,000,000
   33, 22, 10, 65

5. 629,536.   11.   520.   4,103.

6. E   E   O   E   E   O

7. $\frac{3}{4}$ 1 $4\frac{2}{3}$

8. $\frac{6}{6}$

9. a. $\frac{1}{3}$ b. $\frac{1}{3}$

10. a. $13\frac{3}{8}$ $12\frac{2}{5}$ $2\frac{1}{4}$ $\frac{13}{24}$ $1\frac{1}{3}$

    b. $10\frac{5}{6}$ $13\frac{1}{8}$ $10\frac{1}{6}$ $6\frac{4}{5}$ $1\frac{3}{4}$ $5\frac{7}{9}$

11. a. $\frac{14}{20}, \frac{15}{20}, \frac{16}{20}, \frac{13}{20}$ b. $\frac{13}{20}, \frac{7}{10}, \frac{3}{4}, \frac{4}{5}$

12. a. five tenths - .5 - $\frac{5}{10}$ - .50

    b. five hundredths - .05 - $\frac{5}{100}$ - .050

    c. five thousandths - .005 - $\frac{5}{1,000}$ - .0050

13. a. 13.638   12.441   .078
    b. 1.86   .018   22.41

14. a. 1, 2, 4, 5, 10, 20
    b. Suggested answer - 8, 16, 24, 32, 40, 48

15. $47 - 42 = 5$ $21 \div 3 = 7$ $28 + 5 = 33$ $36 + 36 = 72$

16. Six plus eight is not equal to three times five.
    $5 \times 4 < 5 \times 5$

17. $N + 38(- 38) = 71 - 38$
    $N = 33$
    $33 + 38 = 71$

    $283(- 109) = N + 109(- 109)$
    $174 = N$
    $283 = 174 + 109$

    $N - 49(+ 49) = 86 + 49$
    $N = 135$
    $135 - 49 = 86$

    $112 + 289 = N - 289(+ 289)$
    $401 = N$
    $112 = 401 - 289$

18. a.   16   9   12
    b.   12   20   4
    c.   48"   6   9
    d.   75 minutes

19.   2, 3   2, 2 $2^2, 3^2$ 36

20. a.   two to the fifth power   2   32
    b.   ten squared   10   100

21. $2^2 \times 3^3$

	108
2	54
2	27
3	9
3	3
3	1

1. .2.3   .4   .7   .8

2. .600, .370, .504, .630, .400   .37, .4, .504, .6, .63

3. five and forty-three thousandths

4. a. 2.937 b. 6.83 c. .0387

5. a. 2   b. 4   c. 2
   d. 16   e. two to the fourth power

6.
	15	
3	5	
5	1	

3, 5

	18	
2	9	
3	3	
3	1	

2, 3²

7. 3, 5   2, 3²
   2, 3², 5
   2, 3², 5, 90

8. Circled: $8 \times 12 = 96$ $5^2 = 25$

9. $8 \times 6 = N$ $48 = N$
   $27 - 15 = N$ $12 = N$
   $9 + 6 = N$ $15 = N$
   $45 - 6 = N$ $39 = N$

10. $N \times 7 (\div 7) = 112 \div 7$
    $N = 16$
    $16 \times 7 = 112$

    $N \div 9 (\times 9) = 13 \times 9$
    $N = 117$
    $117 \div 9 = 13$

11. $=$ $2 \times 12 = 24$ $6 \times 4 = 24$
    $>$ $6 \times 5 = 30$ $3 \times 9 = 27$

12. $.\overline{22}$ or .222   .6

13. seven and two-thirds

14. $\frac{10}{16}, \frac{12}{16}, \frac{8}{16}, \frac{9}{16}$ $\frac{1}{2}, \frac{9}{16}, \frac{5}{8}, \frac{3}{4}$

15. a. $\frac{2}{12} = \frac{1}{6}$ $\frac{4}{12} = \frac{1}{3}$ $\frac{6}{12} = \frac{1}{2}$

    b. $\frac{1}{6} = \frac{③}{18}$ $\frac{1}{3} = \frac{⑥}{18}$ $\frac{1}{2} = \frac{⑨}{18}$

16. $11\frac{5}{24}$ $4\frac{4}{9}$ 75   57 $\frac{3}{10}$
                        3   5   42

17. a. 8
    b. 9
    c. 1
    d. 5
    e. 3
    f. 7
    g. 2
    h. 10
    i. 6
    j. 4

18.
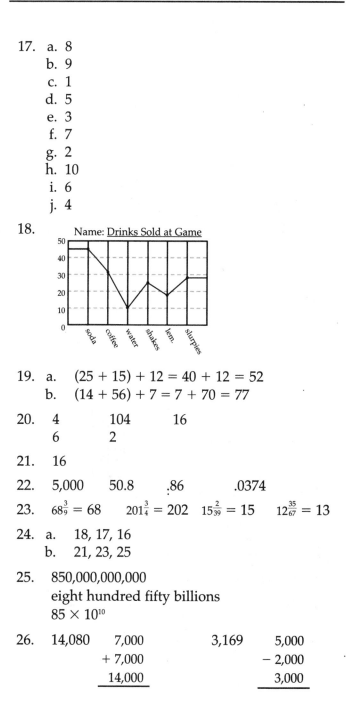

19. a. $(25 + 15) + 12 = 40 + 12 = 52$
    b. $(14 + 56) + 7 = 7 + 70 = 77$

20. 4   104   16
    6   2

21. 16

22. 5,000   50.8   .86   .0374

23. $68\frac{3}{9} = 68$ $201\frac{3}{4} = 202$ $15\frac{2}{39} = 15$ $12\frac{35}{67} = 13$

24. a.   18, 17, 16
    b.   21, 23, 25

25. 850,000,000,000
    eight hundred fifty billions
    85×10^{10}

26. 14,080   7,000   3,169   5,000
               + 7,000   − 2,000
               14,000   3,000

1.   3.897   4.57   5.56   .57013

2.   410   3,620   .87   .0091

3. $.54\frac{7}{8} = .55$ $.090\frac{1}{5} = .090$ $9.7\frac{1}{6} = 9.7$ $20.4\frac{1}{9} = 20.4$

4.   .500   .520   .350   .513
        .35   .5   .513   .52

5. a. $\frac{43}{40} = 1\frac{3}{40}$ $9\frac{38}{24} = 10\frac{14}{24} = 10\frac{7}{12}$ $7\frac{5}{24}$ $2\frac{5}{10} = 2\frac{1}{2}$

   b. $\frac{3}{10}$ 33 $\frac{3}{8}$ $2\frac{1}{2}$

6. $\frac{14}{18}$ $\frac{15}{18}$ $\frac{9}{18}$ $\frac{12}{18}$
      $\frac{1}{2}$ $\frac{2}{3}$ $\frac{7}{9}$ $\frac{5}{6}$

7. a. .875   b. $.\overline{66}$

8. a. >   =
   b. N = 2   N = 12

9.   16   16   27   49

10.
```
        | 12|              | 16|
   | 2 | 6|           | 2 | 8|
   | 2 | 3|           | 2 | 4|
   | 3 | 1|           | 2 | 2|
2², 3                  | 2 | 1|
                    2⁴
```

$2^2, 3$ 2^4

11. $2^2, 3$ 2^4
         2^2
         4

12. a. E   b. I   c. S

13. a. 135°   obtuse
    b. 50°   acute
    c. 90°   right

14.   14 in.   6 sq. in.

15. a. 3
    b. 2
    c. 4
    d. 1
    e. 6
    f. 5
    g. 8
    h. 7

16. a. $A = \frac{1}{2}BH$ A = 12 sq. ft.
    b. D = RT   D = 240 mi.
    c. A = LW   W = 6 in.

17. $3 \times [18 - (2 \times 5)] = 3 \times (18 - 10) = 3 \times 8 = 24$
    $[(6 + 8) \div 7] \times 9 = (14 \div 7) \times 9 = 2 \times 9 = 18$
    $5 + 21 \div 3 - 6 = 5 + 7 - 6 = 12 - 6 = 6$
    $8 \times 2 - 13 + 24 \div 6 = 16 - 13 + 4 = 3 + 4 = 7$

18. a. $\frac{2}{3} = \frac{8}{N}$ (dimes)
                     (quarters)
            $2 \times N = 24$
         $2(\div 2) \times N = 24 \div 2$
              $N = 12$

    b. $\frac{2}{3} = \frac{N}{15}$ (dimes)
                     (quarters)
           $30 = 3 \times N$
       $30 \div 3 = 3(\div 3) \times N$
           $10 = N$

19.   15 $\geq$ 15   13   11   >   9

20.   14 hr. 63 min. = 15 hr. 3 min.

21.   3 ft. 8 in.

22.   2 lb. $1\frac{1}{4}$ oz.

23.   actual - 996   estimated - 1,000

1. a. 832,000,000,000,000,000
   b. 431,000,000,000,000,000,000

2. a. 355×10^6
   b. 241 billion

3. light-year

4. a. 115

   $$\begin{array}{r} 115 \\ -\ 34 \\ \hline 81 \\ -\ 62 \\ \hline 19 \\ -\ 19 \\ \hline 0 \end{array}$$

   b. 139

   $$\begin{array}{r} 369 \\ +\ 139 \\ \hline 508 \end{array}$$

   c. 4,592

   $$56\overline{)4{,}592}\quad 82$$

   d. 43

   $$\begin{array}{r} 43 \\ \times\ 7 \\ \hline 301 \end{array}$$

5. a. 710   160,230   7.32
   b. 3.2
   $7.75 - 2.625 = 5.125$
   $4.6 \times 5.5 = 25.3$

6. a. 4
   b. 3
   c. 2
   d. 1
   e. 5

7. a. 69   b. 1,205   c. XXVI   d. DXIX

8. a. .5   .25   .75 $.\overline{4}$ $.8\underline{}$
   b. .125   .375   .625 $.\overline{33}$ $.1\overline{66}$

9. a. 6
   b. 8
   c. 7
   d. 5
   e. 2
   f. 3
   g. 4
   h. 1

10. $C = \pi d$
    $C = 3.14 \times 7$
    $C = 21.98$ in.

11. 26 in. $A = L \times W$ $A = L \times W$
    28 sq. in. $A = 4 \times 2$ $A = 5 \times 4$
               $A = 8$ sq. in. $A = 20$ sq. in.
               $8 + 20 = 28$ sq. in.

12. a. T, Pr   b. R, Pr   c. S, Py   d. T, Py

13. $V = L \times W \times H$
    $V = 6 \times 3 \times 5$
    $V = 90$ cu. ft.

14. $V = S^3$
    $V = 2^3$
    $V = 8$ cu. yd.

15. a.
    square

    b.
    triangle

    c.
    triangle

16. a. 2
    b. 3
    c. 1

17. a. 10   b. 15   c. 9

18. a. base 10
       10
    b. meter, liter, gram
    c. milli   kilo
    d. yard   quart   ounce
    e. 100, 1,000

19. a. $\frac{2}{24} = \frac{1}{12}$ $\frac{4}{24} = \frac{1}{6} = \frac{2}{12}$ $\frac{8}{24} = \frac{1}{3} = \frac{4}{12}$

    $\frac{4}{24} = \frac{1}{6} = \frac{2}{12}$ $\frac{6}{24} = \frac{1}{4} = \frac{3}{12}$

    b. 12
    c. 1950 – 1
       1951 – 2
       1952 – 4
       1953 – 2
       1954 – 3

1. a. 1,755   6,254   29,175

    $83\frac{5}{7} = 84$ $18\frac{5}{49} = 18$

    b. 9.908 5.86   .433

    $.012\frac{5}{6} = .013$ .03

    c. $14\frac{5}{24}$ $7\frac{1}{3}$ 27 $4\frac{1}{2}$ $\frac{1}{2}$

2. a. even number or 0, 2, 4, 6, 8 0, 5   0
    b. add up to a multiple of 3
        add up to a multiple of 9
        add up to a multiple of 2 and 3

3. | PF | PF | LCM | | PF | PF | GCF |
    |---|---|---|---|---|---|---|
    | ②③ | 2,⑤ | 30 | | ②3 | 2, 5 | 2 |
    | 2²③ | ② | 48 | | ②3 | 2⁴ | 4 |

4. variable

5. a. $x + 39 = 84$

        $x + 39(-39) = 84 - 39$

        $x = 45$

    b. $y \div 8 = 13$

        $y \div 8(\times 8) = 13 \times 8$

        $y = 104$

    c. $\frac{n}{6} = \frac{6}{9}$

        $n \cdot 9 = 36$

        $n \cdot 9(\div 9) = 36 \div 9$

        $n = 4$

    d. $\frac{4}{8} = \frac{5}{c}$

        $4 \cdot c = 40$

        $4(\div 4) \cdot c = 40 \div 4$

        $c = 10$

6. 9, 5, 7, 11   16, 6, 28, 8

7. $\frac{11}{16}$ $1\frac{7}{16}$

8. $\frac{3}{4}$, .75

9. 144   9   640   27

10. $\frac{.5 \text{ in}}{1 \text{ mi.}} = \frac{3 \text{ in.}}{x \text{ mi.}}$

     $.5 \cdot x = 3$

     $.5(\div .5) \cdot x = 3 \div .5$

     $x = 6$ 6 miles

11. 30°   125°

12. M   D   M

13. yard, quart, ounce

14. 10   1,000   100

15. .05   40   7,000

16. a. 6   b. 5
     c. 8   d. 7
     e. 3   f. 2
     g. 4   h. 1

17. a. $P = s + s + s$
             $29 = 11 + 11 + s$
             $29 = 22 + s$
         $29 - 22 = 22(-22) + s$
             $7 \text{ in.} = s$

     b. $P = 4 \cdot s$
             $36 = 4 \cdot s$
         $36 \div 4 = 4(\div 4) \cdot s$
             $9 \text{ in.} = s$

18. a

19. 3″   6″

20. | $C = \pi d$ | $A = \pi r^2$ |
     |---|---|
     | $C = 3.14 \cdot 6$ | $A = 3.14 \cdot 3^2$ |
     | $C = 18.84 \text{ in.}$ | $A = 3.14 \cdot 9$ |
     | | $A = 28.26 \text{ sq. in.}$ |

21. a. 8%   b. 23%   c. 5%   d. 94%

22. a. 45:100 $\frac{45}{100}$ .45   b. 9:100 $\frac{9}{100}$ .09

23. a. .75 75%   b. .20 20%   c. .375 38%

24. a. 9.46 A.M.   b. 6.00 P.M.

25. a. 7:15   b. 21:30

26. a. x = Joseph $x + 3$ = Lisa
             $x + x + 3 = 27$
             $2x + 3 = 27$
         $2x + 3(-3) = 27 - 3$
             $2x = 24$
         $2x(\div 2) = 24 \div 2$
             $x = 12$
         $x + 3 = 15$ $12 + 15 = 27$
     Lisa - 15 dimes   Joseph - 12 dimes

     b. x = Julie $x + 12$ = Mary
             $x + x + 12 = 44$
             $2x + 12 = 44$
         $2x + 12(-12) = 44 - 12$
             $2x = 32$
             $x = 16$
         $x + 12 = 28$ $16 + 28 = 44$
     Mary - 28 cupcakes   Julie - 16 cupcakes

1. a. $(7 \times 100,000,000) + (8 \times 10,000,000) +$
        $(3 \times 1,000,000) + (2 \times 100,000) + (9 \times 10,000)$
        $+ (0 \times 1,000) + (5 \times 100) + (3 \times 10) + (8 \times 1)$
    b. $(7 \times 10^8) + (8 \times 10^7) + (3 \times 10^6) + (2 \times 10^5) +$
        $(9 \times 10^4) + (0 \times 10^3) + (5 \times 10^2) + (3 \times 10^1) +$
        (8×10^0)

2. a. D   20   b. A   13
    c. C   45   d. A   30

3. $9 \times (2 + 5) = 63$

4. a.   14   14
           14        $\times\ 4$
           14   56
         $+\ 14$
           56
    b.   68   (1)   4
          $- 17 = 51$ (2) $17\overline{)68}$
              $- 17 = 34$ (3)
                  $- 17 = 17$ (4)
                      $-$ 17   0

5. a. $\frac{3}{10}$ .3   30%
    b. $\frac{2}{5}$ .4   40%

6. 95%   16%   63%   6%   8

7. 2.25 $2\frac{25}{100}$ or $2\frac{1}{4}$

8. $\frac{5}{8} = \frac{x}{24}$ (balls)
                        (members)
          $120 = 8x$
          $120 \div 8 = 8x\ (\div 8)$
              $15 = x$

9. a. 5 7
    b. 1 9
    c. 3 10
    d. 4 6
    e. 2 8

10. a. $l \times w$ 24 m²
    b. s^2 36 ft.²
    c. πr^2 314 in.²
    d. $\frac{1}{2}bh$ 14 cm²
    e. bh 30 yd.²

11. a. -5   b. 1   c. 15
    d. 9   e. -4   f. -2

12. 2, 4, 6, 8
     (0,2) (2,4) (4,6) (6,8)

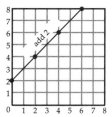

13.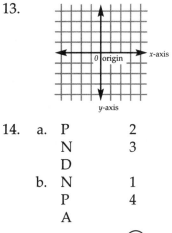

14. a. P   2
        N   3
        D
    b. N   1
        P   4
        A

15. a. Kevin had ⟨35⟩ baseball cards. He sold 17.
        How many cards does Kevin have now?
        answer: ⟨18⟩
    b. The temperature was ⟨8°F.⟩ During the
        night it fell 13 degrees. What was
        the temperature the next morning?
        answer: -5°F

16. a. 9   36
    b. 8   5

17. a. 24
    b. International Date Line
    c. 6
    d. no
    e. 5:00 P.M.
    f. 2:00 A.M.

18. 7 in.

19. a. $4\frac{3}{8}$ b. $\frac{3}{4}$ c. 27.12
    d. 4.6   9 lb. 6 oz.

1. a. five-sevenths
   b. nine thousandths
   c. negative six
   d. twenty-four and one-third percent

2. a.
$$\begin{array}{r} 39 \\ 39 \\ +\ 39 \\ \hline 117 \end{array} \qquad \begin{array}{r} 39 \\ \times\ 3 \\ \hline 117 \end{array}$$

   b.
$$\begin{array}{r} 201 \\ (1)\ -\ 67 \\ \hline 134 \\ (2)\ -\ 67 \\ \hline 67 \\ (3)\ -\ 67 \\ \hline 0 \end{array} \qquad \begin{array}{r} 3 \\ 67\overline{)201} \\ \underline{201} \\ 0 \end{array}$$

3. 2, 9, 8   subtract 4

4. a. 7   b. 4

5. a. 1   b. 3
   c. 7   d. 9
   e. 5   f. 4
   g. 6   h. 2
   i. 8

6. a. $\underline{p}\ \dfrac{8}{20} = \dfrac{4}{10}$ $\underline{n}\ \dfrac{2}{20} = \dfrac{1}{10}$ $\underline{d}\ \dfrac{4}{20} = \dfrac{2}{10}$

   $\underline{q}\ \dfrac{4}{20} = \dfrac{2}{10}$ $\underline{hd}\ \dfrac{2}{20} = \dfrac{1}{10}$
   b. 2:10
   c. pennies, dimes, quarters, nickels,
      half-dollars
   d. yes
      7:19
      probably not

7. a. 10
   b. 5
   c.

8. a. 2:10   2:10   1:10   3:10   2:10
   b. 20   20   10   30   20

9. a. ten
   b. liter, meter, gram

10. 4 decagrams   3 grams   1 decigram
    6 decigrams   1 centigram   7 milligrams

11. a. M   M   D
    b. 1,000   10   10

12. 198.45   20.32
     11.023   9.513

13. a. 8:24 $\dfrac{8}{24}$ $\dfrac{1}{3}$
    b. $\dfrac{1}{3} \times 27 = 9$ dogs
    c. $\dfrac{7}{8} \times 12 = \dfrac{84}{8} = 10$ whole cans, $\dfrac{1}{2}$ of a can

14. a.
$$\frac{3}{5} \times a = 9$$
$$\frac{3 \times a}{5} = 9$$
$$5 \times \frac{3 \times a}{5} = 9 \times 5$$
$$3 \times a = 45$$
$$3(\div 3) \times a = 45 \div 3$$
$$a = 15$$
$$\frac{3}{5} \text{ of } 15 = 9$$

   b.
$$\frac{5}{6} \times a = 15$$
$$\frac{5 \times a}{6} = 15$$
$$6 \times \frac{(5 \times a)}{6} = 15 \times 6$$
$$5 \times a = 90$$
$$5(\div 5) \times a = 90 \div 5$$
$$a = 18$$
$$\frac{5}{6} \text{ of } 18 = 15$$

   c.
$$12 = \frac{3}{4} \times a$$
$$12 = \frac{3 \times a}{4}$$
$$12 \times 4 = \frac{(3 \times a)}{4} \times 4$$
$$48 = 3a$$
$$16 = a$$
$$12 = \frac{3}{4} \text{ of } 16$$

   d.
$$6 = \frac{2}{3} \times a$$
$$6 = \frac{2 \times a}{3}$$
$$6 \times 3 = \frac{(2 \times a)}{3} \times 3$$
$$18 = 2a$$
$$9 = a$$
$$6 = \frac{2}{3} \text{ of } 9$$

15. 9, 3, 3.3

16. 1:3 $.\overline{333}$ $33\dfrac{1}{3}$ or 33%   3:5   .6   60%

    5:8   .625 $62\dfrac{1}{2}$ or 63%   1:6 $.\overline{166}$ $16\dfrac{6}{10}$ or 17%

17. a.   593,000,000,000
    b.   200,000,000,000
    c.   58.675
    d.   83.148

1. a. one
   b. zero, one

2. 2^2, 5

20	
2	10
2	5
5	1

3. 2, 3, 5   2   2, 3, 5^2 150

4. a. 605,000,000,000
   b. 970,000,000,000

5. a. $.3\overline{3}$ 33%   b. 3:4 $\frac{3}{4}$

6. a. ⓐ9 45   b. ②39%

7. $\frac{1}{2}$ $\frac{7}{12}$ $\frac{2}{3}$ $\frac{3}{4}$ $\frac{5}{6}$ $\frac{11}{12}$

8. a. 3.45   b. 46.5

9. 4:24 = 1:6

10. 20
    9

11. a. 3
    b. 1
    c. 6
    d. 4
    e. 2
    f. 5

12. a. 2   b. 3   c. 1

13. a. line GH
    b. parallel
    c. similar

14. >   >   <

15. $24 + 29 + 34 + 12 + x = 127$
    $99 + x = 127$
    $99(- 99) + x = 127 - 99$
    $x = 28$ mystery books

16. $\frac{RS}{XY} = \frac{3}{5}$
    $\frac{6}{XY} = \frac{3}{5}$
    $30 = 3 \cdot XY$
    $30 \div 3 = 3(\div 3) \cdot XY$
    $10 = XY$ $\overline{XY} = 10$ in.

17. 365   10   5,280
    16   9   2

18. a. $D = r \cdot t$
    $174 = r \cdot 3$
    $174 \div 3 = r \cdot 3(\div 3)$
    58 mph $= r$

    b. $P = 2 \cdot l + 2 \cdot w$
    $P = (2 \cdot 8) + (2 \cdot 3)$
    $P = 16 + 6$
    $P = 22$ ft.

    c. $C = \pi d$
    $C = 3.14 \cdot 10$
    $C = 31.4$ in.

    d. $A = s^2$
    36 sq. in. $= s^2$
    6 in. $= s$

19. x = girls $4x$ = boys
    $x + 4x = 25$
    $5x = 25$
    $5(\div 5) \cdot x = 25 \div 5$
    $x = 5$
    $4x = 20$

20. 4, 2, 0, -2, -4, -6
    6,4 4,2 2,0 0,-2 -2,-4 -4,-6

21. 102
    0   40%   60%

22. a. 9   25   64
    b. 2   6   11

23. 9   4

24. a. =   b.   <
    c. >   d.   =

25. a. 8.517   2,424   .03451   970
    b. 2 lb. 14 oz. $5\frac{4}{9}$ 763 $1\frac{44}{81}$

1. a. $1\frac{5}{6}$ $1\frac{1}{4}$ 12   2.48
    b. 72%   9 qt.   4 wk. 6 da.   6 in.

2. a. $\begin{array}{r} 3\,600 \\ \times\ 500 \\ \hline 18,000 \end{array}$ b. $\begin{array}{r} 59,000 \\ \times\ 2,000 \\ \hline 118,000 \end{array}$ c. $\begin{array}{r} 41,000 \\ \times\ 63,000 \\ \hline 123,000 \\ 2\ 460,000 \\ \hline 2,583,000 \end{array}$

3. 300   6,000   12,000

4. a. $2.18\frac{1}{4} = \$2.18$ $4.83\frac{1}{2} = \$4.84$
    b. $6.71 = \$7$ $19.21 = \$19$

5. a. $\begin{array}{r} 75 \\ \times\ .20 \\ \hline 15.00 \end{array}$ 15 days

    b. x = feet
    $$15 = \frac{5}{8} \cdot x$$
    $$\overset{1}{8} \cdot 15 = (\cancel{8} \cdot \frac{5}{8}) \cdot x$$
    $$120 = 5 \cdot x^{1}$$
    $$120 \div 5 = 5(\div 5) \cdot x$$
    $$24 = x$$

    c. x = oranges
    $$10 = \frac{2}{3} \cdot x$$
    $$\overset{1}{3} \cdot 10 = (\cancel{3} \cdot \frac{2}{3}) \cdot x$$
    $$30 = 2 \cdot x^{1}$$
    $$30 \div 2 = 2(\div 2) \cdot x$$
    $$15 = x$$

6. a. 61   b. 21 R3

7. a. 26   24   27
    b. 116   604   222
    c. 1,460   14   47
    d. 6.602   8.62   .18
    e. .009 $1\frac{1}{4}$ $\frac{3}{8}$

8. a. 9:12 $\frac{9}{12} = \frac{3}{4}$ .75   75%
    b. 10:16 $\frac{10}{16} = \frac{5}{8}$ .625   63%

9. a. ABK   AKB   BAK   BKA   KAB   KBA
    b. median   David would be in the middle.
    c. 4:12   33%

10.

	2	5	10	3	9	6
435		✓		✓		
270	✓	✓	✓	✓	✓	✓

11. $A = l \cdot w$
     $A = 7 \cdot 3$
     $A = 21 \ (\times 2) = 42$ sq. in.
     $A = 4 \cdot 3$
     $A = 12 \ (\times 2) = 24$ sq. in
     $A = 7 \cdot 4$
     $A = 28 \ (\times 2) = 56$ sq. in   Total = 122 sq. in.

12. R — G / M — N

13. a. ⌐   b. △   c. ⬡

14. a. $x + x + x + x + 3 = 31$
     $$4x + 3 = 31$$
     $$4x + 3(-3) = 31 - 3$$
     $$4x = 28$$
     $$4(\div 4) \cdot x = 28 \div 4$$
     $$x = 7$$

     b. $$\frac{x}{8} = \frac{3}{12}$$
     $$24 = 12 \cdot x$$
     $$24 \div 12 = 12(\div 12) \cdot x$$
     $$2 = x$$

15. a. $P = 2l + 2w$
     $$20 = (2 \cdot l) + (2 \cdot 4)$$
     $$20 = 2l + 8$$
     $$20 - 8 = 2l + 8(-8)$$
     $$12 = 2l$$
     $$12 \div 2 = 2(\div 2) \cdot l$$
     $$6 \text{ in.} = l$$

     b. $A = s^2$
     $36 = s^2$
     6 ft. = s

     c. x = books
     $$\frac{2}{7} = \frac{x}{14}$$
     $$7x = 28$$
     $$7(\div 7) \cdot x = 28 \div 7$$
     $$x = 4$$

16. $\$14 < b < \$20$
     $b = \$15, \$16, \$17, \$18$ or $\$19$

17. -7, -3, 0, +3, +5, +6

18. a. line
     b. Oct. 22, Oct. 1, Oct. 29, Oct. 15, Oct. 8
     c. Morgan Family Grocery Bills